Daddy's House

Daddy's House

A Daughter's Memoir of Setbacks, Triumphs & Rising Above Her Roots

MILDRED J MILLS

Published by
Hybrid Global Publishing
333 E 14th Street
#3C
New York, NY 10003

Copyright © 2024 by Mildred J. Mills

All rights reserved. No part of this book may be reproduced or transmitted in any form or by any means, electronic or mechanical, including photocopying, recording, or by any information storage and retrieval system, without the written permission of the Publisher, except where permitted by law.

Manufactured in the United States of America, or in the United Kingdom when distributed elsewhere.

Mills, Mildred J.
Daddy's House
    Paperback ISBN: 978-1-961757-27-1
    Hardcover ISBN: 978-1-961757-29-5
    eBook: 978-1-961757-28-8
    LCCN: 2023922577

Cover design by: Julia Kuris
Copyediting by: Nicole Frail
Interior design by: Suba Murugan
Author photo by: Lelund Durond Thompson

This book is a memoir. The events are portrayed to the best of the Author's recollection of experiences over time. While all the stories in this book are true, some names and identifying details have been changed to protect the privacy of the people involved.

www.mildredjmills.com

DEDICATION

In loving memory of Mama and Daddy, whose stories live on in these pages.

I dedicate this book to my parents, Abraham and Mildred Billups, who loved the younger me enough to set me free to realize my dreams. You instilled discipline, structure, kindness, respect, and an unparalleled work ethic, which shaped me into the woman I am today. It took years for me to realize that you gave me the best you had. I am grateful for your gifts.

*I can be changed by what happens to me.
But I refuse to be reduced by it.*

—**Maya Angelou**

*If people are doubting how far you can go,
go so far that you can't hear them anymore.*

—**Michele Ruiz**

Acknowledgements

Writing this book has been a long, arduous journey, and I am fortunate to have many friends and family who supported me across the finish line. From the bottom of my heart, thank you for your encouraging words, phone calls, and inspiration. You were the wind at my back on the steepest climb up the mountain.

My dearest husband, Darryl, your keen eye for catching minor missing details that enhanced my story was invaluable. Thank you for loving and believing in me and being my anchor on every leg of this journey. To my son, Richard, your gentle nudges kept me writing through my darkest days when I wanted to quit; thank you. I thank my daughters—Ashaki and Nadria, grandchildren, and every brother and sister who encouraged me or helped me remember.

To my editor, Nicole Frail, you pushed me to dig deeper, let down my guard, and freely tell my truth rather than shield those I wished to protect. For those reasons, I have a richer story.

Dr. David Hicks: I will never forget your tenderness as my advisor, guiding me through and beyond Wilkes University's Maslow Family Writing Program. How can I ever repay that kindness?

To my mentor, Beverly Donofrio, I sincerely appreciate you taking me under your wing, befriending me, teaching me the true meaning of shaping a story, and guiding me to "The End." You made me see the good in every character, even when I tried not to.

Karen Strauss and the incredible team at Hybrid Global Publishing: thank you for your passion and patience in becoming a partner in making my dream of becoming "Author of" come true.

Lelund Durond Thompson and team, how do you turn a photograph into a work of art? Thank you for capturing my best self through the camera lens and providing stunning images for the cover design artist to work with.

Thanks to every educator—especially Dr. Elizabeth Harper-Neeld and Ashley Sardoni—who ignited a writing spark in me, beginning with Mama and Daddy. I apologize upfront for forgetting anyone and will be offering thanks for years to come; I offer special thanks to a small group who regularly checked on me, some sending me gifts and flowers: Willie Blake, Joseph Bates, Abbie Brothers, Syni Champion, Dr. Richard & Dianne Cohen, Sedare Coradin, Betty Neal-Crutcher, Yvonne Danielly, Theodore (Ted) Gates, Valerie Golden, Doyle Gorman, Marilyn Hayes, Johnnie Horn, Cassandra Johnson, Janice Johnson, Carmelle Killick, Karen Kristie, Renee Logans, Dr. Ayanna Kersey-McMullen, Ellen McTigue, Gwen Lusk, Dolores Mitchell, Dee Pipes, Squeesta Collier-Semien, Cynthia Smith, and Cherise Story. My Sharon Lester tennis team, you girls rock on the courts and in my corner. Kristin Andree and The Renew Team, thank you for enthusiastically checking on me regularly. My Wilkes University cohort and biggest cheering squad, I won't forget how much we've been through together. The women of WIVLA, thank you for warmly embracing me.

Lastly, thank you, God, for giving me the strength to heal, the willingness to forgive, and the courage to tell my truth.

CONTENTS

Chapter 1:	A Mother's Dowry	1
Chapter 2:	Honor Above Resentment	9
Chapter 3:	A Girl in Training	17
Chapter 4:	Thunder and Lightning	31
Chapter 5:	Sex, Life, and Death on the Farm	43
Chapter 6:	Body Changes	53
Chapter 7:	A Stubborn Streak	61
Chapter 8:	Up, Up, and Away	71
Chapter 9:	Crossing State Lines	85
Chapter 10:	The Purple Heart	97
Chapter 11:	Harsh Realities	107
Chapter 12:	Starting Over	119
Chapter 13:	Immaculate Conception	127
Chapter 14:	The Unemployment Office	139
Chapter 15:	Frigidaire Corporation	149
Chapter 16:	Matrimony	155
Chapter 17:	On My Own	173
Chapter 18:	A Painful Separation	187
Chapter 19:	My Son	197
Chapter 20:	New Love and Turmoil	211

Chapter 21:	Marriage and Separation	217
Chapter 22:	Stinging Words	227
Chapter 23:	Hard Drinkin' Lincoln	239
Chapter 24:	Retaliation and Deposition	249
Chapter 25:	Women and Children	259
Chapter 26:	Secrets Revealed	277
Chapter 27:	A Memory Returns	281
Chapter 28:	Precious Lord, Take My Hand	291
Chapter 29:	A Return to Daddy's House	299

CHAPTER 1
A Mother's Dowry

One starlit morning when I was eighteen, a lump like a fist clamped my heart as I rushed out the back door and down the steps with my blue Sears Roebuck suitcase containing everything I owned. I grabbed the door handle of the pink Super 88, where Daddy sat behind the wheel, beckoning me to get in. A chorus of bullfrogs sang harmoniously with the humming engine, and the car's headlights beamed a path across the cow pasture, drawing me forward.

I turned and gazed back at Mama, a silhouette in black plastered against the white cinderblock wall. She stood on the concrete porch, her too-thin pink-and-blue floral shift waving like a flag in the gentle breeze. Tears, illuminated by the reflection of headlamps, gleamed against her cheeks as she watched her namesake walk away, the first of her children to do so. It was June 1969.

I was the third of Abraham and Mildred Billups's seventeen children, born in Wetumpka, Alabama—a small, dusty community in the sticks of Elmore County. Our white cinderblock house sat at the dead end of a red dirt road that ran straight through the woods at the butt end of the earth. I stood there torn between the two people who gave me life: Daddy at the steering wheel and Mama on the porch. When I looked from one to the other at two o'clock that morning, it was abundantly clear I wanted freedom from them both. Yet, I couldn't help but wonder if I was doing the right thing.

I glanced over my shoulder and waved a last goodbye to Mama. She threw open her arms and reached for me. A strong breeze whipped open her flimsy duster and exposed her large breasts, protruding stomach, and big thighs shaped like cured hams. In pitch blackness, this startling sight was like something out of a comedy, but nobody laughed. I asked myself: *Is it wrong of me to leave her?*

I wondered what life would be like waking up mornings not guided by those hands, rough and steady, or encouraged by her gentle voice. I was too young then to grasp the magnitude of the dowry Mama had already given me. She didn't have a penny to offer but had bestowed on me a sense of worth, pride, and independence as much a part of me as my skin color.

I ignored Mama's nakedness and focused on the curly ringlets above her shoulders, creamy skin the color of a banana peel just before the brown spots come, full lips, and raggedy yellow flip-flops held together by a pink safety pin. I had no idea then that she was already eight months pregnant with my youngest sister, the seventeenth and last child she would bear. I drank in her beauty under the crescent moon that hung like a front porch swing, and my heart crumbled, hearing each muffled sob that escaped her

A Mother's Dowry

throat. But no amount of crying would keep me here with my fortress, my friend—my strength.

I raced back up the steps, and Mama folded me into her arms like egg whites into a cake batter. I absorbed her warm, firm body, felt her heartbeat, pressed my face against her cheek, and tasted salty tears. Mama squeezed and held me like she feared I might disappear. "Mildred, I knowed from the day you was born you would be my *first* child to grow up and leave me," she said in a soft-voiced wail that tore at my heart.

But I was past feeling guilty about finding my place in life. Hell, yes. I was leaving my Mama.

I looked behind her at the sagging screen door and whispered, "Mama, I can't stay. I need to make a better life for you *and* me."

I will never forget the resignation on Mama's face as she wiped the tears from her eyes, faced me with her hands on my shoulders, and repeated a passage I'd heard her recite many times: "Trust in the Lawd wit' all your heart and lean not on your own understanding. In *all* your ways, acknowledge Him, and He will direct your path." She chuckled nervously. "I ain' never told you this, but that's my favorite scripture. Proverbs."

Daddy laid on the car horn, and Mama and I winced.

"Do the best you can with what you have, and remember, Mildred, nothing beats a failure but a try. I done packed everything a girl needs in your suitcase." I nodded but didn't speak. With that teaching, Mama gave me her blessing and released her young daughter into the night, covered by God's grace and mercy.

Mildred J Mills

I walked away from Mama wrapped in love, the remembrance of her raggedy-toothed smile emblazoned on my heart. I slipped onto the bench seat across from Daddy and waved through the passenger side window until the car backed away from the house, and I could no longer see her standing on the porch in the dark.

Tears threatened to slip down my face as I thought how, only yesterday, I had sat alone on that same little porch, perched like a cat with a fresh bowl of milk. I remember thinking then that it had been two months since my eighteenth birthday, six weeks since Daddy last beat me, a week since high school graduation, and the first time since I was five that I was *not* in the cotton field on a weekday. I felt twelve feet tall on that June day, lighter than a feather.

On that porch, I'd been ecstatic, knowing that in less than twenty-four hours, I would wave goodbye to the cotton fields of Wetumpka, Alabama, when Daddy drove me to a technical college in Columbus, Ohio. I had locked my fingers behind my head, closed my eyes, and leaned against the concrete wall of the only home I'd ever known. Then, I said to the rising sun, "Kiss. My. Face." Shivers of excitement pinched my nipples as sparrows soared and bumblebees buzzed—unrestricted. Soon, I'd be free from the sights, sounds, and smells of Mama, Daddy, and my fifteen surviving brothers and sisters.

With so many people always buzzing around, I'd thought my home was a place of confusion; I couldn't decide whether to love its beauty or hate its stench. Every time I stepped outside the house onto the little porch, the smell of chicken shit, hog pens, and the maggoty red outhouse spread its arms like a greeting committee. Yet, beyond the pigpen, where the soil was rich and black, the sweet smell of honeysuckles and cultivated fields eased into my bloodstream.

As Daddy backed away from the little porch, just outside the door where my sisters slept, I wanted to soak in every part of the cinderblock house and the family I left behind. I envisioned my seven younger brothers sleeping on one narrow bed or the floor of the screened-in back porch, then glanced through the car's rear window as we passed the front porch, where, as a child, I had delighted in the joy of playing jacks with my older sister, Bunny. The house faded to black amid crackling pea gravel under Daddy's racing tires. I faced the road ahead and thought, *So many porches, only two bedrooms.*

Burrowed into the corner of the Oldsmobile passenger seat, hoping Daddy wouldn't notice me, I gripped my purse so tight my knuckles were white. I should have been shouting hallelujah and jumping for joy that I had graduated high school and was off to a bright future. But I knew I was never more than one wrong word and a U-turn away from being back in the cotton field. So, there I sat, strung tight enough to have a nervous breakdown, trying not to set off the lunatic in the driver's seat.

Daddy flew down country roads, gripping the steering wheel like a lover as we headed toward I-65 North, leaving a trail of red dust in the dark. I closed my eyes, inhaled deeply, and filled my lungs with country smells from the open car windows—fresh-mowed grass, honeysuckle blossoms, pine needles, and skunk. The farther north I rode in Daddy's car, leaving everything and everybody familiar, the more I wondered what aromas would greet me in the unfamiliar territory of Ohio.

With that thought, I was suddenly afraid. I realized that in my haste to be free of my parents, I hadn't thought of what a sheltered existence I had lived in my two-parent home where, despite struggles, they remained together to raise their family. I remembered a story Mama told me when, as a young girl, I asked her how she and Daddy had met and ended up on the farm.

My parents grew up two miles apart and knew each other from church and school. Mama was the youngest of ten, Daddy the youngest of twelve, and both were the first high school graduates in their families. Mama and Daddy married in 1946, a year after he returned from Egypt. He was twenty-five; she was twenty.

In October 1950, after purchasing a sixty-acre farm with Daddy's GI Bill money, they left his mother's house on a horse-drawn wagon, carrying all their worldly goods and my two older siblings: four-year-old Brother and seven-month-old Bunny. Mama was already pregnant with me.

I imagine Daddy at the reins calculating how long clearing the land and building a farm would take, facts that come naturally to a brick mason and carpenter. I envision Mama thinking about me, embracing me, protecting me, the three-month-old pod growing inside her belly. She told me how happy she had been to have a place of her own but how terrified she was of being miles away from her mom (ten miles), moving to an isolated, wild, and untamed place.

Recently, sitting across the dining room table from Mama, I asked how she adjusted to the unfamiliar surroundings and overcame her fear. Mama clasped her hands and smiled. "Eventually, I grew to

A Mother's Dowry

love the peace and quiet and watching things grow." Remembering her words, I was swaddled in a cloak of peace and calm, heading to a faraway place with an opportunity for my own growth. I faced the road ahead. A kernel of hope and satisfaction sprouted inside me with every mile, remembering what I was leaving behind. I knew I had taken my last ass whipping from Daddy. And I decided right there in that car that if Daddy couldn't break me, I would *not be broken*. I also remembered that I had left a praying Mama behind, one who had breathed prayers into my spirit as she held me to her bosom only minutes earlier.

CHAPTER 2
Honor Above Resentment

I grew up believing—as I still do—that Mama had a direct line to God; she called on Him often and with such fervor that I knew He would grant her wishes. Almost every time I walked through our home and found her seated, her eyes were closed in prayer.

Mama prayed about everything. She even prayed before whipping me. I recall the creased face, quivering lips, and sad pleas as Mama lectured me after I committed a punishable offense. This time, I'd hurled a fork at Brother. I had cooked dinner and was setting the table, and he shoved me. I was ten; he was fourteen. I cocked back my right arm like Sandy Koufax and hurled a fork that sailed past his head and through a windowpane, shattering the glass. Mama huffed into the dining room from outdoors in time to witness the whole thing.

"Git out there and bring me a switch," she yelled. "You and your hot-headed temper." I handed her the switch. "Lawd, have mercy, Mildred, this gonna hurt me more than is' gonna hurt you."

I stood eye-level with Mama as she sat on the edge of a ladder-back chair, making this declaration. In my young mind, I thought she was nuts. Why pray for God's mercy, whip me anyway, and claim it caused *her* pain?

I didn't want to add to Mama's agony, so I lowered my head and tried to look repentant, although I wanted to punch something rather than get hit. By the time she was mad enough to whip me, I had deserved it.

"I'm gonna let you slide this time," Mama sometimes said, only to come back weeks later with "I'm gonna beat you for the old and the new" and order me out of the house to pick a switch from a peach tree. I trudged along slowly, looking over my shoulder, hoping she'd get distracted by some other disaster. I even wished God would remind her through Psalm 127:3 that "Children are a gift from the Lord; they are a reward from him." But after so many babies, she likely didn't view them as gifts anymore.

With a peach branch in her hand, Mama became Superwoman. I skipped around, yelping like an excited puppy, while she flailed that switch through the air. It sounded like a swarm of bees, and upon contact with tender little legs, it left an impression. Mama's whippings didn't last long, but she raised her voice an octave during the act. "You know why I'm beatin' your tail?" She didn't wait for an answer, and I didn't offer one. "I ain't gonna let you grow up like you was hatched by the buzzards and raised by the snakes." I still don't know what that meant, but it sounded awful.

Some Friday nights, I was thrilled when Daddy disappeared to places unknown, even though it left Mama home alone with their house full of babies. The house was filled with laughter and

Honor Above Resentment

lightheartedness on those nights. I felt like the little girl I was—free to dream and be anything or anybody I wanted to be, even a butterfly. Mama allowed us to express ourselves freely, not fearing Daddy's wrath. She'd gather her children in the living room, saying, "Let's have a prayer meeting." She'd begin the service soft and slow with a song like "Tell Him What You Want," a call-and-response spiritual, in her off-key voice. Mama would sing, "You know Jesus is on the main line." We'd chime in, "Tell him what you want/tell him what you want." I loved the call-and-response section. Mama would yell "Call him up!" three times, a sound of desperation in her shrill voice. We'd echo the call, ending with the refrain, "And tell him what you want."

I often wondered if those prayer services occurred when Mama craved human touch to fill lonely nights. I now realize she taught us how to pray, share, and bond with each other on those Friday evenings as we clapped, laughed, and sang like we were part of the Hallelujah chorus. Mama called our names in chronological order. "Now it's your turn. What song you wanna sing, or would you like to pray?" She never forced participation yet encouraged us, making us believe we could perform like Mahalia Jackson or James Brown.

After singing, Mama would drop to her knees in front of our old sofa—its floral cover meant to conceal bare wood frames and broken springs hidden like skeletons in a casket. She'd prop her elbows on the couch and rest her chin in her palms. We'd bow our heads, close our eyes, and clasp our hands.

Mama spoke to Jesus like He was sitting on the couch drinking the wine He made from water at the marriage at Cana. Her prayers were almost always the same: "Dear Heavenly Father, I come before you in the humblest manner I know how." She asked Him to bless the sick and afflicted everywhere, the prison-bound and those less fortunate than us. Mama asked forgiveness for her sins by thought, word, or deed, and for things not pleasing in His sight; forgive those who had sinned against her. "Father, throw your long arms of protection around us and keep us safe from all hurt, harm, and danger." Every request sounded more urgent than the last. She wrinkled her face and pleaded with God as if her life depended on it.

"Hallelujah," we'd shout. "Amen." The more we responded, the longer Mama prayed. Sometimes we'd peep from under our eyes at each other, crinkle our faces, and giggle silently. But there was no more giggling when Mama said, "Lawd, let me live long enough to raise my own little chillun so they won't be scattered everywhere. When my work on Earth is done, please give me a resting place somewhere around your kingdom, for Christ's sake. Amen."

As the words to her prayer sank in, I couldn't decide whether to cry or sneak off to bed. I'd look at my siblings, barefoot and dusty, sitting in a semicircle around Mama. We played and worked outside every day, did not own a change of clothes, and only bathed on Saturday nights. Who but Mama would want such a raggedy crew?

Sometimes, Mama spoke to us like she was going away. "I done taught y'all to take care of one another, no hittin' and fightin'. Whatever one got, I expect you to share." She would lower her head, shake it slowly from side to side, and sit silently for several seconds. We stared at Mama and each other with our eyes glazed over like we were destined for an orphanage. No one moved, just sat on the floor with our faces twisted up, lips quivering, and eyes unfocused.

Honor Above Resentment

For the next few days, we were helpful children, no bickering—perfect church scholars.

Years after I left home, I asked Mama, "Why did you wake *me* in the middle of the night to take care of your children? Why not Bunny or Rachel?"

We sat across from each other at the twelve-foot rectangular table that Daddy and his sons wrestled down several flights of stairs at an office building to provide seating when all his children came home. Mama slowly rubbed her palms together in a handwashing motion.

"Well, Mildred, you just had a way with my babies; they responded to you." She rocked gently on a chair and stared through the sliding glass patio door at cows grazing near the lake.

I let that sink in for a moment. "Mama, what does that even mean?"

She squirmed on her chair and looked directly into my eyes. "Well, Bernice wasn't no good with chillun, and Rachel couldn't stay awake." Bunny, whose given name was Bernice and the name Mama always called her, was a year older, and Rachel—a year younger.

I resented having my sleep disturbed, but I took Exodus 20:12, "Honor thy father and mother," seriously as a child, and I still do. I greeted each screaming baby with a sharp pinch to their little fat thigh. What the hell? They were already squalling, and I was tired and filled with resentment. Why was *I called* at five o'clock every morning for the last nine or ten years I lived at home to cook homemade biscuits, grits, eggs, gravy, and sausage or bacon for a house full of people?

Mildred J Mills

Those last years at Daddy's house, I would think, *That is not my husband peering across the hot stove looking for a meal*, and *Those aren't my hungry children with the wet diapers that I rocked back to sleep at night.* Did they call me because I never complained and meticulously performed tasks like a bionic servant? Of course they did! They were no different than an abusive employer, husband, friend, or slavemaster who piled work on a willing spirit until she was ready to snap. But I would bide my time and bite my tongue, focus on one goal, get the hell out of Alabama, and make my own way.

While questioning Mama about choosing me as a caregiver, I asked if she remembered packing my suitcase when I left home at eighteen. Her eyes lit up. "Oh, yeah. I'll never forget it," she said. "I packed needles, thread, a thimble, and everything I thought my girl, who wasn't never coming home again, might need. Oh, I knowed you'd always come back to see me but never again to stay."

I was pleasantly surprised that without ever discussing it, Mama knew precisely how I felt as a child leaving home. Yet, she did not cling or insist that I stay. I asked, "How did you know I would never return?"

"I just knew. You was just a girl but looked like an old woman, tired and ready to go." She told me she understood why I ran away from the burden they placed on me. While writing this book, I remember Mama told me, "Mildred, you was a brave and fearless girl, courageous enough to leave home," a strength she told me she lacked.

Two days before I sat in Daddy's car with my packed suitcase, he'd sidled up to me in the middle of a cotton field full of waist-high

Honor Above Resentment

Johnson grass and gnarly nutgrass that I thrashed with my sharp hoe. He said, "We done come to count on you a awful lot 'round here, Babe. I dunno whether we can afford to let you go to Ohio. Who you reckon can cook and do all the other things we trained you to do?"

I felt a tight ball in my stomach as I hoed and chopped weeds like they were Satan's horns. I lowered my eyes and said, "I don't know," and wondered how that was my problem. I thought, *I'm no special monkey; "train" somebody else.*

"Well, me and Mama gonna talk it over tonight and see what we need to do."

I stared at the ground and chopped even harder. "Yes, sir." *God, help them make the right decision. Please don't make me run away.*

CHAPTER 3
A Girl in Training

Every Sunday until we outgrew the car, the family piled in Daddy's 1949 Fleetline Chevrolet, dressed in our best clothes, and headed to Sunday school at the church his grandfather had built. Daddy floored the gas and flew past any car that dared get in his way. The wind whipped through the open windows and pinned us children to the back seat. Mama clutched her church hat with one hand and the baby with the other but knew better than to open her mouth.

Pea gravel crackled, and a cloud of red dust chased us like a whirlwind when Daddy swung the Chevy into the churchyard and parked in *his* spot under a large oak tree. He was the adult Sunday school teacher, piano player, and head deacon. Only his oldest brother, the pastor, had more power. Daddy grabbed his King James Bible, slammed the car door, and hustled up the steep church steps to meet with the boys' club, his older brothers, in the vestibule where a large rope hung from the church bell. Years later, Mama told me that he and his brothers held formal meetings on "how to keep a woman in her place, namely their wives."

Mildred J Mills

Mama slid off the front seat with an infant in her left arm and hoisted a toddler from the back seat onto her right hip. Eight-year-old Brother closed the car door. He, five-year-old Bunny, and I, then four years old, held hands and strolled behind Mama. A sprinkle of church ladies smiled and spoke. Mama said, "Hey," in a voice sweet as syrup.

Years later, she told me how the church ladies giggled behind her back, seeing her and her children lined up like stairsteps across a church pew. "I heard the whispers: *'I bet she pregnant again.'*" Mama claimed it didn't bother her, but the whine in her elevated voice contradicted that notion. "I was a married woman wit' a husband, after all. Some of them women had chillun and ain't had no husband." When she was really riled up, she tsked her lips, wrung her hands, and wrinkled her brows. "Lawd, sometimes I cried and prayed and asked God how come Teetie and Sista (her older sisters) couldn't have some a dem babies?" I thought she sounded like a woman confined to a life sentence, and I wondered if sitting in church was her escape.

Every Sunday morning, I raced up the steep steps of Mt. Zion Baptist Church, a sturdy white building with a steeple so tall it looked like a stairway to heaven. I squeezed into the same corner spot on the first row of a hard wooden pew behind a potbellied stove.

Aunt Lizzie—the children's Sunday school teacher and Daddy's older sister—marched into church like a bulldozer and snapped open her worn King James Bible. "Good morning, class," she chirped and jammed one hand on a hip until each student responded. Then Aunt Lizzie delved into her favorite topic—the devil. She stomped

A Girl in Training

back and forth in front of us, wearing white, old folks' shoes, and preached hellfire and brimstone, condemning a sleepy bunch of farm kids to damnation.

One Sunday, just as my head rolled back and my eyes closed, a chilling screech split the air when the massive double doors at the back of the church swung open. Every child swiveled around like synchronized swimmers to examine the newcomer.

Wham! Aunt Lizzie cracked a twelve-inch ruler against the top of the pew. "I done told y'all to turn yourselfs 'round and stop lookin' back in church." She smacked the ruler again, just as she sometimes cracked our knuckles. "Keep it up, you gonna turn into church asses, and you goin' to hell." Aunt Lizzie waved her King James in our faces. "Lemme remind you what the Good Book says happened to Sarah when she disobeyed God." She slammed the Bible on the front bench and smacked her hands together. "Sarah looked back and, *Whap!* Just like that, she turnt to a pillar of salt." I envisioned Sarah stuck on a salt block like the ones I saw in cow pastures, licked to death like a white lollipop at the end of a stick.

It was no accident that the young children's class was next to a wide-mouthed wood-burning stove. Uncle Huey, Daddy's older brother, crept to the heater and pried it open with a black fire poker. Sparks crackled and flew onto the wood floor. When the heater was so hot the outside glowed red, the stooped man who resembled Ebenezer Scrooge brushed off his powder-blue seersucker suit, pushed his eyeglasses up his nose, glanced at us, and smiled a wry grin. With every child wide-eyed and focused on him, he slipped away, his reminder of what happens to bad kids accomplished.

Mildred J Mills

By the time I was in third grade and ready to advance to the next class, I had heard so much about Satan that I wanted to stand on that pew and shout, "Show me the devil!" Not a single Sunday passed that Aunt Lizzie didn't narrow her eyes and say, "Y'all know what the devil look like?" No one responded. "He got a sharp, pointy tail, red horns, and a split tongue like a snake—got a hot pitchfork, too. He's nuthin but a deceiver." I couldn't have put the words together back then, but I thought the devil sometimes sounded mean and scary, like Daddy.

At the breakfast table when I was three, and everyone's eyes were closed for grace, one-year-old Sonny grabbed a sausage patty from Mama's plate and stuffed it in his mouth. Daddy swatted his hand hard enough to bring a welt. The sound of his palm against the baby's flesh was like a lightning crack across breaking glass. "Boy, keep your hands off your mama's plate." Sonny's reaction was immediate, a wail that wrapped itself around your heart and left a small callus. Daddy snatched him by one arm and pummeled his backside with rapid blows that sounded like gunfire from an automatic weapon. He slammed the baby back on Mama's lap.

Mama lowered her head and chewed sausage like it was a rubber hose, something hard to swallow. She blinked back tears and rubbed Sonny's back like it was fragile. She tapped her foot and sang softly. "Hush, now, baby, don't you cry." She pinched off a piece of sausage and handed it to him. Sonny grabbed it with chubby fingers and popped it into his mouth. Tears still streaked his face, but he grinned into Mama's eyes, revealing four baby teeth. While she sang, her half-smile didn't hide the rot that had eaten away at her four front teeth.

A Girl in Training

That same year, when I was supposed to be asleep late one night, my bedroom door creaked open, and Mama tiptoed into the room. It was winter. The wind howled outside and whistled across the threshold beneath the back door. She pulled two sticks of firewood from behind the door, stuck them in the potbellied stove, and stoked the fire with a black poker. Mama patted the covers where her young children slept, puttered around the room, and straightened the blankets, checking if we were asleep.

The sound of rocks crunching under tires approached the back door fast and stopped too close to the little porch outside our bedroom. The car door slammed. I heard Daddy laughing and mumbling to himself. He eased open the creaky screen and crept inside.

Mama leaped from behind the door, swung the fire poker, and barely missed his head. She yelled something that sounded like, "You gonna stop that catting around, and I mean it." Daddy snatched the fire iron from her as effortlessly as he could have taken it from three-year-old me. He knocked her backward across the foot of the bed and pressed the poker against her throat. Daddy looked like he was wrestling one of his cows when, with one hand, he yanked his arms out of his olive Army overcoat and flung the coat over Mama's face. She screamed, kicked her legs, and tried to jump off the bed. Then, she lay silent, still as a corpse.

I sprung up in bed with my mouth frozen open, my voice in my throat. Daddy pressed the poker harder against Mama's neck. I wore a white cotton underslip and panties and clutched a patchwork quilt Mama had made. A white-hot flash slapped me, saying, *"Do something."* I hollered, *"Mama, wake up."* She didn't move. I screamed. *"Daddy, you killed my Mama!"*

He startled out of his blind rage. "Gal, shut your God-damn mouth and get back to sleep." My two sisters and a baby brother, sleeping in the same room, never moved or opened their eyes. Mama's underskirt covered her face like a white sheet over a dead body and exposed her naked bottom. That night, I wished I were big enough to gouge his eyes out with that hot poker.

The same year he almost killed Mama, I'd wandered out to the little porch, whistling and looking for Daddy. It was so hot inside that Mama's face and arms looked like melting ice cream cones. "Gone out there wit' ya' Daddy and sit under that shade tree." I jumped at the chance to get outdoors and watch him work. Those brown eyes were focused, and every move of his calloused hands deliberate, like a well-oiled machine—no wasted motion. Daddy and Brother were under the black walnut tree in the backyard, yanking on a makeshift hoist—a massive chain with links that looked like giant horseshoes looped across a pulley mounted on a tree limb. The enormous black walnut tree and a large pecan tree provided shade to cool the house, but they were no match for the Alabama heat in August.

Daddy's khaki shirt clung to his back. His face gleamed with sweat. The muscles in Brother's skinny arms pumped like pistons as he struggled with Daddy, hoisting the engine from the 1949 Chevy Fleetline. I plopped onto the ground under the shade tree—my homemade white dress with tiny green flowers spread out like a picnic blanket around my feet—and cracked black walnuts with half of a brick, fishing delicious meat from the hard shell, eating a few, and stacking some on my dress for Mama.

A Girl in Training

I heard a distant sound like popcorn growing louder and louder as it approached the backyard. A large black car snaked down the dirt road, crunching pea gravel as it crept behind the house and parked so close to the Chevy that even I couldn't squeeze between the two vehicles. A white man popped out of the driver's side of his Chrysler like a jack-in-the-box, close enough that I could have written my name on his dusty brown shoes. I dropped the brick, scooted behind the tree, and struggled to ignore his flabby belly resting on his belt. His shades were so black that my reflection stared back at me from their lenses.

The man wrinkled his face, gazed over the top of his dark glasses, and whistled low, incredulous. He stuck his fists on his hips and said, "Ugh." He looked at the chicken house, cows grazing in the pasture, and at Maude, our horse standing in the stable swishing flies with her tail. He strolled up to Daddy. "Is you Abraham?"

Daddy stood five-foot-eight and was a solid one hundred sixty-five pounds. You didn't want to tussle with a man who made a living as a brick mason, farmer, and carpenter, a man who worked more than sixteen hours every day running a farm. The brown eyes inside his chiseled face zeroed in on a target like laser beams. His fists looked like sledgehammers, and each finger was as big as a frankfurter, the kind they call red hots. No amount of cleaning removed the black grease from fingernails thicker than silver dollars. "Who wants to know?" he asked, barely moving his lips.

The white man walked around Daddy's Chevy and kicked the tires. He said his name, but I don't remember it. I'll call him

Mr. Goodrich. "I'm from B. F. Goodrich. You three months late on ya' payments for them tires."

Daddy leaned back, jerked the chain hard, and grunted. The engine inched a little further from the car. He still didn't look up but spoke in a slow, measured tone. "Well, I ain't got the money right now. Soon as I get it, I'll be sending it on to ya'."

Mr. Goodrich cleared his throat and stepped so close that Daddy wrinkled his nose like he smelled something foul. In a drawl only a southern white man can mimic, he said, "That ain' good enough, Abraham. Ima collect dat' money or dem' tires. Which one's it gonna be?"

One of Daddy's strictest rules to us children was, "I better not *ever* hear of you starting no trouble, but if trouble comes knockin', you better make sure it don't never come back." The trunk of his car stood open. There were wrenches, greasy rags, screwdrivers, and tools strewn everywhere. Daddy jerked his head up and locked eyes with Mr. Goodrich. I slipped behind the pecan tree when the muscle in his jaw clenched.

Daddy let go of that chain, and with a speed and sound loud enough to burst an eardrum, the motor slammed back under the car's hood. Shag, our brown and white collie, snarled and obeyed Daddy's "heel" until the car engine broke loose. Then, the dog split the air with a bark that sent chickens squawking. I hugged the tree and stared at Brother; he stood near the car, unmoving like he had seen a ghost. We both watched Daddy, whose eyes were barely visible slits. He swiped his hands across the front of his khaki shirt and left five grease prints. In three strides, he was at the back of his car. Daddy yanked a tire iron out of the trunk, slung it across

A Girl in Training

his shoulder like a baseball bat, and lunged toward that white man who looked like he was running a football drill, backpedaling faster than most people ran forward.

With a voice low in his throat, Daddy said, "By God, you must can't hear! I said ain' got the money. Now git off my place right now, or there's gonna be trouble."

When Mr. Goodrich raced to the driver's side of his car, a warm trickle rushed down my legs and onto my bare feet. Daddy stared over the top of that tire iron like a double-barreled shotgun. The hairs stood on Shag's back as he bucked and reared like a stallion and tried to get his teeth into Mr. Goodrich, limited only by the length of his restraint.

The man dove into his car, fumbled to jam the key in the ignition, and flipped it in reverse, spinning pea gravel around the black walnut tree. Shag almost became roadkill. That man sped away like a red-faced convict on the run with his hair flying behind him. He hollered out the car window, "You better git that money to us, Abraham, or I'll be back to pull them tires off that car."

I was almost four years old, an age when people think kids won't remember. After witnessing that scene, I knew if B. F. Goodrich never collected a dime for those tires, *that* man would not set foot on our property again. The man with the tire iron and the raging dog was enough to give me nightmares. That was the first time I thought Daddy was crazy. And yet, days later, I would be charmed by his singing or his use of family game nights, when he'd pull out dominoes, checkers, Chinese checkers, and bingo, teaching us to think strategically through problems. I fondly remember the man who showed up on those nights, clapping his hands, speaking softly, and teaching his children strategies for competing and winning.

My best memories of Daddy are of him singing. The following spring, I was four and trailing behind him as he sang "The Battle of New Orleans" or "Amazing Grace." When he said, "We fired our guns, and the British kept a-comin'," my little-girl ears heard, "The biddies kept a-comin'." I didn't know anything about the British, but I knew about our baby chicks. I was a teenager before I learned the difference.

For years after he grew older, Daddy and I laughed about the "biddies." I asked him why he sang that song so often. He said it reminded him of the days leading up to his departure from New Orleans to fight in World War II. He loved telling the story of his long journey on a ship to Egypt. The trip lasted so long that the only food remaining was "camel hips." He rocked gently on his swivel chair with an incredulous look. "I saw this long leg laying on a table, and I asked, what is that?" One of his shipmates told him it was dinner, a camel's hip. "Man, I looked that leg over and decided I don't want none of that." Daddy told the man, "I'll just wait 'til we get where we going to eat my supper." Daddy clapped his hands, reared back, and laughed each time he told the story, remembering how he devoured the camel hips after days with no food.

Daddy surprised me during one of our laughing sessions when he was ninety and I was sixty. "I really enjoyed hearing you whistle when you was a little bitty thang," he told me with a twinkle in his eyes. I had longed to hear those words when I was a child. Sometimes, when I saw him coming from a distance, I'd burst into song or begin whistling, trying to impress him, hoping for a

A Girl in Training

compliment. I had longed to be close, but I also kept my eye trained on him, fearful of his rage and wary of his trickery.

I was learning that Daddy was especially tricky about paying his debts. Like earlier that summer, in August, when the sun was barely up, but the temperature hovered well above ninety degrees. The cotton was ripe for picking. After breakfast, Daddy grabbed me by my arms and swung me above his head. I wrapped my legs around his neck, clutched his head with my little arms, and hung on for fear I would fly off his back.

Daddy tore past the two full-sized beds in the girls' room, the smell of pee as potent as Clorox. The rounded metal headboards with little iron slats, small enough that a child's head wouldn't get stuck, looked more like prison bars than beds where girls slept. I felt a slight shiver as I glanced back, hoping I wouldn't see maggots crawling in the sinkhole in the middle of the mattress again tonight like there were sometimes. Daddy pushed through the lopsided screen door. Green flies darted inside and landed on the beds, drinking from pools where too many babies slept. He loped down the steps of the porch, through the backyard.

A summer breeze bathed my face as I enjoyed a piggyback ride on my handsome daddy's back. His smooth black skin and curly hair glistened in the sunlight. The rhythm of his work boots against the ground was like chords from black and white piano keys. Brother and Bunny ran behind us and struggled to keep up. I wondered why they looked like they were about to be hanged.

At the cotton field, Daddy spun me to the ground, and his six-foot cotton sack appeared from somewhere, and he slid its wide strap around his neck. The bag trailed behind him like a wedding gown train. He smiled and placed me on the bag like I was precious cargo. I crossed my legs at the ankle and enjoyed the cotton stalk parasol above my head, fascinated by spotted monarch butterflies that flitted and kissed cotton leaves. The white bolls were wide like the welcoming hand of God, watching over me.

Daddy bent over, snatched cotton from two rows, and stuffed it through the neck of the sack. I tumbled to the ground when the bag was nearly full, and he never noticed. I dusted myself off, scrambled back up, and hung on tighter while he hummed "Amazing Grace." Fat mosquitoes stung my bare feet, legs, and arms until they puffed up and bled.

Bunny poked along beside Daddy and tugged cotton sprigs like they might bite, sliding them into the bag hanging from her neck like a flowered noose. She stared at her bloody cuticles and sniffled. Thick black plaits stood on her head like the arms of the cross. Her dress, a tattered brown thing, hung off one shoulder. I waved, smiled, and tried to make her feel better. She rolled her eyes and looked the other way.

Seven-year-old Brother looked like an old man laden by the six-foot sack hanging from his back. Now and then, Daddy yelled, "Come on, Boy!" Brother could work like a horse on mechanical things, but his fingers weren't nimble at picking cotton. I peeked through the stalks and smiled. He had a pained expression on his face. *What could make him so sad?* I wondered.

"Boy, go up to the house and draw a bucket of cold water from the well; don't you forget the dipper, neither," Daddy hollered. Brother tore out of the field, happy to take a break and try to please his father. His overall strap flapped back and forth across

A Girl in Training

his shoulder as he raced beyond the hog pen and scooted under the barbwire fence. Black dirt cooled my fingers while I dug holes and avoided hairy black worms.

I had been riding on his sack for three months when Daddy called Brother, Bunny, and me into a huddle. "Let's have a little contest. Babe, I betcha you can pick more cotton than Bunny and Brother." Looking back, I should have been suspicious when he shot me that sly grin. He pulled a buffalo-head nickel from his pocket, held it in his palm, and flashed it before the three of us. It reminded me of how magicians show you the empty hat before a trick. Daddy said, "You beat 'em both, and this nickel is yours."

I hadn't picked cotton before, but I had watched Daddy strip it from bolls, and I was a fast learner. I grabbed cotton with one goal: win that nickel, buy Mama a postage stamp, and have a penny left for a treat—maybe banana kisses or a yellow moon pie. Daddy weighed our cotton and grinned. "I knew you could beat 'em." As I watched him laugh and stuff the nickel back in his pocket, I thought, *It's never too early to learn about competition, and not a bad idea to pay attention to the game runner.* Daddy never mentioned the nickel again, and I sure didn't ask about it.

I never forgot the wide grin on Daddy's face, an ugly one that said, *Fool*. I wanted to whip him with a cotton stalk the way he hit us when we didn't move fast enough, wake up early enough, or didn't do whatever enough. I was a girl-in-training, studying the ways of deceitful and abusive men like Daddy.

CHAPTER 4
Thunder and Lightning

As my departure date approached, the chance that Daddy didn't intend to let me go lingered in my mind. Still, I walked alone, reflecting on my home—a place where I never planned to return. I swung into the open bay of the barn, a faded red structure with a severely sloping roof, except for the area above the car shed, which was flat and an excellent place to dry freshly picked peanuts on the vine. A carport, two animal stalls that opened to another parking area, and a storage room for tools and feed were on the ground level. My favorite part of the barn when I was a child was the hayloft with stairsteps and wide double doors. The freedom to jump several feet to the ground or slide down a plank with my arms spread wide, squealing at the top of my lungs, while gathering splinters in my backside was more exhilarating than a day at Six Flags.

An extended trailer, soon to be filled with cotton, corn, or watermelons, sat empty next to the barn. I rubbed my hands together and felt callouses tough as shoe leather from year-round manual labor. In fall and winter, I tossed corn from the trailer to the barn bare-handed with the rhythm of a heartbeat. While chopping cotton or weeding the garden each spring, I gripped a hoe handle tight enough to strangle a chicken. There was no harsher punishment against a little girl's hands than the stabs and jabs of cotton bolls, ripping cuticles until they bled, but I respected that such hard work created a healthy body and mind in me.

 I poked my head into the stalls on the other side of the barn where Susie, our old black and white Holstein cow, was chewing her cud. She noticed me and rolled her eyes. We have a history. Once, when I was twelve, I sat on a five-gallon bucket and milked that contrary heifer. Susie decided she disliked being milked as much as I loathed milking her. She raised her hind hoof and delivered a sharp kick to my right bicep. A spasm leaped like a frog to the surface of my arm. Milk spilled. I hopped off that bucket, found the closest stick, and swung it across her face. I resumed my milking, and she behaved herself.

 Later that day, I walked past the stall and stared in horror at the red and swollen left side of her face. Yellow mucus slid out of her eye and down the side of her black and white coat. I prayed that the cow would bury her face in a hay bale or fall asleep before Daddy made his nightly inventory round, checking animals and farm equipment. I had eased into bed that night and nodded off when Daddy screamed, "Ant Babe! Get your bony ass out here."

 A pins and needles sensation prickled under my skin. I smelled my own sweat as I walked out the back door, too terrified to fake innocence. A hundred-watt bulb hanging from an extension cord

Thunder and Lightning

above Daddy's head illuminated the pained expression as he examined Susie's eye. "Yes, sir?"

The veins stood out on his temple, and his lips had disappeared into his face. "Look what you done to my cow. You know how much milk she gives every day? Susie is worth ten times more'n you! Go find me whatever you hit her with."

Outside the barn and down on my knees with one hand waving around like a metal detector, I searched for the pecan branch in the dark. Daddy stood with the light at his back, his hands on his hips, and watched my every move. When my hand touched the thorny stick, I wanted to break it in half, but his eyes were trained on me like laser beams. Before I was off my knees, Daddy snatched the stick and grabbed one of my arms, beating every part of my body concealed beneath my clothing. I spun in circles and screamed, unable to escape the blows that lit my skin on fire. The welts on my back, butt, and thighs were immediate. Daddy was a master at burying scars from prying outsiders' eyes, and he always drew blood.

After my stick beating, he said, "You get that bucket and fill it with soapy water, then take a rag and wash Susie's face morning and night until it heals." I couldn't help wondering if Daddy had worked at a torture chamber in another life, for what logical person would devise such creative means of punishment.

Whoever said cows are stupid didn't know Susie. I took that beating, washed her face, and she never raised her hind leg to kick me again, but she gave me the evil eye whenever I approached her. Now, I smiled, air-kissed the old girl, and waved goodbye to the stench of mucky cow stalls surrounded by horseflies, swarming like B-47 bombers, stealing sips of blood before a swishing tail could fight them off.

I hurried past the outhouse and thought to use it again for old times' sake. I stepped into the lavatory and squatted with my feet on the toilet seat, a habit I had formed, fearful of maggots crawling inside a cavity if I sat on the stool.

I closed my eyes and held my breath, pretending the horrific smell didn't threaten to choke me and wished I could will away the memory of a particular horror story. When Rachel, who was quite mischievous, was about nine, she locked three Rhode Island Reds inside the outhouse. Afterward, she and I wandered off to play beside the house when Daddy, who didn't miss much on the farm and seemed to have eyes in the back of his head, was suddenly in the outhouse, fishing the birds out of the toilet with an ice hook. He slammed down the toilet seat, closed the door, and left the chickens inside.

"Rachel, get out here," he hollered. "So, you gonna kill Sunday dinner, huh?" She stared up at Daddy, her body trembling. Dust covered her bare feet and legs, and tears formed dirty tracks down her cheeks. Daddy bent close to her face. "I bet you won't shut nothin' else up in there. I got a good mind to kill you." He snatched a rope from the back of his International Harvester truck and struck her so many times I lost count. "Now get that garden hose and wash that shit off them chickens." She screwed a nozzle on the end of the hose. He closed the door and latched it, pinning her inside. "When them chickens look like they did before you stuffed them in that toilet, knock on this door. You better not knock one minute sooner."

Thunder and Lightning

Water squirted through the cracks of the outhouse, and it sounded like a demolition crew at work between Rachel screaming and banging against the wall and the chickens squawking. I hid nearby, afraid to speak for fear of getting the rope. Daddy opened the door, and Rachel was dripping wet with poop clinging to her dress. My heart broke. She and I were inseparable, like identical twins. I tried to protect her when we were small, but not even I would hug my sister, who was usually feisty and daring but would flee in terror from Daddy's volatile flare-ups.

Years earlier, Rachel and I were huddled on a cowhide bottom chair at the dining room table one stormy afternoon. She was three, and I was four. When a lightning bolt punched a fist across the sky, she clutched my waist and burrowed her face into my flat bosom; a thunderclap rattled the windowpanes. Rain thrashed against the tin rooftop like a drumline, but the storm across the room held my attention.

I thought, *Oh, no. Not again.*

Daddy flew from his bedroom behind Mama like a bull chasing a matador. Strips of torn fabric hung from her nightgown, a flimsy thing that dragged the floor. Her screams cut through the air like arrows toward a bull's-eye as she ran toward the front door. Daddy raced behind her, grabbed a fistful of black curls, and snatched her backward, his work boots a drumbeat across the wood planks. I smelled fear on Mama's breath. She hollered, "Abraham, let me 'lone. *Please, Abraham, leave me 'lone.*"

I don't ever remember Daddy speaking words when he beat Mama. He just kept hitting her. Their worst fights occurred when I was a small child at eye level with his leather belt. I will never forget how quickly he could rip it through the loops and beat us. He looked ten feet tall wearing that belt—black with a silver buckle.

I peered through the slats on the ladder-back chair and shuddered with the guttural screams that I didn't realize came from my throat. Sounds from my four-year-old self, powerless to fight. Mama shot through the living room, eyes wild, arms flailing, looking like a basketball with arms and legs—out of balance. I gripped the bars of the chair back. *"Run, Mama!"*

Daddy snapped out of his crazy place, realizing Rachel and I were watching. He charged toward the dining room. "Get your asses outta here!"

When Mama's eyes met mine, bulging and unfocused, her expression said, "It never occurred to me to run." With Daddy's back turned, she scrambled off the floor and flew out the front door. Her nightgown hung off one shoulder and waved behind her like it was racing to catch up. One swollen breast flapped across her shoulder as she ran down the front porch steps.

I felt sick to my stomach when I heard thunder and lightning, but I still hopped off the chair at a dead run and grabbed Rachel's hand. "Come on, let's go."

"Get back here. You ain't going nowhere." Daddy snatched our arms and raced us to the front door, breathing so hard I thought I heard his heart drumming against his ribcage. He hit the door with his fist and yelled at Mama's fleeing back, "That's right. Run. What kinda woman leaves her chillun?" He had shoved us against the screen so hard it left prints on our faces. "Look at your fool Mama running down that road like a raggedy tramp."

Thunder and Lightning

Daddy stomped back and forth—a madman who couldn't believe she had taken off. "She'll be back. Where the hell she going looking like that? Ain't nobody 'round here gonna take her in, not when they know she done left me with all y'all chillun'?"

Rachel and I screamed, reaching out our hands as we watched Mama grow smaller and smaller. She wore no shoes, and I thought she might catch a cold. Still, my heart danced with joy that she had found the nerve to run and get away from Daddy's fists and nasty temper.

I peered under the slat that separated the bottom of the door from the top with tears streaming down my face. Mama moved up the road like a missile. Dark clouds hung low, and rain pelted her skin. Her wet hair hung over her face like a black veil. I prayed as hard as a little girl could for God to grant my wish that Mama would stay away this time.

I paced near the door and looked up the road all day, but Mama didn't come home that night. For dinner, Daddy served hard black-eyed peas. I longed for the soft ones seasoned with fatback that Mama saved for lean winter days, making you forget they weren't fresh but dried. The burnt cornbread with a mushy center was unfit to eat. No one uttered a word except to say grace around the dinner table that night.

Two days later, Mama still wasn't home. Daddy woke us up just after sunrise to wide-awake farm animals—roosters crowing, cows mooing, and pigs oinking—but each child was in a different state of disarray. Plaits stood at all angles on girls' heads, matted mucus stuck to mouths and eyes, and a pained expression was on everyone's face. The smell from the baby was a tell-tale sign of the last time someone changed his diaper.

But Daddy was wide awake. He marched us out to the barn. "Git in line," he said. We shuffled into chronological order with rigid shoulders and looked straight ahead, resembling tiny cadets with our backs planted against the front of the barn. "Yo' mama gone; say she ain't coming back." *Yippee*, I thought.

"She staying with Aunt Mallie in that little shotgun house down on the old Cain place. Any y'all who wanta stay with your Mama is welcome to go. Raise ya' hand if you thinkin' 'bout going." He ignored my index finger in the air. "Course that old place where she staying ain't nowhere to be raising chillun."

I cut my eyes over at Rachel and kept my hand up.

"Wait. Don't raise your hands yet." Daddy stood before us like he was still a World War II soldier. He stretched himself and towered over six children ages eight to a few months.

"Y'all know Mama just canned a buncha peaches last week? And ya' know how good her canned peaches are, don't ya?"

With visions of sweet peaches dancing before our eyes, we said in unison, "Yes, sir."

Mama knew how to put away for a rainy day, canning green beans, butter beans, beets, corn, tomatoes, apples, fig, and pear preserves. But the canned peaches were the biggest prize. They winked from a clear Mason jar like giant yellow suns split in half with fuzzy brown pits scooped out the middle. She would have won the Alabama Peach Canners Contest if there had been such a thing.

We could have used some of them with so many stomachs growling right then. Yet, Daddy strolled along, stopping long enough to stare at each of us. "Well, whoever go with your mama ain't gonna get none of them peaches. Y'all thas' gonna stay with me can eat many as you want." I wanted to punch him in the stomach for playing us like that.

"Now, who's going wit' your mama?" My hand shot up like a gun with a hair trigger. Rachel and Sonny slid their index fingers up.

"I wanta stay with you, Daddy," Brother and Bunny said.

"Sonny, you ain't going nowhere. You need to learn how to work the farm." Daddy walked close to me, smelling like yesterday's sweat. "Gone in the house. You'll be leaving tomorrow if you don't come to your senses by then. I'll take you over to Aunt Mallie's place."

I was so lightheaded I could hardly catch my breath. Rachel and I hustled into the house and pulled open the lopsided dresser drawer. We were wearing identical dresses Mama made from flour sacks. Hers was white with tiny blue flowers; mine had green ones, and we were barefoot. She and I stuffed a pair of clean panties and socks, a cotton underskirt, one dress, and our patent leather Sunday shoes in a paper sack. We giggled and slid our bag on the dresser with a cracked mirror and peeling top. Tomorrow, we would be long gone.

The smell of bacon and homemade biscuits and Mama's voice coming from the kitchen snatched me awake the following day. I leaped out of bed and ran full force into her, eye level with her big belly. She stood next to the stove with her silky black hair pulled back in a ponytail, looking young and prettier than I remembered. She wore new flip-flops, the color of egg yolks, and a shift that resembled a pink flower garden. The smell of fried food was a breath of heaven in the kitchen. Mama gazed at me and patted my head like I was a puppy.

I tugged at her new dress. "Mama, Mama! Can we leave now?" Daddy stood close to her, wearing a smug smile. He had combed his hair back, making his prominent widow's peak look like the sharp point of an arrow. His khaki shirt was starched and tucked in his pants. I smelled Brut, and it wasn't Sunday.

I studied Daddy's work boots laced up around the bottom of his khaki trousers. A gleam from the black belt with the silver buckle caught my eye. He held a vase, a delicate piece of glass that sparkled like stars. It encased a single rose as red as blood. He set it on the mantel, and Mama couldn't stop smiling. How Mama gazed at that fake rose told me everything I needed to know. I didn't appreciate how they were smiling at each other.

A cold glance that was supposed to be a smile flitted across Daddy's face. "Good news, Babe! Mama thinks it's best if our family stay together." I stared up at him, incredulous. (What Mama thought didn't matter to Daddy then, nor did it ever matter all the days of her life.) He goosed me with the butt of his fist and said, "Now, run tell Rachel y'all can unpack your things." He bent down so close I felt his warm, sticky breath on my face. The pupils at the center of his eyes were black and beady; they reminded me of a crow. He laughed and pinched my cheek—too hard. I had never seen Daddy hold Mama before, but there he was, standing behind her with his arms wrapped around her waist and her leaning back against him, grinning like a schoolgirl. He shushed me along. "Gone, now. Unpack your little things."

My feet refused to move. Rachel ran away or hid from danger when we were children, whereas I stood as stubborn as an oak tree. I defiantly watched, refusing to look away from the Sunday

Thunder and Lightning

school teacher, deacon, and church musician who beat his wife. I needed to tattoo his behavior on my brain, a trigger to haul ass when confronted with eyes like his.

    I stared at Mama, swooning over a fake rose like she hadn't been beaten nearly to death a few days earlier. Back then, I wanted to headbutt her in the stomach hard as I could for letting Daddy trick her into coming back home, spoiling what could have been the happiest day of my life. I didn't know it then, but now, I realize she probably returned because she was pregnant.

CHAPTER 5
Sex, Life, and Death on the Farm

A low, mournful whimper drew me behind the chicken house more than a year after Mama returned. I was five. I skipped through the backyard hunting for kindling wood to start a fire around the washpot, a three-legged potbellied thing so sooty you couldn't tell if it was iron or copper. "We need to wash the white clothes today," Mama told me. It was barely seven o'clock, but the sun peeked over the hill, looking like a sizzling egg yolk. I tiptoed around the chicken house in search of the whimper. Shag, our brown and white collie, was hopelessly entangled with a scruffy stray from another farm. He had clawed a trench in the ground, pulling his female partner backward. With their butts stuck together, she dug her heels in and snatched him in the opposite direction. They reminded me of kids playing tug-of-war. I was happy the female was winning. With each yank, Shag yelped in pain.

I raced into the house. "Mama, there's a pink thing like a rope stuck between Shag and another dog. He keeps crying when the other dog pulls the pink thing." Mama pushed a skillet across the stove, turned off the burner, and grabbed the broom. "Stay in this house, and don't you look out that window or come outdoors 'til I tell you to."

I couldn't wait to get inside and away from whatever those dogs were doing. The way they scratched and pulled frightened and fascinated me, but as a curious child, I hopped on the lopsided bed mattress, sneaked to the window, and peeked through the curtains. I wanted to see why Mama needed the broom.

She rapidly struck the dogs until straw was flying. "You, *get* away from here." The dogs created a dust storm trying to escape the thrashing, but no amount of whaling set them free. They collapsed in the ashes around the washpot and panted like heavyweight boxers who had knocked each other out. Mama huffed up the little porch steps, wiped the sweat from her forehead, and walked through the back door. I was sitting on the bed like I hadn't seen a thing. "Mildred, you can start a fire a little later."

A twinge of excitement zipped through my body. I was delighted the scruffy mutt from another farm had Shag in a fix, tangled up in his own balls. She was the first female I had seen put the screws on a male. Minutes later, I saw her strutting away with her tongue hanging out the side of her mouth, a pleased look on her face. Shag skulked under the house and licked himself.

I now know that sex on the farm was as natural as breathing—the only way to thrive. I was intrigued by the bull, pushing an entire herd of heifers around the pasture one at a time in the spring. I

Sex, Life, and Death on the Farm

wondered if he had favorites or chose the one closest to him. Each winter, there were new calves. I was not fond of the rooster that sneaked up behind an unsuspecting hen and pinned her with his wings, sending her ruffled and screaming across the yard. Yet, baby chicks popped out of eggs regularly. The boar hog seemed the laziest male on the farm. He sloshed slowly through slop and crept up a sow's back, humping slowly. Months later, sprawled on her side, several piglets squealed and pulled at her nipples. Even Mama and Daddy contributed to the labor force with a new baby almost every year.

Sometimes, as a teenager, I felt a pulsation in the pit of my stomach, seeing a bull mount a heifer in an open field in the middle of the day, totally uninhibited. Males on the farm took what they wanted regardless of the sharp snap of a swishing tail or squealing from females, powerless to fight back, including Mama. In all my years on the farm, I saw only one female initiate intimacy.

I was strolling along the red dirt road, kicking rocks and eating cherries I had picked, going to put a letter in the mailbox for Mama. I was seven. Maude, our chestnut brown horse with a white face, pranced back and forth along the fence line beside Old Man Gray's mule, an ugly gray thing. He matched her step for step, separated only by strands of barbwire. The animals locked necks, nickered lips, and gazed at one another like lovers. Maude stepped back, reared into the air, and sang out a loud whinny. She glided over the fence into Old Man Gray's pasture like her front hoofs had wings. Maude frantically swished and lifted her tail, spread her legs, and a geyser of liquid splattered the ground.

Mildred J Mills

My mouth dropped open when a stiff black thing bigger and longer than Daddy's arm snaked out of the mule and swung between its legs. He trotted up behind Maude, licked her fanny, reared up on his hind legs, and looked tall as a pecan tree when he clamped to the horse and started humping. Its rear hoofs sounded like thunderclaps as he rocked and thrust while Maude braced herself and stared straight ahead.

Our neighbor, Old Man Gray, stormed down the dirt road between two barbwire fences yelling and waving a hammer. He resembled a bony white ghost in overalls and a straw hat. "*Where the hell is Abraham?*"

Daddy raced toward the man with his fists clenched, and I hopped into the ditch with my head swinging like a pendulum, watching the two men. "Keep your God-damn horse outta my pasture," Mr. Gray hollered. He swung his hammer, and Daddy ducked and punched him with his fist. I ran home.

"*Mama, Mama.* Daddy and Mr. Gray are fighting. Maude jumped the fence, and the mule got on her back. He kept pushing her. Now, that old white man is mad at Daddy." I talked so fast I could hardly catch my breath. "How come that mule was pushing Maude?"

Mama had been snapping string beans. "Slow down, child." She listened intently, briefly studied my face, and sat back on her chair. Her voice was as calm as still waters. "That mule was just doin' what comes naturally." I stood near her chair, expecting more, but she grabbed a handful of green beans. "Take that letter to the mailbox like I told you." I looked down at the envelope in my hand like it was a sixth finger I had never seen. I was a wide-eyed, naïve child, but the farm animals taught me sex education. I did not know

Sex, Life, and Death on the Farm

then that I witnessed an ecosystem, watching in awe as planting seeds, whether in the ground or animals, resulted in birth, and eventually, every birth ended in death.

In March 1958, Mama gave birth to Carolyn— her eighth child. She weighed more than eight pounds and was Mama's heaviest baby. I stood beside Mama's bed as she introduced the little girl, a child with hair black as coal and the prettiest one I had ever seen.

A few weeks after Carolyn's birth, Mama said, "You're almost seven now, old enough to help me out at night." I had changed diapers and fed babies during the day, but Carolyn was the first child Mama woke me up to care for. I sat on a small rocking chair next to the potbelly stove, changed her diaper, and fed her a bottle that night. I stared at her cream-colored skin and curly hair, cuddling the baby, who studied me with big, brown eyes shaped like Bambi's. I was in love with Carolyn.

On a Friday in late October, when the baby was seven and a half months old, Mama's sister, Honey, came to help Daddy pull feed corn from the field. Fifteen years older than Mama, Aunt Honey was a dark-skinned, plump woman who frowned so much she had twisted her mouth into a chronic O. My aunt looked at us children how a person would stare at a mangy dog she wanted to kick. I shudder each time I think about how that stubby old woman took a broom and muscled a pile of dirt toward her nieces and nephews. "Get your little asses outta my way." Aunt Honey looked like a fat Black witch with dust swirling around her. She shoved her round glasses up the bridge of her nose, bent close to my face, and said we smelled like piss ants. I had never heard of a piss ant, but you weren't supposed to smell like one from the look on her face. I tried making myself scarce when Aunt Honey came around. Even at my age, I envisioned pushing her down the icy back porch steps in the wintertime.

That Friday, Aunt Honey came inside the house to see Carolyn before going to the field. She wore black old folks' shoes, an oversized wool coat, and a wool hat to ward off the October chill. "Shug," she used Mama's pet name, "this child looks puny, and she's hot."

I have but to close my eyes to feel the warmth of my little sister's body against mine or see her plump legs crossed at the ankle as she sucked greedily from a bottle. But I could never bring back the details of her illness and death. Before I left home at eighteen, I asked Mama to tell me what had happened to Carolyn. A faraway look crossed her face. Mama locked her arms across her bosom and rocked slowly back and forth on the armchair like she held a baby as she relived the agony of losing a child. I listened quietly and questioned a God who would allow such a tragedy.

Mama lamented how even after hours of trying home remedies like rubbing the baby with liniment and Vicks salve, Carolyn's temperature continued to rise, and her flesh felt like it was on fire. "Mildred, I ain't never felt so helpless. Then, Abraham said we better get Carolyn to the hospital."

Mama stopped rocking, closed her eyes, and bit down on a scream so long that she began to tremble, and her stifling wails shook me to my core. She told how she clung to the baby and tried to explain how sick she was when the doctor met them at the hospital. She felt diminished when he hurriedly said, "We losing time talking. Let's get her admitted." Mama repeatedly rubbed the

Sex, Life, and Death on the Farm

loose flesh on her arms and described the doctor lowering Carolyn into an ice-filled incubator and telling them, "It's now a waiting game." Mama and Daddy provided a phone number in case of an emergency and left the hospital for a quick bite with friends who lived nearby.

Shortly after the four friends sat down to dinner, laughing and catching up on old times, the doctor called and urged Mama and Daddy to return to the hospital immediately. Mama hung her head like a woman who'd received a death sentence. "Lawd, Jesus, Mildred, Carolyn was dead. My baby died while we was sitting at Harold and Matilda's house eating dinner."

Tears lapped beneath Mama's chin, leaked onto her dress, and left tracks down her bosom. Mama wept openly, recounting the autopsy report: pneumonia had caused the baby's death. Mama chronicled the visit to the funeral home and a casket too small for the child. They had asked their friend—the undertaker—to bury Carolyn on credit after Daddy could not earn enough in one week to pay in full. I sat stoically across the table, trying to be strong for Mama while she moved her hands like she was dressing her little girl in the new pink dress, white patent leather shoes, and white socks she described. She was grief-stricken, unable to remember if she had tied a bow on her dead child's hair. Mama suddenly stopped talking, stared blank-eyed at me, and cackled loudly. I worried that she had cracked up.

"I'm sure you don't remember this, but your Daddy paid the casket off in about a month, and I'm glad he did, 'cause three weeks later, the undertaker died. When he died, you asked me, 'Had y'all paid that undertaker for Carolyn's funeral?'

That tickled me that someone your age would think of such a thing." I did not remember those details but was glad Mama found a way to lighten the moment while I shed internal tears, remembering a baby whose lifeless face I still saw clearly. But I hardly had time to mourn my sister before there were other babies to care for who could also break my heart. After Carolyn, I could not pull up a single face of another sibling I diapered and fed at night. They had all blended, becoming just another chore I performed.

At the funeral, I stood beside Mama, anxious to touch my baby sister again. Yet, I couldn't reach her. I could barely see into the casket. Her face was darker than I remembered. I stood on tiptoes and could barely see the tips of her patent leather shoes, frills on the hem of her dress, and part of the ruffles on her socks. I glanced at Daddy, hoping he would lift me to see her better, but he sat rigidly on a folding chair and held onto Mama. Her voice sounded pitiful—like a lonely wail from a faraway freight train. She clung to twenty-three-month-old Becky—suddenly the baby again—like she could replace the dead child. I was afraid to walk closer to the casket, fearing falling into the gaping mouth that waited to swallow my sister's body.

My five siblings and I stood, shivering and crying, beneath a large oak tree with gray, leafless limbs that reached across the graveyard like fingers in a haunted house. It was cold, a November day, when the wind sang a mournful tune that caused us to cling to each other. I felt a sense of loss but an even stronger sense of strength as my family was bound together in grief, seemingly unbreakable. That was the first time I thought Daddy looked small, human, like a defeated man who realized he needed his family as much as we needed him.

After Carolyn's burial, I returned to my second-grade classroom. My teacher, Mrs. Townsend, said, "Mildred, take your seat at the front of the class." One by one, my seven-year-old friends marched in front of me and read handmade sympathy cards. I put on a brave face while twenty-eight children read words of comfort from greeting cards marked with Crayola crayons and shaky letters crafted from the hands, minds, and hearts of second graders.

Daddy stored the greetings inside the piano bench. I still cherish my classmates' warbly words scrawled across construction paper. They're among the most treasured possessions in my home more than sixty years later. Now and then, I pull them out and read each one. I can see their faces clearly and recognize that many of the authors are deceased. Their words remind me of when we were all young, alive—babies. Yet, I had already felt death's sting.

CHAPTER 6
Body Changes

Days before I hoped to leave home, I saw Mama—*really* saw her—for the first time. I was eighteen, and she was forty-three, sitting on the front porch swing. Tears pooled in her eyes as she rocked her eleven-month-old teething son to sleep and remembered the twelfth anniversary of her mother's death. "Mildred, I don't even have a picture of my mama. *All* I had of my mama was *one* picture, and somebody throwed it away. I guess that's what y'all will do wit' me when I'm gone." Years on the farm had flown by, denying Mama and me the opportunity to see anything but endless days of hard work that buried us.

I stared into Mama's eyes, brown like mine but slightly larger, thinking how I'd never thought about her agony, only about getting off that farm. "Mama, I would never toss you away like trash." But, with tears sliding down her cheeks, I felt her pain, thinking I may be days from leaving her and wondering how that would feel. Cows grazed in the field nearby; the distant sound of a single car passed along the road, and butterflies lit on the vines, climbing up the side of the front porch. I followed her inside when she nestled the sleeping child against her bosom and laid him across the end of her bed.

I stood in the dining room and took in her smells—sweat and cooking odors damp like fog—with the hunger of a savage. I listened to her voice, warm and soft—a bluebird in song, and cherished our time together. Her bare feet on the wooden planks sounded like shoe leather as she walked into the room and sat.

Gazing across the table that day, for the first time, I realized that one could live with a person for years and never see them. While Mama and I shared the same first and middle names and had existed in the same space since I was born, we were as unfamiliar as two strangers engaged in a first dance. We had spent a handful of days apart all of my life. Yet, we hadn't shared an intimate mother-daughter conversation, not even when I began menstruating.

The day I got my period, a few days after my sixteenth birthday, was the first time I baked a chicken. It was the spring of 1967. I had bent over to slide the dish into the Hotpoint. Mrs. Eloise Jones, the home economics teacher, had challenged my class of fifteen girls to prepare a recipe she called oven-baked chicken and rice. I can still hear Mama's laugh, soft like piano keys, when I mimicked Mrs. Jones's high-pitched voice. "Y'all eat too much fried chicken." The entire class poo-pooed the dish, one unfamiliar to most of us. I was probably eight when Mama taught me how to fry chicken, our every Sunday meal. The only time I had it prepared any other way was once a year when she whipped it up with dumplings in winter.

On that spring day, Mrs. Jones, a high-yellow woman with green eyes, stood in front of the classroom, held a ruler with her

Body Changes

slim fingers, and rapped it against the gas stove. Her beige dress hugged her slender body. She was an older woman in her 40s, but boys noticed when she strutted down the hall with high heel shoes and her hips swinging. Her voice, a ripple that resembled a musical scale, rang around the room. "Let's have a contest. At the end of the year, I'll have something special for the girl who makes the best chicken and rice dish and sews the prettiest apron." I could hardly wait to get home and share the news with Mama.

I shoved my way off the school bus and cast my eyes toward the figure, always standing on the front porch when the bus arrived. She stood like a watchtower—hands clasped protectively beneath her belly. A trail of red dust chased me as I elbowed my way ahead of the pack, first to reach Mama, who was waiting to hear every detail of our day. I loved the twinkle in her eyes as she listened to our daily broadcasts, lapping it up like a hungry hostage on a deserted island.

I never considered the effect being home with four or five small children every day for years without even the company of a telephone or television had on Mama. If I had been a considerate daughter, I might have asked what went through her mind standing at the front door, peering up the road as her eight children marched down the school bus steps like legs on a centipede. Did she count each head to ensure everyone was there, or thank God we were safe another day? As a Black mother in the 1950s and 1960s in the Jim Crow South, I thought Mama couldn't rest until she saw us safely home.

The day my menstrual cycle started, I raced the quarter mile from the bus stop to the front porch with arms and legs pumping, out of breath when I reached her. "Mama, there's a cooking contest, and I need to practice." I described the ingredients: chicken breasts, rice, one onion, butter, salt, and pepper.

"Gone in the kitchen. You can cook supper today. We got all them ingredients." I am still amazed at how patiently she listened as we tugged and vied for her attention.

When I stood in the kitchen preparing that meal, I remembered first cooking for the family when I was six or seven. I had stood on a small wooden bench and ran back and forth from Mama's bed to the kitchen, learning culinary skills while she rested after she'd given birth. I can still hear her instructions ringing in my ear: "Run, grab a boiler; sprinkle in a pinch of salt, not too much pepper. Turn on the stove and watch the pot for twenty minutes."

Back then, I enjoyed dashing between the kitchen and Mama's bedroom, creating, but as I grew older and it became my job to cook breakfast for the family while everyone else slept, I resented it. Yet, from those early lessons at Mama's bedside, I learned the magic that would enable me to craft unique dishes as an adult.

But at sixteen, I laid four bone-in chicken breasts on a Pyrex dish like neat logs on a fire. A gentle breeze rustled two frilly curtains through the open window and stirred heat around the kitchen. I salted and peppered the chicken bone side down. I heard Mama's voice from the living room, gentle as a wind chime, engaging in school children's chatter that grew from a quiet conversation to a crescendo of excitement while each shared a story, competing for her attention. Alone in the kitchen, I created.

I spread a cup of white rice on the bottom of the glass, poured just enough water to cover the skin, and arranged onion slices atop

Body Changes

the chicken. I sifted two tablespoons of flour over the breasts and topped them with pats of butter, like yellow dollops of sunshine. I pranced into the living room with the dish in the palm of my hand and slid it past the nostrils of my siblings, who oohed and ahhed and rubbed their empty bellies. Mama studied the layers, top to bottom, searching for improvements. "That looks real pretty, Mildred. Gone and put it in the stove."

I marched back to the kitchen, full of pride. I bent over, slid the dish into the oven, and 450 degrees of heat blanketed my face. I jerked back and felt a slow trickle sliding down my inner thigh. A warm, wet sensation lingered in the seat of my panties. I slipped out the back door, ran to the outhouse, and found blood flowing from where it never had before. I grabbed newspaper (our substitute for toilet tissue) from the floor, wadded it up, stuffed it between my legs, and eased into my bedroom, afraid and unsure of what to do next.

Mama slipped quietly into the room, where I stood wide-eyed in the middle of the floor. "I thought you was cooking dinner, Mildred." Her voice was tender, and her eyes soft. Yet, at age sixteen, I quivered like a trapped rabbit, afraid to tell her I got my period. I thought she would tell Daddy I was bleeding, and he would beat me. For what? I don't know.

My legs felt rubbery, so I slumped onto the bed. I blurted out, "Mama, I started my period today." She sat beside me on the lumpy mattress, and the springs gave a shrill scream.

Mama studied my face. I was too afraid to meet her gaze. We both stared through the bars at the foot of the small bed across the room. "How you feeling, Mildred? I thought it was about that time."

I stiffened and couldn't think of a single word to say. I wanted to scream. "*What do you mean*, you thought it was about time? Why didn't you discuss intimate details like what body changes a girl should expect, moving from childhood into adolescence?" But I said none of those things. The silence about sex education in our home was deafening. "You better keep your dress tail down" was my only warning. I knew about menstruation because of whispers among my classmates. Mama slid off the bed and buzzed over to the dresser, a queen bee at work. I watched through its cracked mirror, her head bobbing side-to-side as she fished rags from a wobbly drawer.

"Come on. Let's get you some clean cloth for your panties." Mama tore old tee shirts and other soft material into neat strips and handed them to me like silk garments for my wedding trousseau. I wanted to have a conversation with Mama. I wanted her to see me and listen when I expressed fear about what a menstrual cycle meant. I wanted to ask how a rag stuck between my legs would affect my ability to run track, play flag football, or softball. But I was afraid to express those wants because of the time when I was thirteen and wandered into the dining room where Mama was ironing a Sunday dress. I had strolled up beside her, surprised that we stood eye-to-eye at five-foot-three, although I later grew to five-foot-six. "Oh, Mama! I'm as tall as you are now." The words were barely out of my mouth when a sound like a clanging cymbal rang in my head, stunning me after she slapped my face. My eyes watered, and my mouth fell open, but I refused to cry.

Mama's face was a dark mask, spewing venom. "*Don't you nev*er bristle up in my face again." That memory held in my mind and

Body Changes

made me afraid to tell her how ashamed I was to pin a rag between my legs because I had no idea how she would react.

The next day, I sneaked into the girl's bathroom at school and prayed it was empty. I stuffed wads of toilet tissue around the waistband of my skirt and in the back of my panties to stash at home and use as sanitary napkins. I didn't embrace the changes to my body after I got my period. I crossed my arms and shielded my breasts that sprouted out of my chest like puffy biscuits with too much baking powder. I refused to make eye contact with men and schoolboys who ogled me, and I could never prevent the fishy odor during my cycle.

Heavenly aromas floated from the kitchen on the first day of my first period. I pulled the piping hot chicken dish from the oven, bubbly and ready to eat. When I came home at the end of that spring with a blue ribbon and news that I had won a trip to Los Angeles, Mama came just short of giving me what I did not, at the time, realize I longed for—a smothering hug and genuine closeness from my mother. Looking back, I see how conflicted I sometimes was about Mama's feelings toward me. While she encouraged me and was proud of my accomplishments, she gave off a "You are not my equal" vibe, stating, "If you play with a puppy, he will lick your mouth" or "Children are to be seen, not heard." And then there was the "There can only be one woman in a house" comment that baffled me then, but today, it makes me wonder if she felt threatened or minimized, watching her girl become a woman.

CHAPTER 7
A Stubborn Streak

As a child, I didn't have the words or thought processes to realize how effectively and efficiently Mama and Daddy had tapped into every resource to run a successful farm. I now know that as much as I craved and did not receive close affection, my parents' uncanny ability to assess talent, piling more work on me than any child should endure, was their most incredible gift.

At age six, I began my first "official" job while standing on the little porch watching Daddy cut two wooden blocks with a handsaw. I stood quietly with my hands clasped before me, studying the piles of sawdust that looked like oatmeal forming on either side of the wood. Daddy glanced up, and I waved. "What you doing, Daddy?"

His brilliant smile radiated with pride. Daddy's gonna build you a chair to see out the windshield, Babe." He opened the passenger door to his Chevy, placed the two blocks side by side across the bench seat, and slapped a plank on top. He patted the board, and his face filled with pride. "Climb on up here." My bare feet pounded against the concrete steps as I raced from the porch to the car and hopped on the bench, surveying a new world. A grin as wide as the arms of God spread across my face. Daddy handed me a yellow No. 2 pencil, sharpened with his pocketknife, and a spiral-bound notebook with a red cover.

"It's official! You're my new bookkeeper and partner. You'll help me keep track of milk route customers, how much they pay, and what they owe." I spun around and studied the inventory: collard greens, string beans, tomatoes, and other fresh vegetables. The biggest prizes—buttermilk, sweet milk, brown eggs, and butter—spread out on the back seat, all grown on our farm.

I sat on my wooden perch, gazing at places and things foreign to me within a few miles of home, outside my boundaries of the church, school, home, and the occasional visit to an aunt. Daddy drove from one house to another along rutted country roads and noted the customers' names, items purchased, and amounts collected. I placed a plus sign next to clients who paid and a minus sign if they bought on credit. I was intrigued by the unpainted shanties with half-clothed children standing in open doorways, skinny dogs snarling and racing to the end of their chains, and lone chickens pecking at grassless yards as we drove onto dirt driveways.

Most customers were ladies who had lost husbands to other women, divorce, death, or were never married. "These people can't afford groceries at Dozier's (the general store). I charge a little less, and they get fresh milk and better food for their chillun," Daddy said. I pretended not to see him stuff every coin and crinkled dollar in his pocket and dared not ask for a single penny to buy a sucker or a banana kiss. But I saw his resourcefulness and how he treated

A Stubborn Streak

every customer with a kind word and charismatic smile, skills I found helpful when I entered the workplace.

One summer, three years after we started the milk route, Daddy said, "Mama ain't no good at picking cotton. For what she doin', she might as well stay home with the chillun." That morning at the breakfast table, steam swirled from grits and gravy, and the sound of spoons scraped plates. I replaced Mama as the pro bono bookkeeper. She lowered her head and bounced the baby on her knee. I was eight.

By age ten, Daddy had expanded the cotton operation from twenty to forty acres, bought a shiny red Farmall tractor that replaced the horse and plow, and regularly hired cotton pickers. Before daybreak each morning, the sound of Daddy shifting gears in the International Harvester truck, heading up the road to pick up hired hands, correlated with me scraping pots and pans and cooking homemade breakfast for my large family.

Daddy let down the tailgate at the edge of the field, and fifteen or twenty people piled out wearing head rags, overalls, and dusty work shoes. There was joy in faces, all Black and all relatives, and laughter in the voices of people making money by the pound. Years later, a first cousin told me, "Those were the happiest days of my life. I had never picked cotton for a Black man. Yet, Uncle Abraham hired us and paid more." At noon, field hands gathered underneath the cool shade of a pecan tree for bologna sandwiches and Kool-Aid, a bonus from Mama.

"Alright, time to weigh up," Daddy yelled every few hours. Workers rushed to where Mama waited under the shade tree with a bucket of water and a dipper, from which everyone took a long cool swig. All eyes focused on the cotton scale, dangling from a hook attached to a tree, and waited for Daddy to say how much they'd picked. I tallied with my ledger and pencil. Cotton pickers gazed suspiciously over my shoulders, ensuring I recorded weights correctly. "Girl, don't you cheat me," an old woman with snuff tucked in her bottom lip said.

Daddy would drive back and forth to the gin, selling bales of cotton, and I calculated and called out numbers. I attribute those early lessons to my computer acumen and ability to reason and manipulate numbers. Every Friday, he paid cash to his workers, who talked about how they would spend their money. His children never asked for or received payment.

Daddy didn't hire helpers at the beginning of the cotton-picking season because he could not afford to do so. Early one morning, when I was twelve, and there were no hired hands, he hustled through the backyard, past the hog pen, and high-stepped over the barbwire fence like a majorette leading a marching band. Six siblings and I had trudged behind him, oldest to youngest, drowsy as house flies doused with Raid. Daddy spread our cotton sacks on the ground like narrow white sheets with a noose underneath a pecan tree at the edge of the field. The August sun was barely up, but the humidity stuck like flypaper. He smiled. "Y'all sit down a minute." We sneaked sideways glances at each other because Daddy didn't offer anyone a seat first thing in the morning.

Daddy ran his hand in his front pocket and whipped out a five-dollar bill. He held it above our heads and said, "Who wants to make five dollars today?" Today, when I think of that moment, I'm

A Stubborn Streak

reminded of the show *Who Wants to Be a Millionaire?* Suddenly, everybody was awake, sitting in a circle like a group of wide-eyed schoolchildren with straight backs and hands in the air. Daddy spoke low like he was enticing a lover. "Well, we gonna have a contest today. Whoever picks the most cotton gets these five dollars." He slid the money back into his pocket. "Babe, we'll announce the winner at supper tonight. Y'all ready?" We leaped from the ground, hung sacks around our necks, spread across cotton rows, and picked like machines, determined to win that money.

At five o'clock, Daddy hollered, "Let's weigh up." I tallied the numbers and tucked the tablet away until dinnertime. Daddy sat at the head of the table with Mama at his right side, each child sitting in age order, and he laid the five-dollar bill beside his plate. "Babe, you got the numbers?"

I cleared my throat and whipped out the ledger. "Yes, sir."

"Alright, how'd we do?"

All eyes were on me, and I could hardly contain my joy. "I picked 225 pounds; Sonny picked 215," and I called numbers high to low, accounting for everyone.

With a devilish grin, Daddy looked at each of us. "*Great day.* That's a *whole lotta* cotton." I ogled that money, thrilled to have it in my hands soon to share with Mama and my siblings. Daddy rocked back on his chair. "Hey. You forgot somebody." A blank look crossed every face; confusion replaced hope. I, *not anyone else*, picked the most cotton.

"What about Daddy? How much did he pick?" he whispered.

An icepick stab in the gut wouldn't have hurt as much. I lowered my eyes and wanted to rip that tablet to bits. Instead, I said, "You picked 230 pounds." The five-dollar bill disappeared back into his pocket. Daddy cleared his throat and glared at each of us. "Alright, starting tomorrow, what you picked today is your daily quota. Come up short? You get a beating at the end of the day. Now, let's eat supper."

I don't remember what was for supper, nor do I remember if I ate it. But I will never forget the sick feeling in the pit of my gut knowing Daddy didn't make empty threats. Like foolish flies, his trusting children had wandered into another of his tricky traps. I dreaded the days when Daddy ushered me into his bedroom and pulled the strap from behind the door. "You didn't git your 225 pounds today," he'd say before beating me. I prayed as earnestly as a child could and asked God to cleanse me of the harsh feelings I harbored against my father.

I was foolish enough to be standing idly in the backyard when Daddy conjured up another bright idea to get more work out of me. I was fifteen. Daddy dashed across the yard in his laced-up brogan shoes and khaki pants with a gleam in his eyes, pulled a greasy rag from his back pocket, and wiped the sweat from his face. "Babe, it's high time you learned how to drive my truck."

I don't think so, I thought.

Daddy patted the old rust bucket and grinned as if it were his dream truck—a brand-new Fleetside Chevy pickup. "Bunny been driving my truck more'n three years now. She can handle my tractor almost good as Brother." I couldn't imagine why this would matter to me.

He stuffed the dirty rag back in his pocket and said, "Get in that truck and back it under this barn."

A Stubborn Streak

A sound like swarming bees hummed in my ears. I had never driven anything. *He wants to see me fail*, I thought. I opened the truck door, stepped on the running board, and slowly pulled myself under the steering wheel, like creeping under a hangman's noose.

With the driver-side door open, I slid onto the bench seat, and a sharp coil speared my backside. I held the wheel with shaky hands and peered over the dashboard, looking for how to move the truck, parked at an awkward sideways angle, even one inch. In front of the vehicle was the chicken house, and directly behind it were three broad beams supporting the barn.

"Put your left foot on the clutch and push it to the floor hard. Step on the brake with your right foot." The way Daddy said this made me want to sing the hokey-pokey song, but I found nothing funny about trying to distinguish the brakes from a clutch. I tried to coordinate my legs and feet on the pedals. My right foot slipped through a hole in the floorboard, and blood trickled down my leg. I reached for the pain in my bare foot and hit my chin on the steering wheel.

I glanced to the side and saw Daddy's fists jammed into his waist. "Get back in that seat, do what I told you, gal, and stop bleeding on my truck." I finally got my hands and feet on all the right parts.

"Push that gear stick in reverse," or maybe he said first. Glancing at the faint indentations on the gear stick, I couldn't determine first from reverse. By some miracle, I guessed right.

"Now, crank it up." The truck whined, sputtered, and coughed before it finally fired up. "Push the gas, soft, with your right foot and ease off the clutch, slow-like." I spun my neck around, hoping the support beams had magically disappeared. They hadn't.

I jerked my foot off the clutch and jammed the gas pedal, and the truck fishtailed and lurched backward, spinning gravel all over Daddy. The International Harvester moved fast, headed straight toward the barn. Daddy lunged into the open driver-side door and shoved me across the seat. He grabbed the steering wheel and slammed on the brakes before I could crash the barn to the ground. "Get your crazy ass outta my truck, and don't you never set foot in it again. If you'd a tore up my truck, I woulda skint you alive."

I slid out the passenger door quicker than he had jumped through the driver's side, laughter in my belly waiting to break loose. I felt like Br'er Rabbit when the fox slung him over the bridge into the briar patch.

Daddy and I locked eyes through the passenger window like two roosters in a cockfight. A voice inside my head told him off and spewed words I would never say aloud: What the hell do you think I am, a machine? None of your sons washes dishes, cooks meals, irons, or makes beds. You expect me to do all those things *and* drive your truck and tractor? Hell, I'm already cooking breakfast for this whole family every morning, and every night, I'm rocking and changing your babies' diapers. And, I'm up nights on end every April preparing your income taxes. I'm *not* gonna drive your damn farm equipment. Now, take that, Daddy!

When I left the farm in 1969, the only thing I knew how to drive was a nail with a hammer.

Before I left home at age eighteen, I asked Mama why she never spoke up while Daddy played mind games and beat her children.

A Stubborn Streak

I told her that even a chicken fiercely protected her babies. "Well, I thought he was kinda rough sometimes, but what could I do? After all, y'all was his chillun. You'll understand better when you have your own family." Looking back, neither Mama's answer nor her inaction surprised me. As a young girl, I internalized harsh thoughts about Mama. I viewed her as a weak woman—someone I needed to help—trying to survive the hell she lived in but unwilling to make the difficult choice to leave, which meant she'd have to figure life out for herself. Even now, I can't imagine Mama would've intentionally injured one of her children. Yet, part of me believes she figured if Daddy was beating us, he wasn't hitting her.

Today, I cringe thinking that the pain endured for days when Daddy struck me, but the mind games and cruelties were lessons I studied like a chess player pondering her next move. The nickel trick in the cotton field was like a bee sting that surprised me, a trusting preschooler. The five-dollar gimmick, one I, as a preteen, should have seen coming, blunted the pain of future cruelties from strangers, predators, and men who claimed to love me. But when I sat in the International Harvester, a teenager with years of studying Daddy, I dared to try a trick of my own, by refusing to drive that vehicle.

At a very young age, I had studied my parents enough to know that, even though they both had qualities I admired, I didn't want a husband like Daddy or to become a wife like Mama. When I stood on the little porch and saw Daddy drenched in sweat, whistling or singing while working tirelessly to support his family, I imagined that man as a desirable mate. But when I watched through the rungs of a ladder-back chair as Daddy kicked Mama repeatedly while she crouched on the living room floor, cradling her belly like an eagle protects its nest, I had no words for the misery wished on him. I decided then I would not allow men to hit my children, and I never have.

But the woman who sat silently at the dining room table and looked the other way while Daddy whaled on her children while they screamed for mercy was no protector. Unlike the soft-voiced, patient mother who waited alone every day on the front porch, counting heads until each child was safely home from the school bus, she was a coward, not someone I wanted to mimic. I now know that as a child and even as an adult, I would love my parents whether they behaved in ways deserving of that love or not. My deep affection for my parents far outweighed their frailties then, and it still does. I also realize I wanted to please them, and I worked hard to do so.

CHAPTER 8
Up, Up, and Away

The summer after I turned sixteen, my hard work paid off. I learned I had won a trip to Los Angeles, California, with the Future Homemakers of America (FHA), the special prize offered by the home economics teacher for baking the best chicken dish and sewing the most creative apron. Mama was excited to pack my new clothes in a blue Samsonite suitcase from Sears Roebuck, including a hat. "I seen in magazines where ladies wear hats on planes," she told me. She plopped this navy-blue thing that looked like a rooftop turbine ventilator on my head and stood back, smiling like I was Jackie Kennedy. "Mildred, you sho' look pretty in that hat." Mama was a hat person, believing a lady half-dressed without her crown. I loathe church hats, so I deliberately left that one in California.

Daddy drove Mrs. Eloise Jones and me to Atlanta, Georgia, where I rode my first airplane. Several "future homemakers" were on the same flight, all from southern states. In those days, pilots shared points of interest along the way. "Ladies and gentlemen, to your right is the Grand Canyon, one of the world's seven wonders." I bounced off my seat and leaned across several girls to stare at the most magnificent sight I had ever seen. A massive hole in the earth with brilliant hues and shapes opened up and left me breathless.

I arrived at The Biltmore Hotel in Los Angeles wide-eyed and curious, staying for four days in mid-June 1967. The trip details are not as vivid as I would like, but I will never forget how seeing the bold white HOLLYWOOD sign planted in the hills of California impacted the trajectory of my life. During that trip, I realized there were many worlds I wanted to see. The city lights stole my heart. On a tour of Knott's Berry Farm, I saw migrant workers for the first time—brown-skinned men with straight hair, speaking a different language. They reminded me of farm workers in Alabama, except they picked strawberries instead of cotton, sweating under a blazing sun with straw hats pulled low on their heads. I was disappointed at a Hollywood movie set where what appeared as marvelous mansions on television were only storefronts, props.

A trip to the Hollywood Bowl, a concave-shaped structure resembling an accordion, took my breath away. I sat on the edge of my seat in the massive outdoor arena, more stunning than anything I could have dreamed of, awaiting a debut singing group. The curtains billowed from the floor and disappeared overhead. Five gorgeous singers with sun-kissed skin walked onstage as a flamboyant moderator shouted their names: Billy Davis Jr., Florence LaRue, Marilyn McCoo, Lamonte McLemore, and Ronald Townson. It was the 5th Dimension. Their pastel yellow, pink, blue, and lavender clothing fluttered like dove wings through clouds

Up, Up, and Away

as they moved their hands and sang "*Up, up, and Away.*" Lord, I jumped to my feet and screamed like I saw Jesus walking on water. When they sang "*Would you like to ride in my beautiful balloon,*" I hollered, "*Yes, I would!*" I had no idea how it would happen, but I started counting my last days in the Alabama cotton fields.

About midway through our stay, my roommate stole all my money from my purse while we slept. The group leaders sent her home, and my chaperone footed the rest of my bill, calling me her "star pupil." She repeatedly told anyone who would listen that she expected I would win the trip for the next two years.

Daddy had other plans.

I arrived home determined to be obedient, work harder, and do whatever it took to ensure more trips to California and my safe voyage out of Alabama after graduation. Within days of returning, while sitting at the dinner table, Daddy said, "Babe, I need to talk to you. Why don't you, Rachel, and Sonny come on outside?" My legs felt wooden, especially when he asked Mama, who had no say in anything, to come along.

Daddy pulled up a cinderblock near the back porch steps and sat where flies buzzed lazily around a damp spot made by dishwater thrown out the back door. I breathed in the sweet smell of gladiolas planted on the opposite side of the steps. Bumblebees hummed and tapped lightly on the flower's red blossoms, and we stood near Daddy, facing the peaceful waters of Lake Jordan.

"Some of the white folks been asking me to send y'all to Wetumpka High. They want you there to help integrate the school 'cause they know there won't be no trouble outta y'all." Daddy could be hell at the house, but he was a well-respected leader in the community among Blacks and whites. From the outside looking in, Daddy was a man who cared for his family, ran a successful business, and was not what white folks called "a troublemaker." Most importantly, his children were never in trouble. "Babe, how you feel about leaving Doby High?"

I could barely think, much less speak. I wanted to tell Daddy I loved that school—the third one I had attended—the friends I had made and the hours of freedom I had to express myself, unlike at home. I did not tell Daddy that changing schools again made me sad. I also did not say how I cherished earning excellent grades in a nurturing environment and being among other students with whom I had lots in common.

But it did not matter what school I attended. I still heard Daddy's voice ringing in my ear during planting and harvesting season. "Your dress tail better not touch your knees before you're back in that cotton field." As soon as we children were off the bus in the fall, we dropped our books on the dining room table, grabbed a sack, and headed to the cotton field, picking until it was too dark to see in front of us.

I was a top student in my class, played trumpet in the marching band, and was one of the few girls chosen to study algebra in the fall. I wanted to win the home economics contest for the next two years, and I feared the unknown. But I said nothing.

We hadn't had much close contact with white folks. I was disturbed whenever I heard talks of the Baptist Street church bombing in Birmingham, Emmett Till's murder years earlier, and other heinous acts against Blacks who tried mixing with whites. We lived in Jim Crow South, Ku Klux Klan country, yet I was safe

Up, Up, and Away

on our farm. Daddy would fight to the death, protecting his home and family.

"They got a whole lot better books and other school supplies at Wetumpka. It's a shame, but they send the best of everything to the white schools," Daddy said. "What you think, Mama?" he asked.

"Well, I rather they stay at Doby, but the man did say he think they'd be safe at Wetumpka High, and they'll get a better education."

Whatever I thought didn't matter. We entered Wetumpka High in the fall of 1967, my junior year.

Walking up the wide front steps of the school was surreal. I had never had a white teacher or seen so many whites in person. The hallways were wide and brightly lit, with lockers, unlike the dimmer hallways of my old school. I looked straight ahead, hesitant to make eye contact with the staring students, mostly friendly, some laughing among themselves and remarking about skin color and kinky hair. I couldn't help noticing the silky locks, unlike mine, and colors I hadn't heard of, like brunette and bleached blonde. I had heard and was offended by the Clairol commercial—blondes have more fun— because I didn't know a single Black person with hair that color. I'd never even seen blonde hair in person except once when I was five.

We'd been on the way to Big Mama's house, a place we didn't go often. But she was old, sick, and unable to care for herself, so Mama and her sisters took turns spending days with her. I was standing on the floorboard in the back seat of Daddy's car, staring out the window at a skinny white girl jumping rope, dust flying from beneath her bare feet. Streaks of sweat trailed across her dirty face, so pale she resembled a ghost. But I was fixated on the hair, a blonde waterfall flowing down her back like corn silk, unlike my kinky braids that could stand firm against tornado winds. "Daddy, I wish I had hair like that little girl."

"No, ya' don't. White folks smell like dogs, and so do their hair." I'd allowed that image to penetrate my mind for the time it took to drive past the child's house before deciding my corn rows were just fine.

Weeks before beginning my senior year, two things occurred that inspired me to embrace my blackness further. During the height of the civil rights movement, soul singer James Brown released his iconic song "Say It Loud - I'm Black, and I'm Proud," and jazz vocalist Abbey Lincoln appeared on the cover of *Jet* magazine with an afro—big and round as a basketball. I shall never forget how excited I was seeing her curly "afro," a word for natural Black hair. I had to figure out how to force mine into that style instead of having Mama straighten it with a sizzling hot metal comb, burning my ears and neck. After washing it with our shampoo—Tide soap powder—I was the proud wearer of a head full of shapeless kinks.

I strolled into the living room to surprise my parents with the newest style. One look and Mama yelled, "Child, what have you *done* to your head?" An instant smile lit up Daddy's face. He clapped his hands excitedly. "*I* think it's *beautiful*. You look just like my mama." I strolled onto campus my senior year at the all-white school with my fist raised, singing, "Say it loud. I'm Black, and I'm proud." I wore my natural hair, the first Black girl to do so, and ignored the wary looks from teachers and students as I expressed my *blackness* in a way I never had before, defying the label "Colored" or "Negro."

Up, Up, and Away

At the white school, my history teacher feigned an inability to say Negro, the given name for Blacks in 1969. In the classroom, she strolled the aisles with an open textbook, reading historical facts about "Nigras," causing the hairs on my neck to stand up. Yet, this same woman—white with sandy-brown hair, cat's-eyed glasses, and chunky legs—invited me to her office in twelfth grade.

"Mildred, what are your plans after high school?" I did not know. She administered a standardized test and later told me I had a high math aptitude. "You reckon your daddy would let you go away after graduation?" Again, I did not know. She handed me a sealed envelope addressed to Daddy, which, I later learned, contained the test results and information about American Automation Technical School in Columbus, Ohio. I am eternally grateful to that teacher who saw something special in me and contributed significantly to my growth at a pivotal point in my childhood. However, offering no proof, some of my classmates believed she and other teachers secretly sponsored a prom omitting Black students.

The one date of my entire childhood was to a prom at a Black school my senior year. I went with a boy Mama and Daddy thought was "good marriage material." Melvin, whose father was Daddy's brick mason buddy and the son of Mama's high school friend, invited me to his senior prom, a date I believe our parents had arranged. I had no input on the date and didn't care whether it happened. I now believe my parents thought they were doing a good thing, but a couple weeks before prom, Daddy asked Mama, "You think that boy oughta come meet the rest of the family?" At the time, I felt like part of the slave trade, something to be bartered for a head of cattle. I sat alone at the dining room table with my parents, feeling totally alone while they ignored me, speaking as if I didn't exist. I wondered but didn't ask why I, not my older sister, was their first girl to go on a date. What happened to Daddy's mantra, "Books and boys don't mix?" I stared at Mama, waiting for her to answer the question.

"Hmmm. I reckon so," Mama told Daddy and avoided my eyes.

Saturday night, a week before prom night, headlamps on Melvin's blue and white Chevy crawled down the road, slicing the darkness like two white swords. I sat, then stood, and my nerves screamed like pinpricks as I wondered what people did on dates. Melvin walked through the front door wearing dark dress slacks, shiny black shoes, and a white collared shirt. He smiled until Daddy gripped his hand and squeezed it hard, a mouse stuck in a steel trap.

Melvin looked like a nervous drunk, hobbling across the floor, pretending his hand didn't hurt, stumbling when a loud screech howled from a loose floor plank. He squeezed into a corner on the sofa and cupped his hands over his mouth, squirming and laughing. I thought the boy behaved like an idiot. Daddy dragged two straight-back chairs in front of Melvin, where he and I sat like a judge and jury. Daddy fired questions at the boy about his family, and I sat with no idea what to say. After the inquisition, Melvin asked, "Mr. Billups, I wondered if I could take Mildred to the picture show tonight?"

Daddy smacked his hand against his thigh and grinned. "Why, sho' you can, Melvin." At least twelve sets of eyes peeped from behind doors or gazed around corners. The baby crawled across the floor, crept up my leg, and onto my lap. Daddy stood up. "Y'all

Up, Up, and Away

come on in here." My younger brothers and sisters raced into the living room, sounding like mice scampering across the wooden planks. "Who all wanta go to the movies with Babe?" Hands shot up like weapons, and there was a chorus of "I do."

Daddy rocked back and forth on his heels with his hands in his pockets. "Melvin, can all these chillun fit in that Chevy?" A sly grin played at the corners of Daddy's mouth.

Melvin's eyes skittered around the room as he stared at the fingers in the air like guns at a firing squad and slinked deeper into the raggedy sofa. "No, sir." Shortly afterward, Melvin lowered his head, skulked across the creaky planks to the front door, and fired up the Impala.

I wanted to race to my bedroom and slam the door, but Daddy tolerated no such behavior in *his* house. Instead, I continued to sit on the straight-back chair and swallow my tears, furious that I had no say in my treatment. My parents, especially Daddy, had drilled honor and obedience into my head from the cradle. He would have crushed a child who dared voice her opinion or speak out against him.

I looked to the dining room where Mama sat quietly at the table, fumbling with a bolt of cloth, listening to every word throughout the Melvin ordeal. "Mildred, I bet you'll like this pattern I bought for your prom dress. I think it's right pretty." Our eyes met. Pity filled the face of a woman who likely saw her daughter following in her footsteps, a voiceless housewife controlled by a domineering man. Years later, I learned she was looking out for my interest. Mama said she thought Melvin was kind, "not someone who would fight a woman." She lowered her head. "You wanna come help me lay out the pattern?" It was then I decided—no serious relationships before I was financially and emotionally stable and none with anyone handpicked by my parents. *I* would control my relationship destiny.

During prom week, Mama fussed over the Butterick pattern every day. She snipped and measured, adjusting a piece of soft fabric, yellow like a baby chick, this way and that, across the dining room table. Mama clucked and worried like a mother hen as she slipped the garment over my head with straight pins holding the seams together. Satisfied that her masterpiece was a perfect fit, Mama pulled a chair up to the Singer Treadle sewing machine shoved in a dim corner of the dining room lit only by a streak of sunlight through small windowpanes hidden behind a China cabinet. She created an orchestra of sounds like horse hooves dancing as she guided fabric under the needle, worked a foot pedal, and stitched seams together.

Pride covered Mama's face, and she touched the fabric like it was a priceless treasure. "Mildred, a girl's prom is the most special time of her life besides the wedding day." My heart broke when she smiled through decaying front teeth. I had no thoughts of marriage or any relationship with a boy. I couldn't bear being saddled with hordes of children and no dental care.

On prom night, Daddy greeted Melvin with a smile and a pat on the back instead of a handshake. Melvin glided across the living room floor and placed a corsage with a yellow ribbon matching my dress on my left wrist, happy to escape Daddy's rough hands. The fragrance from the white carnations, cool against my wrist, took my breath away. No one had ever given

Up, Up, and Away

me flowers. My younger brothers and sisters giggled, shoved, and waved at Melvin, who opened the passenger door for me. Daddy never opened car doors for Mama. Bunny, my older sister, who Daddy sent to "keep an eye on Babe," slid into the back seat. Since this was my first date and not a topic of discussion in our home, I had no idea if chaperones were customary. No other girl at the dance had a "watcher."

My eyes lit up, and I felt a freedom I had never known when we entered the Fountain Lounge venue at Sandtown, the Black high school. Melvin wore a dark tuxedo and white shirt, and I wore a yellow satin A-line gown. A bubbling waterfall greeted Melvin and me with a backdrop of copper coins near the entry. Strobe lights flickered against white walls, creating an atmosphere like a million stars clustered above a sea of eighteen-year-olds, bright-eyed and full of promise. The sounds of shoe soles clicked against the waxed linoleum floor as the rat-a-tat-tat of snare drums had girls and boys dancing the cha-cha-cha to music from a live band.

When Melvin and I danced and laughed beneath the theme "Three Coins in the Fountain" plastered in bold letters around the venue, I felt like Cinderella at the ball. I forgot about my sister. That night, I was free to be a teenage girl, young and full of life. No diapers to change, babies to feed, or little sisters to bathe. I wanted more nights like this.

When the party ended, Melvin and I left the dance floor together, searching for Bunny. She was not at the dance, and no one we asked had seen her for a while. I trembled all the way home, fearing something terrible had happened to my sister. The cinderblock house sat like a white beacon, with the front porch light guiding us when we turned on the dark, bumpy road home.

Daddy met us at the front door, snatched me inside, and slammed it in Melvin's face. My mouth fell open when I saw Bunny sitting on the lopsided sofa, hiding behind a smug look. Daddy shut down any words I had to say when he jerked my arm and squeezed it hard. "Where the hell were you? Bunny said she looked everywhere, and you wasn't at that prom."

I tried to ignore the vice grip that shot pains up my arm. I was torn between anger and confusion as I looked from Bunny to Daddy. "I *was* at the dance," I said a little too loud.

"If Bunny said you wasn't at that dance, you wasn't there." Daddy yanked me into his bedroom and pulled a wide leather strap off the hook behind the door. I felt the sting of betrayal each time it connected with my back through the formal gown. With each blow, stars flashed before my eyes, my dress ripped, and ropes of welts became part of my skin. Still, I stood like an oak tree against a storm. It was the last time he beat me—the only time I didn't bother crying. What better target to practice the toughness he had taught than on Daddy? I thought, since I hoped to be gone in six weeks, Daddy could do nothing more to hurt me.

That night, I swore I would hate Bunny for the rest of my life. I never fully trusted her again. Years later, one of my siblings explained it this way: "Bunny desperately wanted to be Daddy's favorite, but you were the apple of his eye, a position that she desired." When I learned that her given name was biblical, I researched its history and found "Bernice" was described as "one

Up, Up, and Away

of the shameless women of the Bible." With such a name, she couldn't help herself. And then, I decided to forget about hating Bunny, for the Bible teaches that "Vengeance is mine, saith the Lord." Instead, I channeled my energy toward my bright future and prayed daily to a merciful God to grant my departure in a few short weeks.

CHAPTER 9
Crossing State Lines

Finally, after months of wondering if it would happen, I was sitting in Daddy's car, moving farther and farther away from the cinderblock house. I did not think to ask why my parents agreed to my leaving home, and at the time, it did not matter. I only knew I wanted freedom from the oppression I felt. I was a child without a voice and would not have dared question my parents. Yet, as voiceless as Mama was, I believe she drove the decision.

Months before I left home, Mama sat across from me at the dining room table and said, "Mildred, don't be like me, depending on a man for every nickel you get. I wanna see my girls wit' something of their own." That same day, she hung her head and told me how she was pregnant, yanking on a hacksaw, helping Daddy clear the rattlesnakes, foxes, and water moccasins after he bought the sixty-acre farm. "I want better for my girls," she told me.

People say we were lucky to own our home and the surrounding land. Yet, I knew firsthand the downside to a woman living in isolation, unappreciated for backbreaking farm work and maintaining an entire household. I survived years of King Cotton and the most formidable man I know, saddled with a six-foot cotton sack strung around my neck. Looking back on that day, I was emboldened by leaving the farm. I blazed a trail for my younger siblings, who, one by one, left the farm for trade school, the military, or college.

A hundred miles from home, I saw the twinkling lights of Birmingham—the first city—flicker and disappear outside the car windows quicker than shooting stars. The lights were like thousands of angel wings protecting me inside the speeding Oldsmobile. Daddy zoomed up hills and around steep curves, flying to the next town. Butterflies, moths, and anything else unlucky enough to cross the path of his car splattered against the windshield.

Crossing into Tennessee from Alabama, a magnificent bridge suspended high above an expansive body of water, which danced in the wind and shimmered under the rising sun, brought me to the edge of my seat. A vision like silver coins bouncing over a liquid runway took my breath away. I was fixated on the water moving fast in the same direction. "*Oh, Daddy.* What is that?"

"We're passing over the Tennessee River Bridge; the river feeds the Tennessee Valley Authority. You know about the TVA?"

I gaped at the marvelous structure that seemed to stretch for miles. "Oh, yes, sir. We read about it in history class. I never imagined it would be so beautiful."

Daddy's face radiated with pride as he gave me a history lesson. "That TVA is some piece of work, a powerful tool for flood control, and one of the smartest things Roosevelt did while he was president. You know it all started in Muscle Shoals, Alabama, don't you?"

"No, sir. How do you know all this stuff?"

Happy to teach me, Daddy became talkative, impressing his audience of one. "When me and your mama found our place back in 1950, it was nothing but a sixty-acre wilderness of washed-out land with trees everywhere." He chuckled under his breath. "A lotta work went into making it something that could earn money and support all y'all."

Daddy cleared his throat and paused. "You remember me and Brother putting in all the terraces on the hills to keep the water from washing the place away? A lot of my ideas came from reading about the work they done on the TVA." Daddy was an avid reader of *The Farmer's Almanac*, constantly researched information in *The World Book Encyclopedia* that he purchased when I was in middle school, and read every page of the Sunday *Montgomery Advertiser*.

"No, sir. I don't remember you putting in the terraces."

He wrinkled his brow as if in deep concentration. "If a farmer don't know how to protect the soil, he'll starve the land and himself to death. That's how come we rotate our crops with corn one year and cotton the next. I learned about that through the farmers' exchange program."

Daddy tapped his fingers against the steering wheel and broke into a playful rendition of "The Battle of New Orleans."

With a faraway look, Daddy told me, "When I was in Egypt during World War II, the TVA was responsible for building a buncha plants to make bombs and planes for the war." I listened to him talk on and on about farming and the TVA. We were a normal father and daughter, teacher and student for several minutes. I was unafraid to question him, and he openly answered, seeming to enjoy the exchanges.

I couldn't take my eyes off the racing water, moving like it was running from a bad situation. I had forgotten to familiarize myself with the roadmap Daddy gave me to navigate our course to Columbus. I now realize that the map was another teaching moment, as I had never studied or even held one before. (A few years later, those map-reading lessons would come in handy when I drove back and forth to Alabama from Ohio.) If I knew anything, Daddy—the farmer and traveling brick mason—was always prepared. And although he only took jobs in Alabama, Louisiana, or Mississippi, Daddy studied his roadmap like he read his Bible. He would have known the route and could drive to Ohio with his eyes closed. My emotions fluctuated between adoration and condemnation as I listened to the voice of a loving father sitting across the bench seat from me, imparting knowledge and making memories as he drove me across the miles.

I studied Daddy's fingers, large like kielbasa sausages with fingernails black and thick as a fifty-cent piece, gripping the steering wheel of our Oldsmobile roller coaster. I resisted asking him how those fingers could gently stroke piano keys in church every Sunday, play the music that caused church ladies to wail and shout, and then ball into a fist and knock Mama to the floor in a fit of rage.

He whizzed along, softly singing "Amazing Grace." Those lips, full and shaped like ones made for lipstick commercials, taught adult Bible study every Sunday morning. Yet, I had heard them

Crossing State Lines

impart poisonous hisses like: "You'll never amount to nothing. How could you be so stupid?" I thought of James 3:10. "From the same mouth come both blessing and cursing. My brethren, these things ought not to be this way."

Caught up in my thoughts, I leaped forward when Daddy said, "Babe, what's the next major city? We'll stop, gas up, and go to the bathroom." I fumbled on the floorboard and grabbed the map.

At Clarksville, Tennessee, he skidded off the exit ramp onto the slab of an Esso filling station. A skinny white man with brown, matted hair came out to pump gas and did a double take like he didn't often see people like us. He strolled to the driver's side window, propped his hands on the door frame, and stuck his head so close to Daddy that I could smell his foul breath. "Well, well, well. What kin I do fo' you people?"

Daddy slipped his hand under the car seat with one fluid movement but removed it, clenching his fist and hitting the steering wheel softly like a padded drumstick tapping a bass drum. I was scared shitless he would whip out that pearl-handled .357 Magnum and come up firing. The man jumped backward and almost tripped over himself at the sound of Daddy snatching the door handle. Daddy slammed the door and never looked back as we walked into the store.

Back in the car blowing down I-65N, Daddy said, "I never did like the city, Babe. People jammed up on top of one another. It ain't natural." He asked me to hand him a piece of fried chicken Mama had wrapped in aluminum foil with homemade biscuits. "You think you gonna like this place in Ohio?"

I gripped the roadmap, too nervous to eat. What kind of lunatic could sit there chatting like the filling station scene never happened? "Yes, sir. I think I'll like Columbus."

"When I got out the Army, I went to Harlem. Had heard so much about it, wanted to see what all the fuss was about—never seen such filth. Rats all over the place. The smell of rotten trash everywhere." Daddy spoke in a voice I didn't hear often. It was soft, kind, a plea, almost like a lover. "If you don't like Columbus, you always got a place back home."

That day, I stared out the window at a new world: mountains unclimbed, skies blue and welcoming, and billboard invitations to Ruby Falls and Lookout Mountain, Tennessee, places I'd never heard of but sounded like heaven, places I wanted to see. "Yes, sir," I said, but thought, *Is he kidding?* Bring on the rats and funky garbage. It couldn't smell worse than pigpens, animal shit, and rotten mattresses full of maggots and baby pee.

Water flowed from mountainous rocks, black like granite, so close to the Tennessee and Kentucky highways you could reach out and touch them, and "falling rocks" signs warned of potential danger. Trucks belched and crawled like centipedes gasping for breath as they climbed steep hills through the Appalachians. I could hardly contain my excitement when the Cincinnati-Covington Bridge, our welcome mat into OHIO, loomed spectacularly through the windshield. I don't recall the water, but it was calm, peaceful in my mind. The Tennessee River Bridge ushered us out of Alabama, yet it paled compared to this structure. The bridge contained so much steel expanding across several lanes and covering the sides and top that it resembled a massive birdcage with entry and exit doors.

Crossing State Lines

We arrived at the corner of Broad and Grant in Columbus at noon and parked in front of 361 East Broad Street, my new home at the Seneca Hotel. I studied the ten-story red brick building with tiny windowpanes, a place that resembled a prison absent the razor wire. The structure reminded me of trips through Wetumpka riding in a car with Mama while my sisters and I huddled in the back seat.

Mama always brought our attention to several white buildings lined up like caskets and set way back off US 231, the main road through town. She pointed to the buildings with tiny windows surrounded by razor wire and women walking or working the grounds. "Lawd, have mercy. That's Julia Tutwiler Prison, where they keep the women convicts," she said urgently. Mama would shake her head. "They ain't in there for going to Sunday school, neither. *Please,* don't let me have to come see none uh y'all in Tutwiler."

Daddy unlocked the trunk, grabbed my suitcase, and we hustled through the front door of the building. A large chandelier sparkled throughout the spacious lobby, and oak walls were polished to a high sheen. A woman who resembled Granny from *The Beverly Hillbillies* walked out of the front office, extended a pale white hand with age spots, and said hello.

Daddy deposited five hundred dollars for my tuition and room and board with this woman. She shifted her eyes away from the grease stains on the white envelope, explained the rules for living in the dorm, and gave Daddy the keys to my room. I imagine she talked about the curfew, no boys, housekeeping, etc. *She could have told me to hang upside down by my toenails, and I would have complied.*

Inside the elevator, a Black woman sat in the front corner on a three-legged stool. An aroma like honeysuckles and roses wafted through the open door. Bright red paint covered her fingernails and lips. I tried not to stare at her lashes, thick and spread out like a leaf rake, and her bosom—squeezed inside a purple, tightly knit two-piece suit with black buttons. I had never seen a woman who dressed or smelled like her. Later, she told me she wore Chanel No. 5 every day. After I moved in, I looked forward to that scent. It reminded me of birds flying and a day when Daddy set me free; it made me smile.

Daddy and I stood in the farthest corners of the elevator. The woman stared straight ahead and smacked her Juicy Fruit chewing gum. "What floor?"

Daddy clutched my baggage, looked straight ahead, and struggled to avoid staring at her shapely rump spread across the three-legged stool. "Seventh floor, please." She pressed a button, cranked the door closed, and the creaky old box brought me home.

Along the dimly lit hallway were fancy wood carvings. Daddy turned the key and opened my new room, which was huge compared to my bedroom at home. I lingered at the door and took it all in. Brilliant sunshine streaked through the window and bathed the room with light, lying like a halo across the white bedspread. I tried to comprehend that the full-sized mattress seemed twice as large as the one I had slept on with several brothers and sisters. The lovely dresser near the foot of the bed had a wide mirror without a crack. An overstuffed visitor's chair in one corner and a private bathroom capped off my suite.

Crossing State Lines

Daddy eased the door closed, set the Samsonite in the closet, and pulled his wallet from his hip pocket. He counted eight ten-dollar bills and four fives, squeezing each wrinkled dollar so tight between his forefinger and thumb that he could have rubbed a hole in it. He cleared his throat and glanced around the room, seemingly satisfied I was safe. In that seldom heard, kind voice, he said, "Babe, you need to set yourself a curfew. Every night no matter where I was, I made sure I was home at a certain time, even when I was in service oversea." I loved how he always said "oversea" never "overseas." But i*f he thought I believed he followed a curfew, he must have also believed I had a penis.*

"Yes, sir."

He handed me the money. "This oughta last you a while. We'll send more after we harvest the crops in the fall." He never sent, and I never asked for more.

Growing up, Mama called me an old soul, wise beyond my years, too independent for my own good. That day, I was wise enough to know Daddy handed me a gift, a paid-in-full education that would last a lifetime. He was nothing if not resourceful, finding ways to survive times of sparsity and plenty, always providing for the family. The farm was an asset, which increased immensely in 1967 after becoming a lakefront property bordered by Lake Jordan. White bankers lined up to loan him money, hoping he'd default, which he almost did years later. But I'll get to that shortly.

According to Daddy, before Alabama Power (APC) made the dam project public knowledge, the company had tried to strong-arm him into selling his land. He refused to do so. APC built Walter Bouldin Dam less than a mile from our home, buying up most of the property in the area to expand Lake Jordan, a forty-mile waterway. I didn't ask Daddy where he got the tuition money. I was an unquestioning rule follower and obedient child. I accepted the tuition, a gift from my parents, perhaps their way of paying me back for years of absolute loyalty, providing an opportunity for independence.

"Thanks for everything, Daddy." I studied his hands, rough and calloused, hands that had just forked over five hundred dollars for my schooling, easily a year's net earnings on the farm in 1969. With that one gesture, Daddy trusted me enough to let me soar—rise above my roots.

As he prepared to leave, I looked into his eyes, noticing our strong resemblance: slim, lean, strong-willed, slightly different brown complexions with chiseled faces. Mama and Daddy always treated me special, blessing me with the best of both—his face and her name. Every emotion I could imagine churned inside me when I said, "Bye, Daddy." I wanted to reach out, hug him, and have his strength to hold on to when he was gone, but we were not an emotionally expressive family, so I kept my feelings to myself.

At that moment, I felt love and admiration for Daddy, but until he was on the other side of that locked door, I was aware of the power he still held over me and was wary of the call of the cotton patch. Unlike Mama, who cried and whispered words to live by, we stood unspeaking, staring into each one another's brown eyes. I touched his extended hands; goose flesh shimmied down my arm, a connection I had never experienced. "Bye, Babe." He turned and marched away. Stoic. Didn't look back.

Crossing State Lines

I stood at the door and watched Daddy, always the soldier, stride down the hall until those square shoulders rounded the corner. I ran to the window, waving—unnoticed—until the Oldsmobile's taillights disappeared behind a building on Town Street, heading south, back to Alabama the same day. My heart boomed in my chest. I didn't know whether to scream in terror or jump for joy, but I knew I had missed out on so much living. It was time to shake things up.

I slung my homemade dress across the bed, stripped off the girdle, and stepped out of those tight shoes. I flung my half-naked self across the bed and slept the sleep of a freed slave. No screaming babies with wet diapers huddled under me that night. I had no idea how much I would miss the warmth of those bodies and the laughter of my sister and best friend, Rachel. I often thought of her and my brother, Sonny, but never felt guilty about leaving, only joy that the road I had paved was theirs to follow. I *never once* longed for church or Sunday school or the constant threats of going to hell. Yet, my deep faith in God was *never* shaken, not even today. Still, I *refused* to set foot in a religious institution for more than two years after leaving home. But I digress.

CHAPTER 10
The Purple Heart

Each morning in Columbus, I hopped out of bed singing along with the soulful sounds of WOSU FM radio, the "devil's music," according to church folks back home. But those songs flowed through my body like blood in my veins.

One early summer day, while dressing for school, a muted drumbeat followed by the most angelic voice I had ever heard thrummed across the airwaves. Sonny Charles, an artist I had never heard of, whispered words that brought me to tears with his song "Black Pearl." I had been standing at the foot of my bed, ensuring every curl was in place in my perfectly formed afro, admiring the smile of a girl becoming a woman.

I quickly grabbed a pen and paper to jot down words from the song. Tears streamed down my face as I heard what sounded like an anthem to Black women—women who have served others all their lives, women this singer promised to make his queen, women who will never win a beauty contest for "they" won't pick her. Afterward, I woke up early every morning with my ear peeled to the radio.

Mildred J Mills

Hearing "Say a Little Prayer" *by* Aretha Franklin for the first time reminded me that I wasn't wholly disloyal to my upbringing. My parents had taught me to kneel and say The Lord's Prayer each night before bed, a ritual I continued after leaving home until I heard Aretha singing, "The moment I wake up/before I put on my makeup / I say a little prayer for you." After that, I opened my eyes each morning and immediately asked God to be a shield of protection around me, filling my soul with peace and light.

Then, I would race down the steps from my fifth-floor apartment, eager to see what the day would bring. When I hit the streets of Columbus on my way to school, I was enlightened and frightened. One day, I saw a man too drunk to stand alone, weaving and holding onto a parking meter while he vomited blood. I wanted to ask the man why he drank so much, but I knew how to mind my business. Another day, a Black Panther Party member stepped in front of me. "My Sistah, when the revolution come, are you gonna be ready?" he asked. I stared at the man dressed in all black: combat boots, slacks, a long-sleeved sweater, and a beret cocked to the side of his head. I wanted to say, "I don't know shit about no revolution. Get out of my way," but I hurried around the man and avoided that path in the future.

In Columbus, the lengths folks went to mock others' differences were astounding. The constant questions aimed at poking holes in my confidence were endless: W*hy do you speak that way, why do you say drink instead of pop or sack instead of bag; why are you so country?* Each day I adjusted to my surroundings as Mama taught me: "It's better to be thought of as a fool than open your mouth

The Purple Heart

and remove all doubt." I listened and observed, and except on rare occasions, I kept people at arm's length.

The first week of school, Mary Hairston, a blonde-haired Black girl, had ducked into my room and asked, "Hey, you wanna hang out with us at the club tonight?" Sure that I would go to hell for frequenting a nightclub, I lied that I had no money. I reminded her that we were only eighteen, not of legal age for bars. She flipped her hair over her shoulder. "Girl, don't worry about that."

For weeks, my friends (a term I use loosely, for I preferred being alone) had nagged me about going clubbing. In addition to being busy ensuring I would graduate, I was fearful of what my parents called "the den of iniquity."

But after eight weeks of watching them return home giddy and laughing and talking about the people they had met, I said yes to celebrate graduation the following week. Guilt and excitement warred as I eagerly slipped on a pink mini-dress and five-inch red and white platform shoes.

Seven of us girls hustled to the corner of Town and East Broad Street and stood like young streetwalkers, waiting for Mary's older friend to pick us up in her new car. We squealed like the girls we were when a sleek black Mustang Mach II with silver stripes down each side slid to a halt in front of us. "Hey, Dorothy. Hope you don't mind that I brought along a couple of extra girls." Mary said to her friend. Dorothy, a recent Ohio State University graduate, argued that eight people could not fit into her four-seater with bucket seats, a graduation gift from her father. Yet, standing beneath a streetlight, Dorothy examined fake IDs and matched one to each giggling girl before stuffing us like sardines into the Mustang.

Mildred J Mills

That Saturday at 10 p.m., I flashed a fake ID at the door and followed my friends into The Bottom's Up Club. Inside that smoky joint was like being in a sinful paradise, a Garden of Eden. Knowing I would be out until 2 a.m. for the first time—for one brief moment—I thought about what Daddy told me when he brought me to Columbus. "Set yourself a curfew and stick to it." Still, I hurried with my friends to find a chair.

The lights were low. Cigarette smoke drifted through the air like a slow fog; laughter and chatter filled the room. Whiffs of liquor mixed with perfume and cologne. A disco ball spun slowly above my head; its sparkling lights danced around the ceiling and walls like white butterflies. My friends and I settled at a round table at the back of the club where we could watch the stage and everyone walking through the door. I hadn't drunk alcohol before but ordered a sloe gin fizz because, when I asked the waitress what was sweet, she said, "Oh, honey. It tastes just like red Kool-Aid." The first sip was warm and sugary. I giggled and sat back to enjoy a talent show.

An hour later, a sad-eyed man with broad shoulders and narrow hips who looked as tall as Kareem Abdul-Jabbar sauntered to the stage. The man moved like a sleek, black panther. He *owned* the space at the mic near center stage. "I'll be singing 'A Change is Gonna Come' by Sam Cooke," he said in a low, sultry voice. A sensation like liquid fire began at my belly and oozed like warm maple syrup downward. I then remembered how Maude, our horse, had jumped the fence, lifted her tail, and given herself to the mule next door when I was five. I'll remember the swooning feeling—lightheadedness that left me dazed—for the rest of my life.

The Purple Heart

The man closed his eyes, and words poured from his lips like a spring shower on a hot tin roof, soft, steamy, and seductive. I sang along in my head and imagined every word being true as he crooned about an upcoming change. The man sang with restrained pain on his face. *My God, who is he?* I thought.

When the song ended, he locked eyes with me, strolled through the crowd to my table, and reached for my hand. "I'm Arthur," he said. "I couldn't help noticing your pretty afro when I walked in. You alone?" My mouth flapped open. I hadn't noticed that my friends had scattered like roaches and were giggling across the room from another table. "May I?" he asked and sat in a chair across from me.

Words flew easily between Arthur and me as we talked the night away in a corner. He told me he was an ex-Marine recently home from the Vietnam War, and then he leaned in. "You're the picture of innocence in that pink mini-dress. I love those scandalous shoes," he whispered. They were red-and-white, five-inch-high platforms I'd bought just for that night. "May I ask how old you are?" I was eighteen, he was twenty-two, and I wanted to hear his voice every day. So much about him reminded me of Daddy: he was soft-spoken, confident, a war vet with large working-man hands and wiry muscles. But his eyes were warm, unlike Daddy's, which were sometimes colder than a Frigidaire icebox. Arthur sang in a church quartet, worked in a factory at night, and attended college on the GI Bill during the day. "I love my mother more than anyone in the world," he said, stealing my heart. He wanted to be a preacher. While I was nowhere near ready for children, I wanted to have his babies someday.

It seemed the lights flickered too soon, signaling two o'clock. Arthur asked for my address and telephone number but did not offer his. "A lady never calls a man, and a gentleman doesn't expect her to," he told me. I thought those were the most romantic words I'd ever heard.

Stuffed in the Mustang on the way home, my girls wanted to hear all the dirt. Who is he? Where does he live? Is he seeing someone? Did you get his number? One said, "My God. He must be seven feet tall." I giggled and told them he was only six-foot-four. When I repeated his "lady never calls a man" comment, they said, "That jive turkey is married. You'll never hear from him again." He called the next day, asked me out, and picked me up for our first date on the following Saturday, a bright sunny day.

For weeks, every Saturday morning, I gazed from the second-floor apartment window until his silver Buick Riviera eased to the curb at nine o'clock. By the time I hustled out the front door, he was standing like a six-foot-four God with his narrow butt leaned ruggedly against the shiny car, watching me with arms folded across his broad chest and feet crossed at the ankle wearing high-top white Converse all-star tennis shoes. I glided into his open arms and believed the world was safe.

Arthur introduced me to places I had never been. We cruised through Franklin Park, a beautifully landscaped exotic haven filled with flowers and natural springs—a popular weekend hangout where men showed off hot cars and women. At the Columbus Zoo and Art Museum, he patiently strolled through the venues quizzing me about the animals or art pieces' origins. "Did you know baboons come from Africa? Why are their butts red?" I could not answer either question, but he could.

The Purple Heart

In the Park, we sat on a blanket beneath a buckeye tree. With his back against the tree, he wrapped his arms around my waist. I sat between his legs, my back to his chest, and felt the warmth of his breath against my neck. He told me stories about a place called "Nam." "I arrived as a wide-eyed eighteen-year-old Marine ready to kill some gooks." Instead, "At twenty-two, I left the war—an old man—maimed after shrapnel ripped through my leg."

The day he took me home, he led me into a small, efficiency apartment. A round table with two chairs stood beneath a window where a soft breeze ruffled frilly white curtains. The exotic fragrance from gardenias in a tiny white vase on the table reminded me of Mama's flower gardens. Across the room were free weights and a basketball on the floor next to a twin-sized bed. A single picture of an older woman stood on a six-drawer chest. From the look of the high cheekbones and long limbs, I guessed his mother eyed me from the silver frame.

The heat radiating through his white T-shirt felt comforting, when Arthur wrapped me in his arms. "Welcome to my home, Babe. I want to get to know you." I had waited four weeks to hear him say those words and told him I'd like that. He slid his hand up my red mini-dress and stopped suddenly. "What is this? Are *you* wearing a girdle?"

"*Yes*, I'm wearing a girdle. *Why?*" I asked with attitude.

"Those things are for fat women. Why are *you* wearing it?"

"Mama told me it keeps my hips from shaking." Before that moment, I had felt romantic, warm, and sexy. He slid off my dress and stared at the lacy white contraption like it was trash.

"Listen, Babe. You don't need that thing." He threw it in the small trash can next to the kitchen counter. I started to protest and wanted to run out the door, but then I saw the raw, haunted look in his eyes as he continued undressing me. Arthur patted the bed, and I sat. He unzipped his tight jeans, stood before me, and showed me the scar on his left leg. Staring up from the bed, I could only focus on the long legs in the white boxer shorts, thinking a man who looked like that ought to be arrested.

He lowered himself onto the bed next to me, reached into the nightstand drawer, and handed me a rectangular box. "This is yours—my token for this disgusting gash."

Inside the box, formed like a coffin, was an elegant heart-shaped medal with gold trim and George Washington's likeness lying on a bed of purple satin attached to a purple ribbon. "I hate everything it stands for," he told me.

I gently stroked the dark mark that ran the length of his thigh and asked why he didn't cherish the award. His face hardened. "I ain't got no quarrel with them Vietcong. No Vietcong ever called me nigger," he said, quoting Muhammad Ali. I recognized the pain of a young man who had stood on the frontlines fighting for a country that oppressed and marginalized Black men. I had seen similar angry expressions on Daddy's face when he discussed returning to the United States from Egypt after WWII. Daddy had no physical scars and no purple heart—but he was scarred all the same.

Arthur sighed and gently touched the box. "Babe, will you keep me forever near your heart? I'll think of you when the pain from that day shakes me awake at night." I reached for Arthur. He gazed deep into my eyes, folded me tenderly in his arms, and laid me down. Surrounded by lyrics from The Originals' song,

The Purple Heart

"Baby, I'm for Real," the smell of gardenias, a taste of salty sweat, and the feel of power, he plowed virgin soil. We made love on a twin-sized bed with white sheets in a small place hardly bigger than a dormitory room. I wept, filled with joy, filled with him. He was my first.

CHAPTER 11
Harsh Realities

That first year in Columbus, I felt a loosening of the tight reins my parents had on me as I stepped straight out of childhood into adulthood. Only now do I think it peculiar that after years of close confinement and strict upbringing, not once did I call home asking for advice, and never did my parents offer it. Looking back, I realize enduring demanding, repetitive tasks like picking cotton, making meals, and tending babies shaped my body muscles, strengthened my memory and heart, and taught me how to get up every day and accomplish something, like showing up for school and figuring out how to earn my own money.

I had been in Columbus three weeks when one evening, on the way home, a sign posted on a window two doors from my school caught my eye. "Monique Models Wanted." Free training, high pay, and a chance to wear beautiful clothing. With my hands cupped against the large window, I saw a vast wall with life-sized posters of brown-skinned women (and some nattily dressed men) as glamorous as the movie stars on the cover of *Jet* magazine.

I slipped inside for a closer look and was intrigued by the girls' bright red lipstick, long fake lashes, and flawless skin. I had never even worn makeup or thought of myself as beautiful, so I thought, *What am I doing in this place?* Just as I decided to walk out, a stout woman sitting behind a mahogany desk spoke softly. "Those are my models. Two weeks with me, and you can become one of them."

I didn't know what it took to become a model and hadn't thought of being one, but I did know the hundred bucks Daddy gave me was almost gone, and I needed spending money. After two weeks, guided by the competent hands of Mrs. Rosebud Brown, a woman built like a toad but who moved like a synchronized swimmer, I booked my first job as a Monique model for Lazarus Department Stores.

In July, a month before I graduated tech school, I started searching for a full-time job because returning to Alabama or that cotton field was not an option. I asked anybody who would listen, "Do you know where I can find a job? How do you even look for one?" My instructor said, "Go downtown and take the Civil Service Exam." I did, and two weeks later, I had what Mama called "a good state job" as a keypunch operator at the Ohio State University, on condition of completing school, which I did in August.

Before I started my new job at OSU, I cracked open my fat glass piggy bank. I had saved enough money to purchase a round-trip ticket to Alabama for the weekend on American Airlines. When I spotted Daddy waiting for me at the Montgomery Regional Airport baggage claim, the smile on his face froze, watching me strutting toward him wearing green hip-hugger bell bottoms, platform shoes, and a form-fitting red and green psychedelic blouse.

Harsh Realities

I continued working as a fashion model to earn extra money even after I started working. In addition to providing a polished exterior that enhanced my self-confidence, modeling opened unexpected doors. One benefit was purchasing the garments I wore from Lazarus Department Store at a deep discount. My scant wardrobe quickly included the latest collection of bathing suits, mini-dresses, platform shoes, and other clothing Daddy would have forbidden. Through the Monique Modeling Agency, I met arrogant, fun-loving men and women, and on Friday nights, my phone was always ringing. "Hey girl, we gonna hit the club. You coming?"

On a dare from those wild Monique Models—a ten-dollar bet that I'd win Miss Talent—I competed in the Miss Americolor Pageant, something that, along with modeling, I thought exploited women and was beneath me. But my eighteen-year-old self found fashion modeling was easy money and a lot of fun, and I did not believe I would win a beauty pageant for one moment. Still, the competitor in me could not resist the challenge.

At the crowded Valley Dale Ballroom, an enchanting place with a broad stage, chandeliers, theater chairs, and heavy velvet curtains, I competed against fifteen other girls, each judged on swimwear, an evening gown, and a current events question. I wore a white, scooped neck one-piece swimsuit, red and gold brocade evening gown, and peep-toe gold high heels, clothing my sponsor, "The Other Room" nightclub owner, had purchased.

When the moderator said, "And the winner of Miss Americolor Columbus, Mildred Billups," I could barely move my stiff legs, and my jaws ached from that pasted-on smile. I barely remember someone placing red roses in my arms, pinning a banner on my gown, and placing a crown on my head. But I can still hear my friends screaming my name when I won the city title and would represent Columbus in the Ohio state pageant.

Two months later, I competed for the state title in Dayton, Ohio, and won. As I stood backstage, a swirl of energy, wearing tight, bell-bottom hip-hugger pants, rushed toward me and hugged me like we were long-lost sisters. "Girrrlll, that voice!" she said. (I had sung and received a standing ovation for the pageant's talent portion). She told me her name was Syni Richardson from Alabama, and she had just won Miss Black Ohio. "Why don't you move to Dayton and go to college with me?" she asked. I told her I had finished tech school, worked at Ohio State, and sent money home to help my folks. "If you ever change your mind, call me." We swapped numbers, and I hugged her, thinking I wouldn't see her again. But as fate would have it, a foolish choice I made the following year severely endangered my life, and Syni rescued me, brought me to Dayton, and got me into college.

Still, I will never forget seeing New York City for the first time from LaGuardia Airport and competing for the Miss Americolor national title six months after winning the state pageant. I sang "She Didn't Know (She Kept On Talking)" by Dee Dee Warwick to a packed auditorium with such passion that I again received a standing ovation. Flashbulbs lit up the arena, and the crowd roared, erupted in applause, stood to their feet, and hollered, "*Sing it, girl!*" I placed third at the national pageant and won Miss Talent, and Ricketts Enterprises signed me to a singing contract on the spot.

Harsh Realities

After winning Miss Talent, during a singing engagement at a small club in Columbus, I met my roommate, Beverly, who was ten years older and had an eight-year-old girl.

When I told Arthur I had moved in with Beverly, the look on his face was lethal. "Where the hell did you meet that woman?" he asked. "You can't trust her. She's a bull dike." I argued that she was a lovely woman with a young child. I soon learned that Arthur was right. I became the babysitter and cook while Beverly partied regularly in and out of the house.

According to Mama, there is *some* good in everybody. But after eight months with Beverly, I had doubts, especially after the Sunday night I tiptoed downstairs to the refrigerator for a 7-Up and tried to avoid the dope party at the kitchen bar. The dining room was dark; a Jimi Hendrix song blared from the stereo; strobe lights swirled like swords, slashing paths across the walls and ceiling. Cigarette smoke and the smell of weed lurked heavily in the air. Beverly and three men sat on barstools drinking brown liquor, smoking pot, popping pills, and nodding off. A plastic bag that I thought was marijuana was lying on the counter beside a pile of pills and dollar bills. I tried sneaking past the bar back to my bedroom when Beverly snatched me by the collar and pushed a joint in my face. "Loosen up, bitch. Come have a little fun."

Stunned at the assault, I slammed my drink on the bar next to Beverly and shoved her with all my might. "*Don't ever* put your hands on me again." A friend from Ohio State University had walked in, grabbed me around the waist, led me to a bean bag in the living room, and tried calming me down. He then brought my 7-Up.

After a few sips, the room began spinning, my stomach was unsettled, and I vomited. My friend's face now resembled a wildcat, who growled, swiped a large paw at me, and then chased me through tall weeds in a dark jungle. I scampered away on all fours and huddled in a corner, screaming and kicking at voices echoing from all sides of the room.

"You could've killed her. You crazy-ass bitch."

"I told you not to put that shit in her drink; she's just a kid."

"We gotta get her to a hospital."

"No fucking way. We'll go to jail."

I vaguely remember the nightmare—running far and fast from a dark room with strobe lights, beaded curtains that separated the living and dining rooms, and the screaming trip in an ice storm where I stabbed baseball-sized snowflakes with the tip of a black umbrella.

But I clearly remember telling Beverly I planned to find a new roommate and move the following Saturday. "That's funny," she said. "I'm moving out to L.A. that same day."

The Tuesday before moving day, I stepped off the bus in front of my apartment, startled to find the front door wide open. Beverly's car and the moving trailer, parked in front of the apartment, were gone. I hurried inside my empty apartment and stared the cruel claws of deceit in the face. Beverly, a woman several sizes larger than me, had moved out early, disconnected the telephone and electricity, and stolen most of my clothing. The blue Samsonite suitcases I had won in the Miss Americolor Pageant were not next to the door where I had left them packed with my clothes and shoes that morning. My modeling and pageant photos that Beverly

Harsh Realities

didn't take were in the middle of the floor with the trash. The spot where my five-gallon collector's jar full of half dollars and quarters had left a round imprint on the carpet. The apartment was dark except for the streetlight shining through the living room's small windowpanes where the curtains were missing. For the first time since I left Alabama, I felt naked—completely alone.

I spread my remaining clothing on the floor, huddled close to the wall beneath the window, and slept, hiding from the harm that lurked in the dark. Crawling back to my parents for farm work was not an option. My days of hard labor in Alabama cotton fields were over. I decided I'd rather live in a pasteboard box and sleep under a Croker sack before having another roommate.

On our first date, when Arthur withheld his phone number, stating, "A lady never calls a man, and a gentleman never expects her to," I was too gullible to know better. It had not been a problem until now when I needed Arthur and could not contact him by phone or bus because he lived in the suburbs, far away from bus routes. Cell phones and Google Maps did not exist back then. Unlike today, I could not plug an address into Apple or Google maps and find my way to a location anywhere in the country.

The Thursday after Beverly stole my clothes, I abruptly quit my new job at Ohio State. I raced down Livingston Avenue to a pay phone that night and called Syni, whose number I had tucked away. "Does your offer to pick me up in Columbus and bring me to Dayton still stand? I want to attend college after all."

Outside the phone booth, I ran, screaming from dueling shadows tearing at my raw emotions. One clung to me, urging me to forget—hurry—get out of Columbus to a safe place, while another pressed me into darkness, a place like drowning, sinking, forcing me to remember something that escaped me—pain—swimming, thrashing its way to the surface.

I remember standing on the corner of Broad and High streets in Columbus, Ohio, reading *The Boston Strangler* after work. I glanced at my Timex and noted the Livingston Avenue bus was seven minutes late. Sweaty passengers piled out of buses lined up on Broad Street and dashed to the ones on High Street. A sleek white Cadillac oozed to a halt, parked in the bus lane, and blocked traffic. I craned my neck to see who dared to perch in that restricted spot during evening rush hour amidst honking horns, cursing bus drivers, and angry passengers waving the fuck-you sign.

A black-tinted window glided down, and a man with a head as slick and dark as a bowling ball was sitting in the driver's seat. He slid aviator glasses to the end of his nose, and I avoided his shifty eyes. The faint sound of Jimi Hendrix's guitar rippling through "Machine Gun" floated from his car radio. The man was vaguely familiar, but I couldn't place him. I gazed around nervously as bus drivers laid on their horns. "Get the hell out the way, man," they yelled.

The man grinned, and his lips spread across large white teeth the size of Chiclets. "Hey, Miss Americolor. What you doin' at dat bus stop? Lemme give you a ride, girl." Then, I remembered him, a sad, faceless man—constantly alone—lurking dead-center many nights as I strolled to the end of a runway, working as a fashion model on weekends. One night, I heard that same jerky voice from the man whose name I didn't know—but will call Diablo—when he walked to the stage after my show and reached for my hand.

Harsh Realities

"You were good tonight." That night, I wore all white: a one-piece bathing suit, peep-toe shoes, and an apple cap cocked to the side. At the end of the night, I shook his and other fans' hands, whom I occasionally saw in the audience.

Then, I told him, "Thank you," and thought, *What a lonesome man.* Now, here he was in broad daylight.

I stared nervously at the white Coupe de Ville and the man behind the wheel and thought how, months earlier, when Daddy drove me to Ohio, he pointed to a man in a pink Eldorado with white sidewall tires. The guy wore a wide-brimmed white hat and a purple suit. Daddy had told me that only pimps and preachers drove Cadillacs and that he didn't trust either one with a lady.

"The bus is late, but it'll be here soon. I don't need a ride," I told Diablo.

"But you must be hot." He slipped his dark glasses back on and pretended to fan himself.

"No. I'm not hot." Yet, with the temperature near ninety, sweat crept down my back.

He propped his elbows on the open window and rested his chin on his palm. "Come on, girl, loosen up. Why you so uptight? You think I'd harm you wit' all these people lookin' at me?"

I leaped backward, startled when a strange man at the bus stop pointed his finger in my face. "Get your boyfriend outta here," he hollered. Male bus drivers yelled from their windows, "Get in the damn car, already, girl," and "Man, git yo' ass out the way. You blocking up traffic."

Every day, with a book tucked under my arm and joy in my steps, I had ridden to and from work in an air-conditioned bus, ecstatic to be riding, not walking barefoot in a hot cotton field. For the first time since I'd left Alabama, I felt threatened and wished I could ask Mama or Daddy what I should do. I was trapped between the screaming men on the streets and the man speaking softly through the car window. *Maybe he's a preacher, not some pimp out to harm me.* Perhaps I *should* relax. I looked nervously up and down the street. My bus was nowhere in sight. Cars lined up as far as I could see and blared their horns. I hustled into the car to escape the angry men and thought it was just a ride home.

As soon as I closed the car door, Diablo faked a growl and mashed the gas. "See, I won't bite." He skinned his lips back and laughed. I noticed the space where his eye tooth should have been but couldn't see his eyes behind the aviator shades. Frigid air blasted from the air-conditioner. I felt my heartbeat beating frantically against my chest, but I sat back and tried to relax against the white leather seats. "I live on Livingston Avenue. The address is—"

"*Shut up.*" The door locks cracked like a pistol being cocked. It seemed that time slid into slow motion. Outside the car window, people hurried along downtown Columbus sidewalks to favorite restaurants or bars. Tires squealed when Diablo did a U-turn in the middle of Broad Street, pinning me to the back of the seat. The speedometer hit sixty-five in a thirty-five, and I screamed. He slapped me hard across my mouth. Then I noticed the glint of a little pearl-handle pistol lying between his legs and reached for the door handle. "Ack a fool. I'll *fuck you up.*"

The man drove two blocks and swung into the circular driveway at the Christopher Inn on East Broad Street. A bellman, whom I hoped would help me escape, approached the passenger side door

Harsh Realities

like a prison guard but didn't open it. He gazed through the window and slid his tongue slowly over his large lips, and Diablo stalked around the front of the car, handed the man a fistful of dollars, and snatched open the passenger door. The smell of garlic, rotten onions, and cheap wine from the nearby alley hit me in the face like an assault rifle.

Diablo, tall and muscular, grabbed my elbow, ushered me outside the car toward the lobby, and threw his arm around my waist, holding me close like we were lovers. He smiled outwardly but muttered, "You *better* behave." His blue gators and my platform shoes sang staccato notes like hammering woodpeckers, pecking at the marble floor.

I felt my world spinning out of control as I took in everything inside the hotel, a fancy place I had admired from the bus stop every day. I had dreamed of dining in its top-floor restaurant, an upscale place overlooking downtown Columbus. Diablo said a familiar hello to people at the bar or lobby but kept moving. I shuffled along like a prisoner in leg irons, my eyes darting side-to-side, trying to attract attention from anyone seeing me in distress. But he hustled me down the hall toward the elevator. And then, silence stole my secrets until the day laughter recovered my memory. What happened to me in that hotel was a trauma I buried deep in my bones, forgotten for over thirty years.

At eight o'clock that Saturday morning, only fourteen months after Daddy dropped me off in Columbus, a single tear slid down my cheek. I watched Syni's green Pontiac pull to the curb from my living room window—hoping against hope to see Arthur's car. I remembered him leaning against the Riviera that glistened in the sunlight, me running young and free into the safety of his outstretched arms. I remembered how, for days, I had cried myself to sleep, longing for any sign of Arthur—a phone call or visit—after Beverly drugged me. Then, I got angry and cursed the disconnected phone and my not having his number. With no car or other way to contact him, I swallowed my tears, pasted on a smile, and slipped onto Syni's Grand Prix passenger seat with my remaining clothes in a garbage bag.

    How could it be that my budding love affair, modeling, singing career, and the job of less than a year had ended? It all felt like a mirage. I fled Columbus, Ohio, where I grew up, became a woman, and found my independence. But now, I couldn't shake the shadows of bad memories lost in the rearview mirror as I rode to a place of pretension. I became a college theater major—a pretend girl hiding behind a façade—and began a new life in Dayton, Ohio, where I could laugh again, love again, in an environment that sheltered me from devastation so unbearable that it had shattered my memory.

CHAPTER 12
Starting Over

Throughout the summer of 1970, *The Dayton Daily News* featured me in several articles with photos, including "Miss Americolor of Ohio Named" and "Miss Americolor Ohio Moves to Dayton." A smiling close-up appeared in a piece titled "Miss Ohio Americolor Rebounds from Letdown." Another read, "At 18, Mildred Billups was a shiny-eyed newcomer to Ohio from tiny Wetumpka, Ala. Now 19, she is Ohio's Miss Americolor, third place winner in the national contest, and just about fed up with the beauty contest business." I also mentioned that I would attend Wright State University in the fall.

On a crisp October day in 1970, my first day on campus, I met a boy. I was rushing along the sidewalk from the registrar's office with other students, and he stood in my path like a church greeter near a set of double glass doors. He swung open the door and smiled crookedly, revealing a gap between his two front teeth. He stuck out his right hand and told me his name was Peter. "Are you looking for your friend Syni?" he asked.

I gave him an uneasy smile but couldn't recall having met him. Before I could answer him or object, he offered to help me find Syni and whisked me into the noisy cafeteria where students chatted, laughed, studied, or played cards. He waved and shouted to almost every Black person in his path. "Hey, this is Mildred Billups, Miss Americolor," information I had not shared with him. Heads turned as he hustled past tables, introducing me like he was a tour guide pointing out a historical statue. And then it hit me; Maybe he followed newspaper headlines. The most recent article had appeared only three weeks earlier.

After that first meeting, every time I looked up, Peter offered to introduce me to people "so you can make friends" or taught me to play bid whist, a card game "everybody that's anybody knows how to play." I learned he was a music major; I'd recently won Miss Talent USA singing in the beauty pageant. His parents were born and raised in Alabama, where his grandmother still lived; he suggested they would give me a ride to my hometown when he and his folks visited her. With so much in common, we became close.

A month after school started, I moved into the dormitory and gravitated to the spacious lobby, high ceilings, and bright lights that energized the place. Somehow, I sensed I was safe among the young people who hung out in chairs or on the floor, playing cards or with their heads deep in thick textbooks. Peter, who already lived in the dorm, was buying a Reese's Peanut Butter Cup at the snack stand near a Steinway piano. He had sunk his teeth into the candy when he noticed me, then waved me over to meet some students. "Me and Mildred gonna provide a little entertainment this evening," he said, something I had not agreed to. He boasted

Starting Over

like we were headliners at a concert. I enjoyed singing, so I grabbed the microphone and joined in.

Peter sat at the piano, playing Jackson 5 songs, and I chimed in, singing like Michael. Several students introduced themselves, and I was grateful to meet new people my age, away from predators like Beverly, who had made sport of drugging me and stealing my clothing.

That fall, in addition to my studies, I worked a public relations work-study job that I loved, once escorting Roger Mudd—a CBS broadcast journalist—from the Dayton airport to Wright State University during its "Artist and Lecture Series." When the handsome, charismatic man I had seen numerous times on the news walked off the plane into the cramped gate area and said hello, I couldn't believe my good fortune.

He dove into subjects like one-term limits for Congress to prevent their constant re-election worries. When Mr. Mudd teased that visiting Wright State and its water tower had been a lifelong dream in addition to Rome and Paris, students jumped to their feet in a standing ovation. I stood on the periphery of the auditorium, quietly observing his interaction with the crowd, and dreamed of traveling, commanding such an audience someday, and even seeing Paris and Rome.

For Christmas break that year, with money from my work-study job, I bought a one-way airplane ticket home to Alabama to visit my family. The last time I saw them was July the year before, almost eighteen months. When I walked down the steps from the airplane onto the tarmac at Montgomery Regional Field, a smile split Daddy's face as he stood at the gate waving from the window. I hurried inside, and when he thrust out his calloused palm, I wanted to throw my arms around his neck, something I had never done, so we pumped hands and grinned at one another. On the ride home, he asked, "How was the trip?" about the weather and other mundane topics until we turned on the red dirt road toward home.

Crackling pea gravel brought my younger sisters and brothers storming out the front, back, and side doors up the red dirt road to meet the car, racing it back to the house. My heart zipped along with them as we grinned, waving ecstatically at each other. Some were too young to remember me, their only sibling who had left Alabama. (Brother had moved out but lived close by.) They knew I existed because of my letters home, graduation picture on the piano, phone calls, and Mama's constant reminder that "You have a sister in Ohio."

I had missed home and family last Christmas and excitedly anticipated walking back into the spacious place I had relived over and over in my mind for the past eighteen months. But once inside, I couldn't remember it being so cramped and cluttered. My childhood Christmas smells of apples, oranges, and cornbread dressing were gone. In their place were noisy children everywhere. I had an eighteen-month-old baby sister and three siblings under five years old. Sprigs of soot and ashes from the fireplace clung to the walls and ceiling. I went into the cramped kitchen where Mama was sweating and wiping herself with her dress tail and fell right in place. I helped prepare a dinner of fried chicken, rice and gravy, cornbread, and green vegetables. The mouth-watering chicken from the yard I had remembered tasted gamey and tough, unlike

Starting Over

the tender pullets I now bought from the grocery store, kept in the refrigerator, and fried in an electric Teflon skillet.

On Christmas morning, I handed Mama and Daddy greeting cards with money and unwrapped the clothes they had bought me from Sears Roebuck: boots, a winter coat, and a sweater. A week later, the walls began to close in after sleeping with my brothers and sisters, whose unwashed hands, feet, and small bodies pressed against me like sardines. I was ready to return to the solitude of my dorm room. Daddy had fired shots into the dark, welcoming a baby new year—1971. New Year's morning, at the breakfast table, surrounded by his sixteen children and Mama, he said, "It's so good having you home, Babe. You sure you don't wanna stay? When you need to be back?"

With all the eyes around the wobbly oval-shaped table trained on me, I searched for words to avoid hurting their feelings. In the short time with my family, I realized I enjoyed being alone and no longer fit in the tight space I'd left all those months ago. "I had no idea I'd missed you so much," I said. "But I've gotta get back and do schoolwork. Can you drive me back tomorrow? That way, you won't miss church Sunday."

The following day, Daddy and I left Alabama in pitch darkness and pouring rain. I sat in the passenger seat, staring out the windshield at the severe weather through which I could barely see the car's hood. Daddy flew through the Tennessee and Kentucky mountains, driving more than ninety miles an hour, whipping around curves and trucks, sometimes slipping off the highway's edge only to jerk the wheel back on the road. I was terrified but said nothing. I prayed, asking God to be a shield of protection around me from Alabama to Ohio, where, when I stepped out of Daddy's car, I decided I would never allow him to drive me again. I should have spoken up and told him his reckless driving terrified me. Even though I was an adult, living on my own, I was only nineteen and still feared the long reach of my father, especially while in his presence.

In Ohio, light snow had made the roads slippery but not so slick that Daddy slowed down until he slid in front of Hamilton Hall, unlocked the trunk, handed me my suitcase, and said a quick goodbye. I didn't bother watching him leave. I could hear his tires spinning across campus as I walked into the warmth and safety of the dormitory lobby.

To calm nerves that screamed like notes from a Jimi Hendrix guitar, I slipped Miles Davis's jazz album, *Bitches Brew* onto the stereo and laid across the bed when the telephone rang. "Hey, you wanna spend a few days with my family? Momma said I could invite you to stay over next weekend before school starts." I told Peter I'd love to see his family, whom I'd met at Thanksgiving and had not seen since.

The following Saturday morning, I slipped on Army-green crushed velvet bell-bottoms, a mustard-colored sweater, and a Sears Roebuck winter coat and boots—the clothing Mama and Daddy had given me for Christmas. I stood in the dormitory lobby and watched light snow fall like a white blanket. It covered the horseshoe-shaped driveway and wrapped a glistening shawl around evergreen trees near the sidewalk. Colorful lights twinkled on a large blue spruce tree near the entrance. Christmas carols played softly in the background. I had heard the engine straining

Starting Over

in the distance like a whirring helicopter long before I saw Peter drive up with black and gray smoke shooting from beneath his lopsided Ford Falcon. I slid onto the front seat, happy to see my friend. After slipping and sliding like a rookie on ice skates, the tires finally caught, and the car moved forward. He told me the vehicle, an eyesore with a fresh coat of powder blue house paint, could not go more than thirty miles per hour, which had us both cracking up.

Before the weekend was over, giddy as two kids stealing from the cookie jar, we tiptoed downstairs to the basement and had sex for the first time on a twin bed jammed in a small, cramped space amidst pink insulation stuck between wall beams. When it was over, I felt like I had been set on fire and left to burn.

I didn't realize my disappointment showed until Peter turned from me, pulled the sheet up to his neck, and apologized for being "inadequate." "I bet you were just nervous," I said. The pained expression on his face made me fumble for words. I quoted whoever said, "It ain't the size of the ship, but the motion on the ocean." I told him there would be other times. Still, I wanted to kick myself for trying to spare his feelings when I was so sexually dissatisfied.

CHAPTER 13
Immaculate Conception

Intimacy was the last thing on my mind for the next several weeks as I began a never-ending menstrual cycle. Dr. Washington, my OB/GYN, removed my intrauterine device (IUD), allegedly the cause of the bleeding. When my period continued, he performed a D&C. After the procedure, with my feet still in the stirrups, the doctor stood beside me like a stern-faced father. "Miss Billups, no sex for six weeks. Your uterus is wide open. The chances of getting pregnant are extremely high." I didn't know what a uterus was, but I knew the meaning of pregnancy. Having rocked, fed, and diapered enough babies to last a lifetime, I wanted no part of babies or husbands.

The only time I saw a penis from February, when the female problems began, until July, when I learned I was expecting, was two days after the D&C. On Saturday night, April 10—my twentieth birthday—Peter, who had failed out of school, sneaked up the stairs to my dorm room to shower and dress for a fraternity party. I was in bed resting, drained from weeks of bleeding. We showered together; he went to a party; I went back to bed. An article I read in *American Pregnancy* suggests that if you or your partner have semen or pre-cum on your fingers and touch your vagina, this could allow sperm to enter, resulting in pregnancy without intercourse.

After a visit to Dr. Washington in July, his examination and a urine test confirmed I was approximately three months pregnant. When I told people the "I did not have sex with that boy story," they would give me a look of pity. Only my mother humored me. She chuckled and said, "Mildred, young people can look at one another and get pregnant."

When I told Syni I was pregnant in July, she said, "Girl, you don't want no baby by Peter Lee." She offered to pay for an abortion in New York City, where they were legal, "so you won't ruin your life." I didn't know anything about abortions in New York or anywhere else. But having heard horror stories of women maimed or killed in dark alleys after failed abortions with clothes hangers, I considered my friend's offer. The fear of Mama and Daddy identifying my mangled or dead body in a dark alley chose life for my unborn child and me. Roe v. Wade (a.k.a. the right to choose), the Supreme Court decision providing a woman the final decision on whether to give birth to her child or abort the fetus, was passed on January 22, 1973, a year after I gave birth. In 1971, I didn't choose abortion out of concern for my safety. I don't know what choice I would have made had abortion been legal in Ohio. Sadly, the US Supreme Court overturned Roe v. Wade on June 24, 2022, revoking that right.

A few months after Mr. Mudd had visited the campus, I informed my manager, the program director at Wright State, that I was pregnant. He frowned and glanced over the top of his wire-rimmed readers. "We can't have a pregnant girl escorting dignitaries around our campus." He leaned back on his big office chair with his feet cocked on the desk and instructed me to stay hidden inside the office for the next two months. At the end of the summer semester, he terminated my employment. I did not return to college in October for the fall semester.

I was six months pregnant in late October when the phone rang, and it was Arthur. "I searched *everywhere*, but I *finally* tracked you down. Why the hell did you leave Columbus without telling me?" I had not heard from him in more than a year. Hearing his voice took my breath away.

"*Arthur*, I can't believe it's you. I thought I had lost you forever. Where *were you*, Art, when my crazy roommate spiked my drink with LSD? You were right that I couldn't trust Beverly. That crazy woman stole my clothes and left town, leaving me stranded in an empty apartment with no electricity in the middle of July." I wanted to curse him and, at the same time, curl up in the safety of his arms. Instead, I whispered words so painful I could hardly get them out. "Art, I'm having a baby. It's due in January."

"*What? You're pregnant? Are you married?*" His baritone voice had risen an octave.

"I'm not married," I told him, so shame-filled I thought I would break.

"What kinda motherfucker knocks you up and doesn't marry you? Babe, I want you and your baby. Just tell me where you are, please." My heart broke when he called me Babe, his name for me when we made love. I couldn't hold back the tears when he threatened to kick Peter's ass. I wanted nothing more than to be with Arthur and share a child that was ours.

Tears flowed for the love I had for Arthur and not for Peter, for Arthur's babies I wouldn't have, and because Daddy would never meet this brave, hardworking man he would have admired. I wept because every child should know their father, and neither my spiritual nor moral values permitted such deceit. I could not have lived with myself had I taken Peter's baby from him. But I cried even more because I felt stuck where I didn't want to be, remembering the day Peter and I learned I was pregnant.

I had gone to my OB/GYN complaining of a high fever, loss of appetite, fatigue, and weight loss two months after he'd performed a D&C. When the doctor cleared his throat and asked, "Miss Billups, is it possible you could be pregnant?" I felt like I had been gut-punched. I staggered out of his office and slid across the bench seat of the severely dented 1960-something Buick station wagon Peter had borrowed from his father. Staring through the windshield of the raggedy car, I thought of shattered dreams as Peter drove back to his mother's house. "The doctor asked if I thought I might be pregnant, and he ordered a pregnancy test," I told him. "The nurse will call Friday with the results."

Peter glanced toward me and said, "You wanna get something to eat? We could stop at the Dairy Queen." I stared at him—bewildered. My boyfriend, a chubby man-child with hunched shoulders, was slumped forward, gripping the steering wheel, gazing at the scenery outside the car window like a tour bus driver. He said, "You didn't eat this morning, remember? I thought you'd be hungry." I don't know what I had expected Peter to say, but that

Immaculate Conception

wasn't it. In retrospect, it made sense that a carefree nineteen-year-old boy, sleeping in his parents' basement, where they met his every need and gave him no responsibilities, would be more interested in a Dairy Queen stop than talk about the doctor's visit.

I was hungry for the first time in weeks and handed him wadded-up dollars from my purse to pay for food. After devouring a chili dog, food I didn't usually like or eat but at that moment craved, I felt lightheaded, and my stomach contracted violently. Peter pulled to the side of the road, and in one retching moment, I spilled everything in my guts along Gettysburg Avenue. Back then, I was unfamiliar with morning sickness and had no idea vomiting could be associated with pregnancy. Years after I left home, I asked Mama, who always looked the same to me—pregnant or not—if she ever experienced morning sickness. "Only with Brother," she told me, "And I craved Argo starch until the day he was born."

Today, I am astonished at my ignorance and innocence as a child. I accepted my mother as she was, stout, never realizing she was pregnant. We celebrated each new baby for a moment when Mama called us to her bedside and said, "Meet the new baby." I was thrilled if it was a girl, and we outnumbered the boys. I remember asking why she named my baby brother John Francis in June 1968. "We're honoring the Kennedy brothers, John and Robert," she said. Senator Kennedy was gunned down four days earlier. Once I asked why she made me, not her oldest daughter, her namesake, Mama said, "She just didn't look like a Mildred to me." When I asked what "A Mildred" looked like, she said, "Your sister favored ya daddy's people," which made me realize the care Mama placed on naming her children.

I found myself pregnant and unmarried—far off the path I imagined for myself. Emotions swirled, and I was unable to form a cohesive thought. The metallic taste of bile clung to my mouth. Peter made small talk, seemingly unconcerned and unaware of the magnitude of potential pregnancy or becoming a parent. I was twenty years old and three months; he was nineteen, three months shy of being twenty. I did not want to be pregnant or forever tied to Peter. He had no job, wasn't looking for one, wasn't motivated, had not grown or matured since I met him nine months earlier, and had drifted into a place of complacency. I was sickened that one phone call from a nurse three days later could change my life forever.

"Art, our time has passed. Who knew my not having your phone number would cost us?"

"Babe, I'm giving it to you now. *Please* call me. Call me collect. Just call me."

Arthur and I held the phone, sobbing like mourning doves, each reluctant to sever the last thread binding us. I was trembling, trying to remember something painful lurking beneath the surface, something I needed to tell Arthur, something I feared would crush me.

For the last six months of my pregnancy, morning and night, I hugged the toilet bowl and hurled anything I ate until I arrived at the emergency room two days before I gave birth. On that day, Peter had held my arm and supported me as I waddled through the icy parking lot into the hospital on a cold January morning with heavy air that smelled like snow. The security guard, wide-eyed and nervous, met me at the door. "Miss, what seems to be the trouble?"

Immaculate Conception

"I think I'm in labor." Peter turned and walked back to the car as the man hustled me onto a wheelchair, rushed to the elevator, and wheeled me into a narrow, brightly lit space on an upper floor where the next forty-eight hours were like something out of a horror movie.

A large dark-skinned woman placed a wash pan and several white towels on the counter near my bed and handed me a hospital gown. "Put this on with the opening to the back." I stared nervously at the puffs of steam hovering above the aluminum pan and a plastic bottle with an extended nozzle. The woman draped a crisp white sheet above my knees at the foot of the bed. "Draw your feet up on the table and spread your legs." She pulled back the cover, scrubbed my privates with a hot, soapy towel, mowed off my pubic hair with the precision of a surgeon, gave me an enema, and walked out of the room. I had never felt so naked or humiliated. I curled into the fetal position and tried to drown out the screams and curses of women and girls from nearby rooms.

After receiving an epidural, I nodded off with the strong smell of Pine-Sol and anesthesia stinging my nostrils. I woke up to the sound of a large nurse hustling down the hallway, snapping the metal on a brown clipboard. She clumped to my bedside and asked, "Are *you* Mildred Billups?" I heard judgment and contempt.

I managed a weak smile and wiggled like a turtle on its back, trying to sit up, but my swollen belly stood in the way. "Yes, I'm Mildred."

The woman gripped an ink pen in her right hand and never made eye contact. "How many other children *you* got?"

"I don't have other children." I bit my tongue as my baby kicked. HARD.

The woman shoved her readers to the end of her nose. "Humph, a proper one. You tellin' me this your first child?"

"That's *exactly* what I am telling you."

"Not married, are you?"

I glared at her double chin and the beehive hairdo, a flaming red nest perched on top of her head. "No, I'm not, but the father and I are together." Somehow, I felt I needed to explain to this woman that I didn't want to get married.

She laughed and pointed a red fingernail at my face. "Yeah, and I'm the Queen of Sheba! You just like the rest of 'em coming in here every year; another baby, another daddy."

I reared up in bed and glared at the woman. "Lady, *you don't know me*, but you're *dead* wrong!"

With a dismissive hand flip, she said, "That's what all y'all say. See you next year, *Miss* Billups." I wanted to hurl a shoe at the broad back, retreating down the hall with her stockings shrieking like crickets as her thighs rubbed together. I slumped back on my pillow and cursed myself for allowing someone I would never see again to upset me. And then, a doctor I had never met came to my bedside.

"I'll be delivering your baby," the dark-skin man with straight black hair said with the emotions of a slug.

Sadly, I realized that all the faces belong to strangers when you're on welfare. I longed for my grandfatherly doctor, who had grudgingly convinced me to accept public assistance after my seventh month. "Miss Billups, my fee is extremely high, and the hospital bill will be enormous. Why go into debt when the government is willing to help you?" Then, he placed his large hand on my shoulder and stood close like a caring father. "I have faith in you, Miss Billups. I'll see you again when you're back on your feet." The doctor handed me forms, which I took downtown to become a welfare recipient.

Now, examining me, the no-name doctor jammed a finger inside my pelvis as if to punish me. I felt dirty, flush with shame. He asked if I was in pain. I turned my head and gazed at the ceiling. "I feel pressure, but no pain."

I was alone on my bed. Shrill screams pierced the air like Halloween monsters. I wondered how Mama had given birth to seventeen babies with nothing but prayer and a loyal midwife to dull the pain. I longed to hear her voice, see my friends, or any friendly face, and craved the smell of anything but the sterility of that hospital room with fluorescent lights casting dim shadows across the gray walls of my cramped room. I desired to meet the little one growing inside me, a child who had stolen into my life just as her father had. As the epidural dulled my pain, I closed my eyes and thought of significant recent changes in my life, including how one night, the scripture "A child is a gift from God" came to me in a dream. I had heard the verse in passing but had never used it, but its appearance comforted me.

Before I was pregnant, I did not want a child or a serious relationship until much later. Yet, I chose against abortion, a choice that led to me losing my job and independence and dropping out of college. I clung to the thought of my child being a gift to avoid the devastation I felt walking into that place, answering personal questions like, "Where is the father? Is he employed? Do you have any income? Can your parents help?" I felt like a failure, answering no to each of those questions.

I was even more humbled when I arrived for an exam at the clinic. It was a large open space with pregnant women and girls hollering at small children, who ran around the room chasing each other. When I returned each week, I saw a different doctor and never saw the same one twice. My mother's words resonated as I sat in that wide, unfamiliar space. "In every situation, hold your head high even if you have to die hard." She also said, "Never let the world see you with a hung down head and a sorry look on your face." It took every bit of pride in me not to feel sorrow and sadness for my predicament or not cry my eyes out sitting in that dark, musty, crowded room full of unmarried pregnant women. Although I felt ashamed, realizing I was not better off than anyone else in that room, I chose to think positively. Suffering a few indignities was a small price for avoiding substantial medical bills when I brought my baby home. But I knew then that I would not be in such a place again.

After forty-eight hours of labor, my water broke. A smiling nurse rushed through the door like an angel in a floaty white dress and nurse's cap. "Let's get you to the delivery room, sweetie! We're gonna have a baby. Aren't you excited?" she asked. As a twenty-year-old welfare recipient of three months, a college dropout with no job about to give birth to an unplanned child, I felt many emotions. Excitement was not one of them.

That morning at 4:32, a fresh-eyed nurse with a sunny disposition placed my child across my bosom with the twisted umbilical cord still attached. "Meet your baby girl, Miss Billups." I looked my baby over and found ten pink fingers and ten tiny toes.

"Welcome to the world, Ashaki Niambi," I said. I held her close to my heart and whispered, "Your father and I searched books of African names at Wright State University's Bolinga Center and chose this one just for you. It means Beautiful melody." She started screaming. Within hours, Peter slipped into the room as quietly as a ghost. When the crying child spotted him, a man she had never seen or whose voice she'd never heard, she flailed her fists and locked eyes with him. I felt empty and alone, realizing this child was no longer solely mine but someone I must share.

My first day as a mother felt like a failure. I shared the most intimate moment between a mother and child, holding my daughter to my breast. I wept. She wailed uncontrollably, unable to latch on. "The child is hungry. Here, give her this," a nurse said, emptying a can of Similac into a bottle and shoving it into my hand. The woman did not ask my opinion or offer breastfeeding advice but tossed me a pitying look as she marched out the door. Tears welled in my eyes, remembering how easily Mama sat on a rocking chair, propped her bare feet on the top rung, secured on her lap, a fat baby that latched onto one breast while milk seeped onto her dress from the other, and shelled peas.

Within days, my rock-hard left breast throbbed and was severely swollen, and piercing pains shot through my arm, neck, and shoulder. I visited the clinic twice and saw two welfare doctors who seemed mystified about why I was in such agony. Three weeks later, a third doctor hospitalized me for "exploratory surgery," only to discover that engorged milk glands caused the pain. When I asked the doctor why he chose surgery rather than a less intrusive measure to treat swollen milk ducts, he walked from the room as if I had questioned his integrity, which I certainly had. The sight of the five-inch half-moon gash running from the top of my underarm to the bottom of my breast sickened me. I gave the anxious woman reflecting at me from the mirror a good talk. "You did *not* survive years of King Cotton to allow callous treatment to have you wallowing in pity, surrounded by doubt. Get off your ass and move it."

Beginning the following day, I worked out as soon as I woke up and before bed. I lifted weights, did sit-ups, leg lifts, and jumping jacks, strengthening every muscle, whipping my mind and body back into fighting shape, looking forward to the day I would be back in the workforce.

CHAPTER 14
The Unemployment Office

On Monday, April 10, 1972, I sprang out of bed, staring in the face of my twenty-first birthday and sixth month on welfare. I glanced around the fifty-dollar-a-month one-room apartment on the second floor of a two-story duplex where I had tried to make a home for myself. A full-sized bed against one wall had a lumpy mattress that almost sagged to the floor. I glared at Peter, sprawled across it like a pile of dirty laundry. He snored loudly with his legs spread apart and hands folded over a large stomach that rose and fell with the steady rhythm of ocean waves.

A card table and three folding chairs were near the room's only door, a setup where I dined, entertained, and lounged. The fourth chair stood in the middle of the creaky wood floor, holding an old black-and-white television with a bent clothes hanger for an antenna. Before I could walk into the tiny nook that hid behind a half wall pretending to be a kitchen, I heard a muffled noise across the room and hurried to my daughter. When I noticed the tiny balled-up fists and pink cheeks as my child turned her head and continued sleeping. I smiled, admiring the antique white crib with gold trim, a pretty piece of furniture I had bought before I lost my work-study job six months earlier.

I had placed her crib near the only bright spot in a dark room, where natural light filtered through a small window and fell across her bed like a security blanket. I clasped my hands and prayed for the woman I hoped she would become, a wise and gentle person like her grandmother. "Sweet girl," I thought to myself, "a favorite piece of advice from your grandma is, 'Do the best you can with what you have right now.' A welfare check, a one-room home, and sharing the bathroom with three other families *are* my best for now. But mark my word, little one, before you grow your first tooth, I will work my way out of this place and put you in a good home."

I walked outside the room, across the hallway, and into a bathroom shared by four families. On my hands and knees with Ajax, scalding hot water, and a giant sponge, I scrubbed the piss, shit, and scum of people I have long blotted out of my memory from the floor, sink, toilet, and bathtub. After scrubbing the bathroom clean enough to eat off the floor, I bathed and walked back into the apartment. I pulled my navy-blue pinstriped slacks and blue blouse from a hanger behind the door and threw them across the foot of the bed near Peter. I stormed across wood planks into the tiny kitchen, snatched two olive green skillets off a shelf, plopped them on a two-burner hot plate, and placed a pound of bacon in the larger pan. After grabbing eggs, milk, butter, and cheese from the apartment-sized refrigerator, I slammed its door. Peter rolled over with a baffled look on his face. "What *you* all fired up about?"

The Unemployment Office

Bacon sizzled in a skillet; I cracked an egg against a bowl. "We need to get out of here and find jobs. Sitting around waiting for a welfare check is no life for healthy, twenty-year-olds." I whipped eggs so hard that a portion of the yolk flew out of the bowl. Whenever I walked into a grocery store, I felt shame standing in line with a basket full of groceries, pretending I was not using food stamps. To ease the humiliation, I acted like I had whipped out a wad of cash, paid for my groceries, and whistled all the way home, proud to be a tax-paying wage earner. I thought of Daddy saying, "We don't accept charity." He had refused government handouts regardless of how tough things were on the farm. I slung scrambled eggs, bacon, and toast on two paper plates and set them on the table.

Peter crawled out of bed and sat across the card table from me, slathering butter and grape jelly on white toast. He slapped his thighs together slowly like buzzard wings, a lusty look on his face as he prepared his breakfast.

I lost my appetite when the bottom of his Ban-Lon shirt crept up over the substantial bulge around his midriff. "Do you know what today is?" Not waiting for an answer, I said, "It's my twenty-first birthday—not the life I had imagined for myself." I shoved the folding chair away from the table and grabbed my plate. "The state of Ohio paid me and Ashaki's hospital bills and all the medical care for the past five months. How does that make *you* feel? The state doesn't owe us anything."

I stood up and tossed my breakfast in the trash can. "Something gnaws at the pit of my gut every time I see that welfare check and those food stamps in the mailbox. My parents raised me to earn a living, not have it handed to me."

Peter glared at me as if I were a trail of uninvited ants at a picnic. "What are you talking about? You think you too good for welfare? I know plenty folks on welfare and using food stamps. Why *you* worrying about it?"

I spun around, ready to fight. "Do I *think* I'm too good for welfare? *Hell, no*! I *know* I'm too good for it." We stared across the room like angry roosters in a cock-fighting ring. "My child will *not* grow up on welfare. I'm getting the hell off public assistance if it's the last thing I do."

With a dismissive wave of the hand and a loud slurp, Peter sucked down a cold glass of milk—mockery written all over his face. He sat back on his chair, folded his arms, and scowled. "So, what *you* gonna do, rob a bank? I don't see nobody lining up to hire no woman with a three-month-old baby, *do you*?"

"You don't see much hanging around here sleeping late, hooked on westerns and mystery movies, waiting on a welfare check. *My* welfare check."

I slipped into the bell-bottoms and blouse, slid my feet into size eight pumps, and hurried down the steep stairs on feet that felt light as wings. I stepped outside to fresh buds peeking through maples and oaks, just waking up from long winter naps, and moved swiftly along the sidewalk, inhaling springtime to sparrows singing bird songs. Tender sprouts of grass peeked out of the cold earth. At nine o'clock, while I hustled down Salem Avenue, inhaling exhaust fumes and listening to honking car horns, I wondered what my parents were doing.

I figured Mama will have already cleaned up the kitchen after feeding her family that had dwindled to thirteen, packed lunches

The Unemployment Office

for eight school children, and tended to four babies still at home. I imagined her starting a fire around the washpot, washing greasy work clothes all day, and hanging them on the clothesline to dry while she pondered what to prepare for dinner. Daddy will have plowed several acres before going to the government job where he now worked to supplement his farming income. After returning home in the evening, he would do the same, working from dusk to dawn to provide for his family. *How could I have had a baby with an unemployed man who isn't even looking for a job?* I thought. Remembering my parents that day, I realized how much I relied upon their teachings of setting routines and accepting responsibility to get me through each day, something I cling to as devoutly as I hold to my faith, even today.

It had been two and a half years since Daddy brought me to Ohio, handed me one hundred dollars, and paid for my technical school education. He had said, "If things don't work out, you will always have a place back home." I refused to consider that offer for many reasons, including because my parents had given me all the tools to succeed and sacrificed greatly to ensure that success.

I marched a mile to the unemployment office, determined to change my circumstances. I stopped short inside the building—hordes of angry-looking people stood in a room that seemed bigger than a concert hall. Lines swung in every direction and wrapped around each other like a busy freeway system.

I approached a lady sitting across the room at a black wrought-iron desk. "Can you tell me which is the unemployment line?" She rolled her eyes and pointed to the longest one. I crept forward for hours while people around me grumbled and complained. "They better not cut off my unemployment check. There ain't no jobs out there for a cat like me," said one man. Another tall, skinny guy with few teeth and eyeglasses as thick as a Coca-Cola bottle said he was in the same boat.

When I finally reached a wooden door at the front of the line, I peered through a small glass pane into the eyes of a Black woman whose stiff upper lip said, "Don't *mess* with me!" She stood behind what looked like a bulletproof window, wore a sideways wig and ruby red lipstick, and stared out of beady eyes that would discourage troublemakers. "What can I do for you?" she asked in a dark, low voice.

I straightened my spine. "Is this the right place to find a job?"

The woman's eyebrows shot up. "You looking for *work, not* unemployment benefits?"

"Yes, ma'am. I'm looking for a job." I had never heard of unemployment benefits. We stared at each other with puzzled looks.

"Well, you're the exception. Everybody in here want benefits; don't wanna work. Always making excuses about why they can't find employment." She poked out her bottom lip. "Humph. To tell the truth, they ain't looking for no job."

I didn't care what anyone else was looking for; I was there with one goal in mind—to find employment and get to work.

"Have you ever worked before? What kind of experience do you have?" she asked.

I told the lady I had keypunch experience and had worked in a public relations role during college. For a brief moment, she stared at me through cat's-eyed glasses with silver chains hooked around

The Unemployment Office

both ears, and then she hopped off her chair, walked out of her tiny cell, and closed the door. The lady took me by the hand. "Follow me, honey."

I pretended I didn't hear the curses from people waiting in line. I hunched my shoulders and sneaked an apologetic peek at one lady who spat "Bitch" right in my face. I didn't look at anyone else.

The lady brought me to the first woman I had met across the room. "This one is looking for work. She's got keypunch experience *and* some college," she whispered. "I better get back to my line. Good luck to you, honey." I loved how old Black ladies used terms of endearment (baby, sugar, honey)—and with sweet voices—to encourage anyone trying to better themselves.

The lady at the wrought-iron desk stopped pecking on her typewriter. "Where did you go to technical school? Did you finish? What college did you attend? Where were you employed? How long ago was that? Did you collect unemployment benefits?" The woman couldn't ask questions fast enough and pointed me to a chair beside her desk. "I need to make a call right quick." She rode her finger around the black rotary dial so fast I thought she'd break a nail. "I got one for you who's just what you've been looking for, and she has keypunch experience, some college, and finished computer school." The lady placed her hand over the telephone receiver. "Can you be in Moraine City tomorrow at two o'clock for an interview with Frigidaire?"

"I've never heard of Moraine City, but I'll be there tomorrow."

She hung up and folded my hands gently between hers. "Look, honey. Buses don't go out to Moraine City; you need a car. Find a way to get to that interview. That's a *good* job." She looked around like there were spies in the room. "Don't tell 'em I told you this, but they pay $795 a month—good money with excellent benefits." She jotted down the manager's name and directions to Frigidaire, a division of General Motors (GM). I clutched the note like a gold nugget and stuffed it inside my bra.

My high heels on the sidewalk sounded like a busy woodpecker on a pine tree. I took the twenty steps to our second-floor room two at a time and rushed through the door. Peter and Ashaki were lying across the bed asleep with the TV blaring. "Wake up! You won't believe what happened today. I need to be in Moraine City tomorrow for an interview. I can get a job at Frigidaire making $795 a month." He gave me a blank stare, but I couldn't stop talking. "We can hire a babysitter, and you can find work. Can you borrow your dad's car?"

He yawned unenthusiastically and sat up in bed. "How you gonna get to Moraine City every day if you get that job?"

I wanted to scream, hit something. "Just let me *get* that job, and I'll *show* you how I'll get there. Would you please call your dad?" I wanted to say, "If I have to start walking the night before, I will be standing there ready to work every day when the doors open."

That Friday, my first telephone call after receiving the offer was to the social worker. "I have a job at Frigidaire beginning Monday, May eighth. I won't need welfare anymore."

"Honey, these opportunities don't always work out; you'll need childcare when you start work," she told me in a soft, concerned voice. Then she said I should collect Aid for Dependent Children (ADC) for a while, just in case.

The Unemployment Office

"Lady, thanks for giving me a hand up. God knows I needed it. The job *will* work out, and *I'll* pay for my daycare."

"Good luck. Call if you need anything in the future."

I hung up the phone and fired up the hotplate. While the burner heated up, I could not help thinking how easy it would have been to become dependent on a welfare system encouraged by a kind white woman who meant well. I tore her contact information from my address book, stuck it against the red-hot burner, and watched blue flames erase her on a wave of gray smoke as I reminisced about my new job. I couldn't wait to share the news of my employment with Daddy the following weekend when phone rates were low. I valued his opinion and respect and wanted to redeem myself for disappointing him with my pregnancy. With a wide grin, he would clap his hands and say, "That's my Babe," proud of the girl from whom he expected great things, but I would lie by omission about my welfare stint.

CHAPTER 15
Frigidaire Corporation

That first day, I bounded up the steps to work at 3:30 p.m., half an hour early, and Dan, the data processing director who interviewed me, stood at the top of the stairs. He extended his hand. "Well, hello, Mildred. You're early today." I told him it was a habit from eighteen years on a farm. A warm smile split his face. I was even more amazed when he offered to escort me—a lowly keypunch operator—on a tour through the entire Frigidaire facility.

Dan had an easy way of walking with his hands in the pockets of his black slacks and a soothing voice like a kind father. As he strolled through the vast room with high ceilings and bright lights and introduced me to his leadership team, noting his genuine concern for people, I understood why he would embrace me. He asked about employees' families and mentioned wives and children by name. "How's Billy doing on the baseball team?" or "Give Betty my best." He introduced me as "Mildred, our newest keypunch operator. She's working on a college degree."

Mildred J Mills

A long hallway split the rectangular-shaped room in two. A door leading downstairs to the factory was at one end of the hall, and a large cafeteria was at the other. An all-male management team with desks lined up on the sunny side of the aisle was sitting next to the windows. They spoke quietly into black telephone receivers, smoked cigarettes, and studied reports. I couldn't help noticing that administrators were all women, shuffling papers, occasionally stopping to whisper and laugh among themselves. A noise like revving motorcycle engines rifled through the air where a group of middle-aged white men wired computer boards and fed punched cards through sorters, collators, and decollators. At the same time, two huge printers spat out reports on green and white-lined paper. The only Black man in the whole place wore wire-rimmed glasses and puffed on a curved pipe with a thread of smoke twisting toward the ceiling. The men laughed, joked, and studied me. I wore a burnt orange midi-length dress with a split to the knee and black pumps. The pool of keypunch operators was hunched over their machines near the kitchen with their backs to the windows. The all-women group craned their necks when I strolled past with the director.

When Dan opened the metal door at the opposite end of the hall, I gasped as heat and humidity from the slick black factory floor slammed into me like steam in a wet sauna. I ignored catcalls, shrill whistles, and outrageous wails from men dressed in oversized orange coveralls, safety glasses, and steel-toed work boots. The staccato sound of machinery shoved parts along an assembly line and reminded me of a conductor directing musicians with a wrist snap and a baton's rhythmic wave. At the same time, I marveled at the men whose eyes were on me, but their hands and arms moved in unison, pistons snapping parts together, pushing finished Frigidaire appliances out the other end. Even with the doors and windows propped open, the oppressive heat in the plant was so intense that I saw two unconscious men stretched out on what the director called a "meat wagon" and carted away to an onsite nurse or doctor. *I never want to know what it feels like to work in such conditions.* It reminded me of the cotton field.

Our eyes met at the end of our tour, and Dan gripped my hand firmly. "I expect great things from you, Mildred." I watched this man return to his office, a large corner room where a wife and two blonde-haired children smiled lovingly at him from silver frames on a cherry wood desk. His office window overlooked the parking lot, allowing him to spin around on his chair and observe employees coming and going. Dan's encouraging words caught me off guard, but I knew he would never look through that window and see me racing to work late or leaving early. It was then that I realized the quiet man with the crew cut, square suits, and horn-rimmed eyeglasses had given me a tour of my possibilities if I was willing to do the work.

Promptly at 4 p.m., as the first shift team vacated the space, I slid into my keypunch station, more fulfilled than in months, and clicked my way through eight hours. Women around me moaned and complained about "rambunctious" children, "cheating" husbands, the "boring" job, or whatever, but nothing they said could dampen my spirits. I was a tax-paying member of society with a solitary goal—to keep my head down and work my way out of the keypunch pool one stroke at a time into a position where people laughed freely rather than grumble.

As ecstatic as my day had been, more than once I held back tears, yearning for my four-month-old. We had only been apart three days since her birth; I missed her staring into my eyes, sucking greedily on Similac formula, and fighting to stay awake as I sang "Rock-a-Bye Baby" and lulled her to sleep twice a day and at bedtime. In the weeks leading up to my first day of work, I had established a feeding, napping, and bedtime routine so Peter could manage her while I worked, and she would quickly adapt to a babysitter when he found a job. I could not wait to press her warm body against my breast and kiss her rosy cheeks again.

When the clock struck midnight and signaled the end of my first day of work, I hopped off my chair like a sprinter off the block. I trotted along, elbowing my way through double glass doors and down wide concrete steps with other office workers who stampeded out of the building like a herd of cattle. Folks who had appeared lethargic and slumped forward at their desk had sprinted past me at warp speed. I rushed beyond the security gate and through the parking lot, searching for my boyfriend's beat-up Buick station wagon. I spotted him standing beneath a telephone pole where bugs swirled and crashed into each other like reckless drivers on a racetrack. Peter swayed side to side with the bright light perched above his head, rocking our daughter in his arms. At that time, I thought about dogs peeing on trees to mark their territory. That gesture would have infuriated me any other time. But I ignored Peter, too excited to see Ashaki.

Frigidaire Corporation

I reached for my child, and when she heard my voice, she snapped her head around, stared at me with terror, and let out a frightening wail. She buried her face in her father's chest and continued screaming loud enough for passersby to stop and stare. I would not have been more stunned had she slapped my face. My four-month-old pulled away from me; her father shielded her against his chest like I was a threat.

The total weight of this rejection, wounds that had recently begun to heal, and the indignities I had suffered over the past year flared up and threatened to break me. They ruptured like my gut had the day I learned I was pregnant on a torrid July afternoon in 1971, a day I purged everything I'd eaten bent over the berm on Gettysburg Avenue, but I refused to be broken.

After my first day of work, the first absence from my daughter, I slid across the bench seat using the muscles I worked hard to build and pulled the child from Peter's arms while she writhed, stiffened, and screamed. I noticed the smug look on his face as he feigned surprise at her behavior. "I know you said not to hold her all day, but she cried every time I put her down, so we took naps together. Are you mad?"

"*Of course*, she cried when you put her down. That's what babies do. She's already manipulating you." I wanted to snatch off my high-heel shoe and clobber him over the head. He was actually grinning when he said the child knew nothing about manipulation. Still, I sensed Peter enjoyed the temporary distance between my daughter and me, punishment for ignoring his suggestion that I remain on welfare and stay home to care for the child.

"Unless she is wet, sick, or hungry, *please* don't pick her up. You are encouraging bad behavior." Peter said I was jealous that our daughter preferred him over me, and I couldn't believe we were having this conversation. I shoved the screaming child back into his arms and massaged the headache that started at the base of my neck and spread to my forehead. The baby turned her head, faced the driver's side window, and clung to him like a koala bear, a rejection that speared me to my core. I stared through the windshield at pitch darkness, thinking that my beautifully named child was a manipulator, as was her father.

At eight o'clock the following morning, hours before my 4 p.m. second shift, I rolled out of bed, pulled back the curtains, and watched morning stretch her arms and yawn awake. A sparrow pulled a worm from dewy grass near the sidewalk, and the sun reared its head through the rustling leaves of the giant oak tree across the street. Peter's father's dented Buick sat slumped near the curb like a knocked-out heavyweight boxer with a bashed-in face. Knowing he had been up half the night watching westerns on television, I flicked on the light and shook him awake so the bright sun hit him between the eyes. He rolled over and glared at me. "We're going apartment hunting today. I also need to practice parallel parking for my driving test." He pulled the covers over his face and attempted to sleep. I yanked back the bedspread. *"Get out of that bed."*

CHAPTER 16
Matrimony

On my third day at Frigidaire, the pipe-smoking Black man I'd seen the first day approached me. "I noticed your husband and baby in the parking lot the other night." He told me he had two preschool girls and would be upset if they were out that late. "Where do you live? Maybe we can carpool." I was thrilled to learn we were neighbors, living only two blocks apart. When I said I wasn't married, a twinkle of mischief played around his eyes as he stirred the tobacco in his pipe with a small metal rod. I quickly added that I would pay for my rides.

I couldn't wait to share the good news when Peter picked me up that night. "What do you know about this man? Why is he offering you rides?" Peter asked.

"Are you *kidding* me? The man has worked at Frigidaire for three years. He is married and lives in the neighborhood. You should be relieved to keep this raggedy car off the highway, have more time to look for work, and get the baby to bed at a decent hour."

By the end of May, three weeks after I started work, I had rented a lovely two-bedroom apartment in a decent neighborhood and passed the driving test. Every day, I floated up the stairs, breezed through the front door of our second-floor apartment, and cherished the crushed velvet sofa and chair and matching coffee and end tables with crushed gold inlays on the doors, items I had purchased with my own money. I thought heaven must look like this. I loved that place—the first decent and comfortable home I had acquired. A glass-top dinette set brightened the room, giving it a light, airy feel. I woke up on Saturday mornings and fired up the stereo so loud the walls pulsated. I spun through the place like a genie on steroids, dusting and mopping until everything sparkled, moving farther away from the welfare man.

Weeks earlier, when I had called Mama and Daddy to share the news of my new job, apartment, and phone number, I couldn't bear to tell them I had spent the last six months on welfare. *Why burden them with a temporary situation that I had moved beyond?* "Babe, I ain't surprised you'd have such a job." Daddy's brilliant smile radiated through the line like a warm shawl on a cold day.

"I'm so proud of you, Mildred," Mama said softly, reassuringly.

Now, every evening, the carpool man from work tooted his horn, and I raced down the steps and out the front door, thrilled to go to work. I delighted in the power of having money in a bank account, resources to pay my way, and go shopping for food and clothing. When I stepped through the Elder-Beerman Department Store's doors and paid cash for a new skirt or blouse for myself and clothes for the baby, I experienced a new level of independence.

Matrimony

Leaving the apartment each day, I saw Peter standing at the door, bouncing the baby in his arms and staring as though I would never return. On our rides to and from work, the man often complained about his "lazy wife," a stay-at-home mom. "You and me oughta dump our 'dependent' partners and run away together," he once said. I sat quietly for a few moments, letting that thought sink in.

"Should I show up at your home and ask your wife if that arrangement is acceptable?" Afterward, he puffed on his pipe, collected gas money, and never made another pass.

Peter borrowed his father's Chevrolet and drove us to Reichard Buick on Salem Avenue at the end of May. The bright sunshine streaming through the showroom's floor-to-ceiling windows glistened against every vehicle. My high heels sounded like the ticking hand of a grandfather clock as I wandered around the showroom, studying shiny cars. The salesman mostly ignored me and focused on Peter, who had dressed like a young professional. "What you got your eye on there, Buddy?"

Peter pointed to a champagne-colored car with headlights like pleading eyes. "How 'bout that Riv out there? Now, that's sharp." Besides the cross-shaped symbol on a Chevrolet, I didn't know one car from another. I mostly listened, trying to learn about the cost of a necessary investment that would eat up a good chunk of my check.

"Yep, she's a beauty, but she ain't cheap." The gray-haired white man who wore a dark suit told us it was a 1970 Buick Riviera with very few miles. "Where ya' working, Peter?"

He chuckled and nodded in my direction. "*She* works at Frigidaire. It won't be no problem buying that car."

I snapped my head around. "May I speak with you?" Peter wandered over, looking confused. "That's the most expensive used car on the lot. We don't know anything about buying a car. We're supposed to look first and then talk to your dad."

Peter had that gleam in his eye of a man noticing a hot car or woman. "That's a fine ride out there. If we don't buy it today, it might be gone tomorrow." I didn't know anything about budgeting, but I'd learned how to count. "Let's look at a cheaper car," I said.

The salesman meandered from one used automobile to another, answering my questions about mileage and reliability. In the end, I drove his father's Chevy, and Peter pulled out of the lot behind the wheel of the Riviera. I justified the purchase by telling myself he would soon find work, ignoring Mama's voice in my ear. "Watch yourself, now. Save a little for a rainy day."

When our car doors slammed in the driveway, Peter's mom and dad, babysitting our child, hurried outside to the front porch, and his father gawked at the expensive Buick. "How much did you pay for that car?" Peter said the price. His father shook his head, called him stupid, and walked back inside.

His mother grinned and turned toward me. "Now y'all can get married. You got the job, an apartment, a house full of furniture, a new car, *and* you already got a baby. It's time."

I wanted to scream: "*I* have a job. Your son *does not*. Why would we get married?" But I stood solemn, hemmed up against the wrought-iron railing in a corner on the front porch.

That day in May was not the first time Mrs. Lee had suggested we marry. The last time, I was seven months pregnant. She'd invited us to dinner, and I'd brought dessert—coconut cream and lemon meringue pies. After dinner, she'd pulled her hands from elbow-deep sudsy dishwater, wiped them on an apron, and gave me a stern look. "Y'all *need* to get down to that courthouse and marry before it's too late." *Too late for what?* I'd wondered. Tension began in my lower back like a pulley and tugged my shoulders up around my ears. Peter was across the room digging a tablespoon into the coconut cream pie.

Although I wanted to scream, I'd closed my eyes and spoken slowly. "Mrs. Lee, I. Don't. Want. To. Get. Married."

She'd snapped the dishcloth off her shoulder and glared at my big belly. "Well, you *look* like you *need* to get married." Peter had wandered into the living room, flopped down on the sofa, and stared at a football game on the color television.

I wanted to tell her to mind her own business and ask her why she wasn't pushing her son to get a job, but my Southern upbringing bridled my tongue. I thought, *Get thee behind me, Satan, and don't push.* "Thank you for dinner. We're heading home." I'd hugged her and said goodbye. On days like that, I needed *my* mother.

I hadn't called Mama when I was seven months pregnant, but I did call her now. My stress quickly eased when her voice smiled through the phone like wind chimes on a breezy day. She asked about Ashaki, her first grandchild whom she had only met through photographs. She updated me on my fifteen siblings, telling me about each one, like how school was going or where Brother was working. She asked about Peter and his parents.

Every nerve in my body snapped to attention as I spewed my frustrations, hot like a Type-5 forest fire, at my quiet mother, who always listened. "Mama, I am sick and tired of hearing

Mrs. Lee talk about us marrying. Why do I need to get married? She never talks about Peter finding work, and I'm not sure he's even looking." I imagined Mama at the dining room table, listening to every inflection of my voice, yet waiting patiently to impart words of wisdom. I missed sitting across from her, looking into those brown eyes and the arcs of her high cheekbones when we talked. After a few moments of silence, I knew Mama was contemplating the advice I had heard her repeat many times in the past, "Think twice and speak once."

"Mildred, raising my girls, I always wanted to see y'all grow up, marry a good husband, and have one or two little chillun. I won't tell you who to marry cause once you marry somebody, you're the one who got to live with him. Ever since you told me you was pregnant, many a night, I have laid here worrying about you raising that baby by yourself."

Damn! It stung to hear I had caused Mama restless nights. Growing up, I was with her, working around the clock: feeding, diapering, washing, cleaning snotty noses, and suffering at Daddy's hand. "Mama, I am so sorry I have worried you."

"I'll worry a little less now that I've heard from you. I realize long-distance phone calls are expensive." She chuckled and said, "His mama ain't your mother-in-law, but it ain't no picnic having one telling you what to do all the time. I actually like ole Peter. He seem real nice on the phone, and he sure *loves* talking 'bout Ashaki."

"Mom, he *is* nice and dotes on his daughter, but he's not motivated. Peter is your man if you want to throw a party, play cards, or plan *any* social event. Partying does not pay bills, Mama."

Matrimony

She paused a long time. "Mildred, I never thought of you not being married when you had your first child. Now, I don't mean that in no kinda bad way. But you don't always have to be so independent; you gonna need somebody to help you raise that baby. I can't do it 'cause I got my own house full of chillun in Alabama." She asked if Peter was a good father and cared for the baby while I worked. "If you looking for somebody like your daddy, there ain't many men that work as hard as he do. You see, I didn't grow up with no daddy in my house; maybe that's why I didn't want my chillun to grow up without one."

That talk was our first mother-to-mother conversation, and it elevated our relationship. It brought me closer than ever to Mama. Her words haunted me and caused me to examine my before- and after-pregnancy feelings for Peter and question what I expected from him.

Pre-pregnancy, I enjoyed the social aspect of our relationship. Peter had introduced me to card-playing—something Daddy had forbidden in our home. He taught me to play bid whist, which is still my favorite card game. As partners, we were almost unbeatable, and I enjoyed his fraternity parties. He was fun and friendly in our budding friendship, someone I liked hanging out with. I had felt safe and not pressured to be in a serious relationship.

After I became pregnant, the ground shifted beneath my feet when my work-study job and life in the dorm ended. I had to grow up fast. I was in mourning when I saw my friends continue their carefree campus lives, edging toward educational and professional goals. I had to think about a grown-up life as a mother. *Where* would I find a job? Who could I trust to care for the baby? During my pregnancy, I did not expect anything from Peter. Once the child was born, I believed we should share financial responsibility. As my due date approached, Peter was generous with his time, willingly taking me wherever I needed to go. I relied on him for transportation to doctor's appointments, after which he stayed over. Before I'd realized it, he was sleeping at my place most nights.

After my baby was born and diagnosed with jaundice, she remained hospitalized for a week after I was released. Lying in my one-room apartment without my baby, I was inconsolable the first night. I wondered how she was doing and whether she cried for me. Peter was supportive and assured me that she was okay. He drove me to Miami Valley Hospital every day to visit. When Ashaki was released, I walked down the hospital steps holding her close, and Peter fussed over us, ensuring we were safely in the car. His driving us home from the hospital on a snowy afternoon and me holding our baby in my arms was special—like we were this little family, sharing tender moments and caring for each other.

Hearing Mama say she never expected me to be an unwed mother—something I knew in my heart—and memories of those special, close moments with Peter softened my heart. I believed I was too young, unprepared, and unwilling to marry. I didn't consider matrimony a necessity for being a good parent. But I was convinced to try marriage and raise my child in a home with two parents. In a Carole King song, she sang about feeling the earth move under her feet and her heart trembling when someone—perhaps a lover—was around. I did not feel those emotions when I was with Peter, but I thought he was a good, reliable person.

Matrimony

If we both worked hard, I believed we could have a successful marriage, which we discussed after my conversation with Mama. He promised to get serious about finding work, and two weeks later, Peter's father found him a part-time job, working two hours a day replenishing vending machines at Standard Register.

While Peter worked each morning, I spun through my sparse surroundings cooking, cleaning, and preparing diapers, bottles, and clean clothes—things he would need for our daughter while I worked. I so enjoyed my uninterrupted time with Ashaki. Her preference for Peter, the carefree singer, over me—the one demanding structure and discipline like a set bedtime and feeding schedule—was clear. Her face lit up when he walked into a room or she heard his voice.

On July 15, 1972—my wedding day—the sun hung high in a cloudless sky. A brief summer shower quickly evaporated. At the sound of every engine purring down Walton Avenue, I raced to Peter's parents' living room window. I snatched back the curtain and gazed up and down the street, looking for Mama and Daddy, whom I had not seen for eighteen months. They were coming to my wedding. I was beyond excited about our reunion but was concerned that Daddy had called ahead about car trouble after purchasing gas in Kentucky. I was beyond excited that Rachel, my maid of honor, who lived in Kansas City, Missouri, and worked for TWA, had flown in a few days early to help me prepare for my wedding.

When that 1965 black and white Chevy Impala Super Sport sputtered into the driveway, she and I leaped from the front porch to the ground, skipping all four steps. Car doors flew open, and nine or ten people piled out like babushka dolls tucked into a tight space. I met Daddy's broad smile and squeezed him tight before running around to grab Mama, who held my three-year-old baby sister. I attached myself to Mama like an appendage while we held back tears. That was the first time I remember hugging and being hugged by my parents.

Mama pulled mismatched flat sheets and other gifts that smelled like Alabama from the car's trunk, smiling and announcing which folks back home had sent what. "Now, this is from Sister; this one's from Honey," and so on. Touching each present, I felt the hand and saw the faces of aunts and cousins from Alabama, people who had loved me since my birth, encircling me into that tight-knit place called family—a place of belonging. Our parents bonded immediately, laughing and talking like old friends.

Peter's mom stood behind the wrought-iron railing on the front porch, bouncing a drooling Ashaki against her bosom, welcoming my family. His dad hustled to the driveway and extended a large hand toward Daddy, greeting him like a relative. "Hey, man, pull on back so we can see what's the problem. Sound like you got some bad fuel." The two men jacked up the car in the driveway, drained the gas tank, refilled it, and took it for a spin. They rolled back to the house, grinning, proud to share their Alabama roots and a mechanical talent in common.

Peter and I were married in his childhood home, surrounded by our parents and fifteen close friends and family members. Daddy and I stood in the warm kitchen surrounded by glistening wood paneling, white Frigidaire appliances, and cakes for the wedding reception. He faced me and asked warmly if I was ready to go before offering me the crook of his arm. Strength and warmth radiated over me as I threaded my hand through that triangle and held on while Daddy escorted me into the living room and "gave me away." Yet, I could not forget his words the night I told him I was marrying Peter: "You deserve better." Today, when I see those wedding pictures, Daddy, Rachel, and I are as stoic as funeral-goers. Rachel stood by my side, resembling an identical twin. We wore gold satin dresses—hers with a Nehru collar and mine scoop-necked with silver trim.

The most delightful moment of my wedding day was seeing my parents dancing together. Daddy held Mama close—his arms around her waist, her hands on his shoulders. They moved slowly around the dance floor like strolling through a park, gazing into each other's eyes, smiling and whispering. Mama looked happier than I had ever seen her. During the father-daughter dance, Daddy tucked five hundred dollars into my hand. "This is for *you*," he whispered. "Me and your mama want you to have something from us." I took the money and held back tears, knowing I had let him down by marrying Peter. I appreciated how hard he had worked to care for his large family yet gave me extraordinary opportunities to succeed. I was their first child to leave Alabama, give birth, and marry.

The two families sat together at Marable Party House, the reception hall, bonding over their granddaughter. They passed her around like a Christmas goose at the dinner table. She posed like a princess in a full-length gold dress with pinched pleats and tiny yellow buttons, cooing and kicking her small feet, showing off lacy white socks and high-top Stride Rite shoes.

Mildred J Mills

The reception hall was decorated with black and gold streamers on the walls and black plates, napkins, cups, and tablecloths on the tables. Even the cake was frosted black and gold, matching our wedding colors—honoring his fraternity. Peter had chosen "I Only Meant to Wet My Feet" by The Whispers for our first dance as man and wife. I'd never heard the song, nor had he expressed those sentiments. The reception was lively, with him and his fraternity brothers stomping around the floor like they were on a college campus. I only now recognize how much I sacrificed for Peter's happiness that day, forfeiting an off-white gown in favor of his desired black and gold fraternity colors. I was determined to do my part to make our relationship work. Friends and family wished us well, and we began life as man, wife, and child, absent a honeymoon.

Monday at 4 p.m. sharp, I hopped on my keypunch machine with Mama's voice whispering: "Anything worth doing is worth doing to the best of your ability." I poured all my energy into my marriage, family, and job, determined to succeed at all three.

DADDY MID-TWENTIES IN
WWII UNIFORM

MAMA AGED NINETEEN 1945

THE CINDERBLOCK HOUSE WHERE I WAS
BORN & RAISED

AGE FIVE

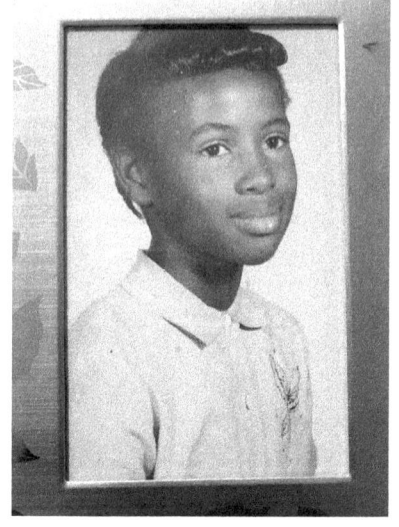

TWELVE-YEARS-OLD

MILDRED 1967 LOS ANGELES
TRIP SIXTEEN YEARS OLD
(FAR RIGHT)

THE SUMMER BEFORE 12TH
GRADE HIGH SCHOOL
SENIOR PICTURE
SEVENTEEN-YEARS-OLD

FASHION MODEL - AGE EIGHTEEN

SWIMSUIT CONTEST

MISS AMERICOLOR OHIO 1970

WSU student cuts records, keeps fingers crossed for success

MISS TALENT USA – 1970 - NINETEEN YEARS OLD

MAMA'S CHURCH HAT

MT. ZION BAPTIST MY CHILDHOOD CHURCH

MAMA & DADDY'S 50TH ANNIVERSARY WITH THEIR 15 CHILDREN

DADDY WISHING BABE LUCK

DARRYL & MILDRED (OUR WEDDING DAY)

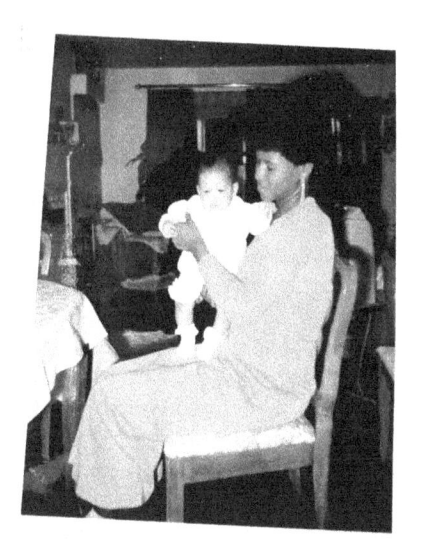

MOTHER & DAUGHTER (ASHAKI)

MOTHER & SON (RICHARD)

THIRTIETH ANNIVERSARY

MILDRED J MILLS - AT PEACE
SEPTEMBER 2023

CHAPTER 17
On My Own

Four years after we married, I stood before a judge in a tiny room at the Montgomery County courthouse in Dayton, Ohio, flanked by my dear friend and witness—Syni—and my legal counsel, Dennis Hanaghan. Peter did not show up. The judge sat like a teacher behind a rectangular table, a slim, silver-haired man wearing eyeglasses and a black robe. When our eyes met, he squinted and looked down at the decree in front of him. "I thought I recognized you. It's been a while." I remembered him as one of five judges at the state pageant I competed in six years earlier. Now, here he was, the lone judge at my divorce hearing. Then, I beamed and walked across a stage, wearing a swimsuit and formal wear, and displaying my singing talent, hoping to win his vote. Now, I wore a strained smile and wanted him to grant me a divorce.

Peter had cheated on me, I'd cheated on him in revenge, and one evening after work, our marriage finally crumbled under a mound of debt, infidelity, and misery. Almost two years after our wedding, Peter's uncle had finally found him a full-time job as a meter reader at the power company. He wore heavy uniforms to work, contributed little to the household, and hung out with his frat brothers. Money was tight, and I was looking for ways to cut expenses.

One evening, when I took a large basket of dirty clothes to the laundromat across the road from my apartment and watched my quarters disappear into the washer and dryer slots, I totaled the money I could save if I divorced Peter. I thought, *Mine and the baby's garments are small and don't cost much to clean. I could free up seven dollars a week if I didn't have to wash and dry his heavy uniforms. The grocery bill would decrease substantially by not feeding such a greedy man.* I folded the clothes and headed upstairs.

"Peter, is this marriage working for you?"

He was reared back on the crushed gold sofa, watching television. "What are you talking about?"

"It's not working for me. Let's end this marriage while we're young enough to find compatible partners. I'm miserable."

"We should stay together for the sake of the child. I'm not going anywhere." He walked to the television and turned up the volume.

I told Peter, "The child will grow up and leave us, and we will still be miserable. I want to file for a legal separation," which I did two weeks later.

He stayed out later each night, sometimes returning so late I had to take the baby to daycare, so I was not on time to work. I believed his antics were deliberate, an attempt to punish me and show how dependent I was on him. At work, I was dependable, hardworking, and accepted all the overtime offered to pay our bills. Peter's behavior threatened my job security, yet he refused

On My Own

to leave or reliably come home to take the baby to the sitter. So, I forced the issue while he was asleep one night. I pried the metal open and slipped his house key off the O-ring. When he closed the door behind himself the following morning, he locked himself out of my apartment and our marriage.

Judge Arthur O. Fisher asked me if I thought I could save the union and if not, why not? "Your honor, we married because of an unplanned child, but there are physical and emotional incompatibilities we could not overcome. I am miserable in this marriage. We both deserve more than we can give each other." He then asked my witness and counsel to speak.

"Judge, this marriage should've never happened. Look at my friend. She has too much going for herself to be married to Peter Lee. I'm glad she's getting divorced," Syni said. My attorney called Peter a lazy loser, a meter reader who lacked ambition.

The pain and shock I felt when the judge slammed down his gavel and pronounced me "released from the obligations [of marriage], and hereby divorced" surprised me. That one action dissolved four years of matrimony in less than five minutes. It felt like a stake through my heart. As reluctant as I had been to wed Peter, I thought divorce was a failure, something I was unaccustomed to. I had no romantic feelings toward him and wanted nothing more than to end the relationship but hearing them trash him felt wrong. He was a good person, just not the right one for me. And so, on Friday, June 16, 1976, my marriage ended due to "gross neglect of duty and extreme cruelty." I was awarded $25 a week in child support payments and a one-time $150 alimony check toward legal expenses, a mere pittance that did little to help me financially.

But to quote my Mama, "Peace of mind comes wit' a high price sometimes."

Leaving the judge's chamber that day, I had peace of mind and was glad to be free of a marriage that had limped along too fragile to survive youth, financial woes, and irreconcilable differences. But I needed something to lift my spirits. So, I went house hunting, although I had not saved a dime to buy a house.

I picked up my five-year-old from daycare and rode through Upper Dayton View rather than make our daily trip to the park. This ritzy neighborhood with custom brick homes was where teachers and other successful professionals settled to raise their families. I wondered how I, as a single mother, could afford one of those places when, at age twenty-five, my greatest asset was a dream.

For years, I had driven up and down Philadelphia, Princeton, and Cornell drives, the main streets surrounding that community, while rushing to work, daycare, and church, too busy juggling life to explore. But that day, I drove slowly down each street, mindful of children pedaling tricycles on the sidewalks in the quiet neighborhood with manicured lawns, wide driveways, and detached two-car garages on tree-lined streets. I chuckled, thinking how each month after I had paid my rent and utility bills and bought groceries, with barely enough money to make it to the end of the month, I dared to envision myself in my own home and a swing set for my baby in the backyard.

As I drove down the last street in the neighborhood, planted like a beacon on the front yard of the next-to-last house was

On My Own

a For Sale sign. I hit the brakes, cranked my yellow Opel GT into reverse, and jotted down the realtor's name and number, thinking, *Why not?*

For two weeks, I drove past the two-bedroom brick English Tudor with a basement numerous times and pestered the realtor with questions on how to qualify to buy a house. "Why don't you come by and see the place?" he asked one evening.

I excitedly parked at the curb beneath an oak tree, grabbed my daughter's hand, and hurried up the sidewalk. As I approached the front porch, I was astonished to recognize the realtor, a short, stout Black man, studying me. The deacon from my church, whose name I've lost through the years, smiled and grabbed my hand. "Mildred, I can't believe it's you I been speaking with all this time. On the phone, I thought you were some old white woman." We both laughed, surprised at such a chance meeting.

A dainty, gray-haired lady I'll call Mrs. Cohen greeted us at the front door, wearing rimless eyeglasses and a blue cotton dress with a white ruffled collar. I gazed past her into a spacious living room. Over her shoulder was a formal dining room with a bay window and a small, bright kitchen with a sink overlooking the neighbor's backyard. Mrs. Cohen wrung her hands nervously as we walked through the immaculate home.

In the living room, she gently stroked parts of a wood-burning fireplace with colorful fish and other creatures made of precious stone woven into its hearth. Strolling from the living room through the dining room and kitchen, I imagined my own furniture in that house and where I might place each piece.

Mildred J Mills

In the full basement, I smelled fresh paint on the smooth, gray concrete floor. The cinderblock walls reminded me of home—Alabama—a place I had not called home for years.

A Maytag washer and dryer standing side-by-side near the bottom of the steps made me long to make this house my home and laundromats a thing of the past. I studied every part of that house and tucked away memories while I continued to dream of owning such a place.

Mrs. Cohen seemed to read my mind. She stopped, reached for my hand, and said, "My husband and I traveled the world, collecting precious pieces for our home." Her beautiful brown eyes traveled to every corner as she held on to me and strolled through the unfinished basement. "When we built our home in 1941, we wove treasures into every room, reminding us of places we traveled together. I shall never forget our trip to Auschwitz, Germany," she told me.

I recognized the pain in the lady's eyes when she walked me out the front door, pointed to the keystone at the home's highest point, and described having it shipped to Dayton from some faraway place. When I turned to leave, she gently said. "Will you join me for tea this Saturday morning?" I gladly accepted.

That Saturday, when I rang the bell at 1408 Ruskin Road, Mrs. Cohen opened the door, and the smell of cinnamon filled the room and rushed out to greet me. She ushered me to the dining room table, where steaming hot cups of Lipton Tea awaited us. Sitting catty-cornered from each other, Mrs. Cohen sandwiched my right hand between her warm, frail ones with blue veins and age spots, lovingly stroking it as a mother would her child.

On My Own

"I don't want to leave my home," she told me. "My husband died last year; I'm in my seventies and can no longer care for the yard. Now, my children are forcing me to sell."

I sat quietly, unsure what to say to a mother who felt diminished, old, and whose children threatened to withhold support unless she bowed to their will.

Suddenly, I was racked with guilt, embarrassed, and ashamed of myself for invading her home. I started to speak, apologize for being there, and bid her farewell. But then, she lowered her head, a tiny gesture that broke my heart when she told me it was time to let go of the cherished memories of her home and her late husband. Goose flesh raced down my arms when she squeezed my hand and said, "I want you to have my home. I can tell you'll take care of it." She told me how so many people had stomped through her house, but unlike me, they would never appreciate what she and her husband had built.

We sipped our tea and ate the sweet cakes she had baked, and she reminisced about the joy of raising children in such a beautiful neighborhood, where most of her friends were now gone, either dead or had moved to the suburbs.

I told her about my divorce, large family, and how I grew up picking cotton on my father's farm. She asked me about my job and applauded my bravery to strike out on my own. For the first time since I had met her, Mrs. Cohen smiled. "Come; I must show you my beautiful gardens."

She rose from the table and hustled me out the back door, down four concrete steps to a large asphalt parking area. I studied the detached, two-car brick garage with a freshly painted brown door and small windows. I imagined my 1970 Opel GT parked in that garage and me never again having to scrape snow and ice from the windows in winter.

The backyard was as magical as a botanical garden. A giant oak tree hung over the garage, and the sweet smell of lavender filled the air. I had never seen or heard of such a thing, but Mrs. Cohen pointed to a blossom-filled lavender tree behind the garage. Even more stunning was a garden full of deep pink peonies, another unfamiliar flower. The plants, propped up and supported by a wire fence, stood more than two feet tall with blooms like little heads of cabbage. At the bottom of the long-sloping yard was a ditch with a rippling brook that separated her property from the adjoining neighborhood. I had no idea how to purchase a home. But as I walked down the sloping driveway back to my car, I dared to dream of wrapping Christmas lights around the massive blue spruce tree at the corner of the front yard.

Back at my apartment on Beechnut Street, I dusted, polished, and shined every piece of my modest furniture, including the gold crushed velvet sofa, matching chair, coffee, and end tables with crushed gold inlays. I envisioned those pieces in a place where the landlord couldn't raise the rent or ring the doorbell with or without prior notice. And then there was a knock at the door.

My landlord was at the far end of the peephole, carrying a large bucket with a snake to fix the broken garbage disposal. Inside, he marched ahead of me like he owned the place, which he did. I remember him snaking something out of the clogged sink and how excited I felt about applying for a Fannie Mae home loan, something

On My Own

I had never heard of until the week before. "You know, Tim," I said. "I'm thinking about buying a house."

That man shut off the running water, jammed one fist on his bony hip, and slung his long blonde hair out of his face. "Nobody's gonna sell you a house. You'll never qualify," he said with finality. He grabbed his tools and continued fixing the garbage disposal. Too stunned to mount a comeback, I stared at the back of his head and remembered how, five years earlier, an old Black man had fired me—an unmarried college student—from my work-study job when he learned I was pregnant.

Warring emotions inside me wondered if these men thought my gender, color, or marital status made me less than others. I was insulted and furious, and that hard slap in the face set a fire under my backside. *Never underestimate the power of rejection*, I thought. I started counting the days until Tim would collect his last rent payment from me.

By the middle of September, after working all the overtime I could muster, collecting bank statements, paystubs, and proof of child support payments, I was approved for a mortgage loan and had a closing date. But the day before closing, after I paid my rent and utilities and bought food, I was five hundred dollars short, and payday was three days away. Yet, I wrote the check anyway, refusing to be denied, then hustled another one to the post office and mailed it.

Afterward, I called my younger sister, Rachel, my ride-or-die dearest friend, who was as happy as I was about my house and explained my dilemma. After she got over the shock that I would write a check without funds to cover it, we hollered, laughing like the young, determined women we were. She was even more shocked when I asked her for a $500 loan told her I had already mailed her a check. "Now, you can cash it soon as you get it," I told her.

"How did you know I had five hundred dollars?" she asked, incredulous. I said I knew she would get it if she didn't have it to ensure I could buy my house. That's the kind of relationship she and I had. She wired the money the next day, delaying her rent payment.

At the closing, Mrs. Cohen sat beside her son with her head bowed like a widow burying her husband again, and I invited her to visit anytime. Sadly, I never saw or heard from her again.

So, on October 1, 1976, less than four months after my divorce was final, I purchased my first home, a $25,000 two-bedroom brick and stucco Cape Cod. Rachel, who worked for TWA Airlines and could fly for free, was my first visitor.

Two months later, my dear friend, Squeesta Collier, visiting from California, excitedly said, "Mildred, *you bought a house*? I didn't know a woman could buy a house." Then she told me she had been waiting for Prince Charming to buy her a home. After briefly noodling on that thought, I told her, "I didn't know a woman *couldn't* buy a house."

I now realize that it was only one year before I bought my house that the Equal Credit Opportunity Act of 1975, which made it illegal to discriminate against women due to race, sex, age, or marital status, had passed. Only one year before that, banks required a married woman's husband to cosign for her and could arbitrarily refuse credit to unmarried women. I might have *never* applied for a home loan if I had known these facts. I didn't realize then that I was

On My Own

a trailblazer, testing the edges of newly acquired women's rights. Two years later, passing the Pregnancy Discrimination Act of 1978 made it illegal for employers to fire women due to pregnancy, childbirth, or any such female problem.

After Peter and I separated, I thrived in my career. Being responsible for dropping off and picking up my daughter eliminated my late arrival chances. Within the first twelve months, management transferred me from the second shift keypunch position to the day shift, and two years later, I was promoted to the input-operations department. I was GM's first employee outside of Detroit headquarters, promoted to the Salaried Employee in Training (SEIT) position to learn the inner workings of data processing on the fast track to an executive-level job. I advanced to a different area every six to twelve months, including the data center, computer and network operations, and programming, with progressively more responsibility and higher pay.

Four years after leaving Peter, I believed my personal and professional life was wonderful. I was with a man I thought I'd spend the rest of my life with, and in 1984, he and I had a beautiful son, Richard. But I'm getting ahead of myself.

In late 1984, months before I completed the SEIT program, General Motors purchased EDS from Texas billionaire Ross Perot to consolidate its disparate computer systems. This move adversely impacted the compensation of thousands of GM employees, including me, who were forced to separate. Transferees would experience cuts in retirement, health insurance, tuition reimbursement, and other perks they depended upon. To deter class-action lawsuit threats, the corporation offered one year's salary lump sum plus twelve months of health insurance to "unhappy personnel" who wished to resign rather than accept forced separation. Employees had thirty days, including the Christmas break, to accept or decline the severance package, allowing ample time for workers to find other jobs. Terminations would be effective at the end of January.

I was not unhappy with my job and had not intended to resign. I loved the company, the people, and my work and believed I would retire from General Motors. I was working quietly like a spy in my five-foot-high four-sided cubicle, dressed in a navy-blue business suit and high-heel shoes, when I overheard giddy white men discussing the golden opportunities such a windfall of cash offered. "I'm going to put together my résumé over the holidays," one said. When an older gentleman told him, "That's enough money to send my kids to college," my ears perked up.

I was thirty-three, divorced, with a ten-month-old toddler and preteen daughter, a mortgage, car payment, and daycare. Even with an excellent job and salary and paying my bills timely, having more than a few hundred dollars in savings was challenging.

I sat at the kitchen table that evening, staring through a plate glass window overlooking the fenced-in backyard with a covered patio, sandbox, and swing set. I studied every number on the explanation of benefits letter from GM like it was the bar exam and my life depended on it, which it did. After taxes and retirement, I would net approximately $25,000 from my $35,000 salary, enough money to fatten my bank account and save for *my* children's college. I slept the entire night fitfully, praying I would find new work without spending the money I hoped to save, but where would I begin?

On My Own

The following morning, I hunted down the man who had mentioned the résumé. "What is a résumé, and how do you put one together?" I asked. I outlined my job experience overnight, found possible positions in *The Dayton Daily News* classified ads, and mailed a compelling letter to several potential employers. Two weeks later, I accepted a computer operations position at Hobart Corporation.

After thirteen successful years, my illustrious GM career ended on Thursday, January 31, 1985. To treat myself, I took off the entire month of February, a much-needed vacation, to recharge and reflect on the new life ahead.

I sat on a crushed velvet swivel rocker, wrapped in a terrycloth bathrobe, nursing my son, and smiling into his deep brown eyes, and every muscle in my body was relaxed. Leisurely waking up every day and not have to pump my breast, pack a diaper bag, and nurse him before racing out the door to daycare and work was the greatest gift I had ever given myself. The furnace kicked on, warming the house against light snow falling outside. I swayed gently in the burgundy chair, priding myself on being bold and quitting my job. But with so much time to think, I realized that while my professional life soared, my personal life was a mess. But I had thirty days to make other bold moves: confront issues that needed facing, including my feelings concerning my daughter.

CHAPTER 18
A Painful Separation

Two months after my son was born, my ex-husband asked to speak with me when he brought our twelve-year-old daughter, whom I had full custody of, home after a custodial visit. Ashaki barely spoke as she walked past me and up to her second-floor bedroom. "Mildred, I don't know how to tell you this, but Ashaki wants to live with me, my wife, and our three kids." He told me he planned to sue for custody because the child was "unhappy." *Unhappy, and he's planning to sue for custody?* I couldn't believe my ears. I thought the lawsuit was more about the thirty-five-dollar-a-week child support he paid, a ten-dollar raise I had received over ten years, and Ashaki's envy of her new baby brother.

"Peter, she's unhappy with structure, discipline, rules, a parent who holds her accountable and is not a pretend friend. Did you notice the 'unhappiness' amped up after my baby was born but never with your new wife and children?" I reminded him that Ashaki was unruly and required constant attention and a firm hand, which I'd given her all of her life. No amount of pleading with him to do what was best for our willful but gifted daughter, who had lying and thieving tendencies and refused to take no for an answer, worked. "Peter, our daughter recently stole her best friend's little brother's lunch money. I revoked her telephone privileges by unplugging the telephone, locking it in the trunk of my car, and taking it to work with me," I told him. "But she defied me by borrowing a neighbor's phone, which I discovered when I called home, and the line was busy." I'd dialed home an hour later, and she answered the phone. I told him that when she stole the child's money a second time, I lost it and spanked her out of anger and frustration, which did not change her behavior.

"Well, she wants to live with me and my family. I already called the lawyer."

At nine o'clock Monday morning, I contacted Mr. Hanaghan. "Mildred, by Ohio law, if a noncustodial parent sues for custody of a child twelve or older, *that child* can choose where she wants to live. It's the worst damn decision I've seen in twenty years of family law practice, but there is nothing we can do about it."

I was devastated, and no amount of begging Peter not to totally uproot the child mattered. Peter, who had converted to a Jehovah's Witness after we separated, disconnected her from all things familiar, including her school, church, and mother. Instead of allowing Ashaki to finish the last two months of the year at Precious Blood Catholic, he enrolled her in a public school voted Dayton's worst.

Oh, how I loved and doted on my child from the moment I held her to my breast and wept as she struggled to latch on, unable to simultaneously nurse and breathe through a tiny, flat

A Painful Separation

nasal passage. At home, I clung to her—a possessive and overly protective mother. I'll never forget how Peter's sister pulled her from my arms. "Let somebody else hold the girl. You're not the first woman to have a baby." As accurate as that statement was, I never knew it was possible to love someone so unselfishly, and I wanted her all to myself.

I praised every accomplishment and encouraged creativity. When Ashaki kicked her legs, cooed, and followed the spinning mobile above her crib with bright, brown eyes, I said, "You are brilliant." When her chunky legs pounded the linoleum floor as she raced into my outstretched arms and walked alone at eleven months, I clapped like she had run a marathon. For weeks, twice a day, she and I sat side-by-side in a cramped water closet, me on the toilet and she on her potty, me reading a novel and she holding a book of bedtime stories, pretending to recite what she had heard the night before. (She was reading me bedtime stories by the time she was three.)

I lived for the excitement in her eyes each summer when I said, "Get dressed. We're going to visit your relatives." She jumped for joy, thinking we were off to her Alabama grandparents' house. Oh, how we both giggled when I said, "We're going to the Cincinnati Zoo." Every year after school ended, my chunky child turned a golden brown and sprouted muscular legs from swimming and playing at the YMCA summer camp. I brought Ashaki to church and Sunday school on her weekends with me. Deacons lauded her as a Biblical scholar, capable of learning and quoting scripture better than many adults, but as she grew up, I noticed my child had a dark side.

Mildred J Mills

The summer Daddy taught her a church solo, Ashaki stole a toy mouse. She was three; her father and I had recently separated. I pulled into the gas station to top off my canary yellow Opel GT and stock up on our favorite snacks: Mikesell's potato chips, Cheetos, Pepsi, and apple juice for our first Alabama road trip alone. Ashaki brought a gray squeeze toy to the cash register. "Mommy, will you buy me this?" I told her no and to put it back where she found it.

More than a hundred miles into the trip, a squeaking sound shrieked through the car and filled me with dread. I gripped the steering wheel and pulled off the road, thinking I had car trouble. I whispered, "*Now, Lord*. You did *not* bring me this far to leave me." I quickly glanced in the rearview mirror and caught the wild eyes staring from the platform in the back of the car. "What was that noise, Ashaki?"

"I didn't hear nothing." I opened the passenger side of the two-door vehicle, and the rubber mouse's beady eyes and whiskers were sticking from beneath the driver's side seat.

I smacked her hand. "Why did you take that toy?" I asked, alarmed at how easily she had lied.

"Because I wanted it," she said defiantly. Tears streamed down her red face.

I was unprepared for that response, expecting an apology, not defiance. "Ashaki, we've talked about the Ten Commandments, especially 'Thou shall not steal.' You *will* return that toy after spending your first summer alone with Grandma and Grandpa."

My parents, especially Daddy, doted on their first grandchild. She was bright, articulate, and charming. "She reminds me of you, Babe, so intelligent," Daddy often told me. While the eight

A Painful Separation

children still living at home had to work in the field, Ashaki did not. I recently asked her about her summers in Alabama.

"Mom, Grandpa would bring me honey buns and let me sit in the truck while the other kids picked cucumbers," she told me. She laughs when she says, "And they would get so mad at me." When I described the tiny house I grew up in and Daddy's strict discipline, she said, "I have never seen Grandpa as anything but kind. He treated me well." She also did not experience the two-bedroom house I knew. Daddy expanded the home a few years after I moved to Ohio. He sold lakefront property and added three bedrooms and a carport. I'm happy my daughter has fond memories of her grandpa and that she spent time on the farm with her young aunts and uncles, the youngest only three years older than her.

One month after I dropped her off, I parked in the shade of the pecan tree, and Daddy hurried across the yard to greet me. "Hey, Babe. I taught my granddaughter a church song. We *sure* enjoyed her. She's just about smart as her mama." I was barely out of the car but couldn't help noticing the joy in his voice and the radiant smile plastered across his face. Daddy's response to his only grandchild was unexpected since he seemed opposed to grandchildren when I had announced my pregnancy, and I had never seen him treat his children with such tenderness. I wanted to share the mouse incident but didn't want to spoil his good mood. I hoped the theft was a one-time incident.

Back in Ohio, Ashaki cried, begging not to return the toy, but I marched her up to the counter, where she apologized and promised not to steal again. I hoped this would instill in her that stealing was wrong. That night, we added forgiveness of sins to her prayer.

Later that evening, Ashaki couldn't wait to share with me and her Grandma Lee "I Know Prayer Changes Things" by Mahalia Jackson, the song Daddy had taught her. That Sunday in church, Mrs. Lee stood Ashaki on a chair in the choir stand, handed her a microphone, and in a voice filled with punch and knowledge beyond her three years, my daughter led the song, remembering every word. The entire church stood up, clapped, and sang along. Filled with pride, I thought of the scripture, "And a child shall lead them." I thought the powerful words to the song and teaching her right from wrong were enough to keep her honest.

Yet, when she was five, Ashaki stole several Kennedy half dollars from a gallon-sized piggy bank in my bedroom and, when confronted, denied doing so. After catching her two weeks later, hiding under her bed, peeling silver wrappers from Hershey's kisses, and stuffing some of the coins back in her purse, she again denied taking the money, cried, and shouted, "You never believe me when I tell you something."

I thought of how comfortable I felt sitting across the dining room table from Mama, so I asked Ashaki to come and sit with me. I spoke to her as kindly as I knew how. "Ashaki, please tell me what's wrong. Why do you choose to lie? Nobody lives in this house but you and me. You had to know that I knew you took the money."

"I didn't want you to think I was bad," she said. Tears flowed again even before she began crying.

I was surprised because I had never referred to Ashaki as bad but referenced her behavior as disobedient. Lord knows she kept me on my knees, praying, "Father, show me how to parent my special child; help me live the life I speak about, and please, let me be a

A Painful Separation

good example for her." I was concerned about Ashaki's sneaky habit of taking things and chronic lying rather than accepting no for an answer. When I spoke to Peter about her behavior, he dismissed it. "I only see her every two weeks. I will not discipline her. If you got problems with the girl, you deal with them." I told Peter he would regret the day he chose not to discipline his daughter. As concerned as I was about her behavior, I was encouraged and hopeful because she was also bright, likable, and charismatic, traits I hoped would win out as she matured.

In fifth grade, Ashaki was the only Black child in her class. Yet, she ran for and was elected student council president. She wanted to be a calligrapher, something I had never heard of. I bought her a calligraphy set, and teachers raved about her talent. I was moved to tears the first time she presented me with a poem using her new tools. I embraced her tightly. "Ashaki, with your talent, you can be *anything* in the world you want if you apply yourself." The light in her eyes was like stars as she beamed with pride, happy to have pleased her mom.

That same year, my daughter begged, "Mom, I've always wanted to play saxophone. Please, will you buy me one?" It was the first time I heard she wanted to play any instrument. Yet, she told me how one of her young aunts in Alabama had shown her the basics when she spent summers with her grandparents. Remembering the joy I had felt playing trumpet in school, although it was not in my tight budget, I happily rented her a used instrument. After hearing any tune once, I was amazed at her natural talent and ability to play it by ear. But I had to push and prod her, and even then, she seldom practiced and lost interest after a year.

When she began middle school at age twelve, Ashaki asked to try out for the cheer squad. I bought her a uniform. On the evening of tryouts, she stole another girl's 18-carat gold necklace from the locker room, was caught wearing it the next day, and lied that it was a gift from her grandmother. The child's parents brought charges, and Ashaki was placed on probation. As punishment, I removed her telephone privileges and locked the house phone in my bedroom when I went to work. She hacked the door lock with a steak knife, defying me.

I called Daddy, desperate for any disciplinary advice he could offer, anything that might help keep my daughter out of prison, a place she seemed hell-bent on going. "Daddy, it's too bad a parent can't put their kids out before age eighteen," I told him.

He laughed, and I heard through the phone the familiar hand clap he used when he was excited. "Maybe not, but you can make 'em so uncomfortable they'll pack up and leave on they own." I felt better after I spoke with Daddy. I knew his idea of "uncomfortable" would land me in trouble with the law, but I chuckled, remembering how one of his sons had slipped off the farm and joined the Army rather than enduring Daddy's tortuous discipline.

I had never felt such discomfort as when, a few months after she stole the bracelet, Ashaki raced up the stairs after school the first day I brought her baby brother, my newborn son, home. She suddenly stopped inside his bedroom door, and her mouth dropped open. She stared into his crib, unspeaking for what seemed like minutes as he lay on his stomach, tiny fists balled up, asleep with the angelic posture of a newborn baby. "I didn't know he'd be so cute. Why does *he* have dimples? And look at his beautiful black

A Painful Separation

hair." Her dark expression and cold eyes sent chills down my spine. I thought she could harm her brother. "It's always been just you and me. Why did you need another child?" she asked.

I hadn't known what to expect from my daughter, but her comments and tone were alarming. When I learned I was pregnant, I sat with her at the dinner table and explained that she would be a big sister. Later that night, I heard her whispering and giggling on the phone with her friends. "My mom is *disgusting*. Can you believe she's having a baby?" Her words stung. It sounded like she was discussing a stranger or someone she disrespected, not her mother. I had no idea what to say without screaming in anger, so I said nothing.

But I said plenty that day in my son's bedroom. "*This* is your brother, Ashaki, and I love you both equally. He's just a baby—*my baby*—and he's not going anywhere. I hope you will become the loving and selfless big sister he deserves." Within days, Peter sued me for custody.

I had packed her bags a few weeks later, and her father, as the custodial parent, picked her up at my front door. Warring emotions twisted at my insides like sheets through a wringer washer when I watched my daughter hurry away from me like an escaped convict and into her father's minivan. She was thirteen. I had never been so simultaneously elated and deflated or wrestled with such a strong push and pull toward my child whose behavior—I couldn't deny—often haunted me, reminding me of the Rhoda Penmark character in *The Bad Seed*.

But the day my ex-husband picked her up, I locked the front door, held tightly to my sleeping infant, and asked God for the wisdom and knowledge to raise a kind and loving son.

CHAPTER 19
My Son

My son was conceived on a blazing hot Fourth of July in 1983, five years after I first met his father.

One evening in 1978, I hustled to my second-shift data center job at the farthest end of the building in an impenetrable vault built to protect General Motors' computer intelligence. I hurried down the windowless hallway with low-hanging fluorescent lights, leafing through the night's job report, sizing up my workload, when I turned the corner and gazed into the greedy eyes of a man with a mouth full of bright teeth. He reminded me of Little Red Riding Hood's wolf. He abandoned his conversation with a woman in a wheelchair and looked me over, head to toe. I looked down to check that my navy-blue pencil-legged wool slacks and satin blouse were fastened. When he opened his mouth to speak, I rolled my eyes, looked straight ahead, and kept walking. I quickly entered the security code, opened the computer room's metal door, and slammed it shut, locking out unauthorized personnel.

Within minutes, the tall, slim man was bent over, pressing the buzzer, and peering through the small sliding window like a Peeping Tom. I snatched the glass open and glared. Undeterred, he adjusted his brown tweed jacket and eyeglasses and introduced himself. "I'm Casanova King, a day-shift programmer at Delco Products, but I need to get this job run tonight. Can you help?" His brown eyes searched mine like spotlights that had located their target.

The man was handsome, a slightly shorter version of Arthur—six-foot-two with a head full of curly black hair—but I was not his Sunday dinner and didn't appreciate his brazenness. "The woman you spoke to in the hallway is the job scheduler. Schedule your job through her."

"The lady said you could help me. It's the end of her shift. I'd certainly appreciate it if you could push this job through for me. Here, take my number." I didn't appreciate his bossiness or how he stared at me. With his left hand, he grabbed an ink pen from his shirt pocket and smiled. "Call me tonight; I'll be waiting, okay, Mildred?" He scribbled his home and work numbers on a sheet of paper, and I shook the hand he extended, pissed that he knew my name and I hadn't given it to him. I had no intention of contacting that man. I was startled when, the next day, he popped into my path like a Jack-in-the box. "What are *you* doing Friday night?"

None of your damned business, I thought. I handed Casanova the report and kept walking, but he followed behind me. "Say, Mildred. May I have your phone number, please?"

"You may not." I strolled away from Casanova, unsettled by his aggression. But in the coming days, the scripture "We have not because we ask not" was a recurring theme in my mind. I wasn't

My Son

in a serious relationship, but I thought I would be interested if the right person came along. I noticed he wore a college ring on the second finger of his left hand. Still, something about his hungry eyes unsettled me. It seemed I'd seen eyes like his before and distrusted them, but I gave him my number two weeks later, thinking a conversation wouldn't hurt anything.

We spent hours on the phone for the next several weeks, laughing, flirting, and getting to know one another. Casanova's voice was warm and engaging, and he was primarily a good listener. His smile seeped warmly through the phone line when he described a man with whom he taught Sunday school, an older gentleman who was also a mentor. He attended college on a basketball scholarship and earned a Bachelor of Science in math. He coached boys' basketball at his high school alma mater and a Little League baseball team.

"You almost sound too good to be true. Tell me something about you that would surprise me and one of your less than stellar qualities."

"I grew up in the projects, a community I will always give back to, and my grandparents were my greatest gift." Even though his parents divorced, and his father was absent from his life, Casanova's paternal grandparents' home was a safe place where he often spent nights. I was deeply touched by the joy in his voice as he recalled doting grandparents who showered him with love. "Their doors were always open for my two siblings and me." His infectious laugh rang across the line. "Well, I don't know if it's a less than stellar quality, but I'm a greedy man, Mildred. I don't like to share." I appreciated that Casanova used my name often.

He and I spoke or saw each other almost daily, even after he left General Motors to form his own company. After we were a couple, I introduced him to my daughter, who spent every other weekend with her father. She adored Casanova. He treated her affectionately, often holding long conversations about her day. He had the innate ability to speak to her at her level, which she loved. Before long, we attended the same church, where I sang in the choir, often led solos, and taught Sunday school. I cherished the weekends we all spent with his sister and her family, watching his nephew play baseball, and the holidays when I invited his family over and cooked turkey and dressing, collard greens, potato salad, cakes, and sweet potato pies. Some evenings after work, Casanova and I had epic tennis battles and walked away from the courts, soaking wet and angry, fierce competitors seemingly willing to fight to the death.

One evening in late June of 1983, Casanova called. "Hey, you wanna play before the sun goes down? Maybe later, we can meet at my place." At the courts, he handed me a skillet I had left at his home. "I'm kinda scared to give this thing to you. With that bad attitude of yours, you might hit me over the head with it 'cause I'm gonna put a whipping on you." I stuck it in the trunk of my car. We laughed, battled it out on the courts, and I headed home soaking wet.

I pulled the skillet from my trunk as the automatic garage door slid down. My sweaty left elbow touched the metal door frame, and an electrical current knocked the pan to the floor, raced down my left leg, and shock waves sizzled the bottom of my left foot. I was on birth control pills, but blood trickled down my legs as I walked up the stairs; my menstrual cycle started several days early. My OB/GYN suggested I toss the remainder of that twenty-one-day packet and begin a new one in seven days, which I did. Later, an electrician examined the door and found a shortage. "The rubber on the bottom of your tennis shoes is the only reason you weren't electrocuted."

Monday, July fourth, Casanova called. "Hey, Mil. Let's throw some hot dogs and burgers on the grill at my place and watch the fireworks later tonight. Maybe we can start a few sparks of our own before nightfall," which we did more than once.

Two months later, at my annual well-woman appointment, I complained that I had not had a cycle since the shock. "Well, you're not pregnant. I just examined you," the older white gentleman said with conviction.

"My cycles come like clockwork, always last three days, and I haven't missed one in years, not since I started taking the pill," I told him. The doctor commented on my tight abdominal and pelvic muscles but humored me and ordered a blood draw to rule out pregnancy. It was the middle of September. When the doctor called and gave me a due date of April 1, he said he would have wagered a hundred bucks that I wasn't pregnant. I would've let him keep his hundred dollars for a different outcome.

When I told Casanova the news of my pregnancy, you could have hung meat across that chilly phone line. He was silent so long that I thought he had hung up. "How did *that* happen?"

"Do you really want me to answer that question?" I was as unprepared for such news as he. I told him I had never wanted to be pregnant or have another child out of wedlock. But I was in no mood for his suspicious and accusatory tone. "Call me when you want to discuss this rationally."

When I was five months pregnant, after not hearing from him for weeks, I drove by Casanova's home one morning on my way to work because he seldom initiated conversations or visited me anymore. The last time we spoke, I suggested we move on. "I won't subject myself to someone who doesn't want me," I told him. "I can and will raise our child alone, but I expect financial support once the baby is here." He claimed he didn't want to break up but insisted basketball and other activities took up most of his time and left him exhausted. His routine hadn't changed in five years, *but suddenly, he was tired*? I believed he was lying.

When his ranch-style white brick home at the end of a cul-de-sac came into view, and just before I turned onto his street, the garage door began to snake open slowly. I held my breath when I saw *two* cars parked side-by-side. The kitchen door leading into the garage opened, and Casanova's shiny black shoes crossed the threshold, followed by a pair of high heels. At the same time, my heart almost stopped; I slammed on the brakes, got my shaky legs on the accelerator, and backed out of his view. I watched, bewildered, as he and this woman braided themselves together like a plaited horse tail, kissing and laughing.

I had no claim on that man, but I felt like the world's biggest fool for being involved with a philanderer. I wanted to run away and hide, but I refused to let him get away with the lies. I cranked up the car and headed straight for his driveway. Suddenly, the garage door was rewinding its way down. Casanova came out the front door and

My Son

met me at my car. I saw in his eyes what he hid well when we met: darkness, lies, and deceit. "What are you doing here?" he asked.

"Why did you lie when I asked if you wanted out? You've been too exhausted to have a conversation for weeks, and now I see why." He asked if he could meet me at my house. I agreed. I don't remember the drive home, only the blind rage at myself for being too busy and trusting to notice Casanova making a fool of me. I juggled church, Sunday school, my daughter, lawn care, career, and college courses. But it seemed Casanova juggled women.

Reflecting on our time together, I remember Casanova was always "busy" when I visited my parents, whom he had never met, which should have raised my suspicions. As we became closer, I learned that he was skittish about riding or driving long distances or flying due to the required travel while playing college basketball. He mostly stayed close to home. There was only one time during our relationship that I asked him to travel to Alabama with me.

On Tuesday, September 15, 1981, my nineteen-year-old brother, Michael Ray, drowned in the lake that borders the family farm. I was thirty. After work that evening, I unlocked the back door and raced up the steps to answer the ringing phone. "Babe," Daddy said with strange hoarseness in his voice. "I just called to let you know Michael drowned at the lake today."

"Michael?" I was confused, thinking how Sunday I had spoken with my nineteen-year-old brother, who had recently graduated high school. He answered the phone, and when he heard my voice, pretended to be a young fellow flirting with a girl, and we laughed a lot. The conversation had been refreshing, for although I still had eight younger siblings at home, I seldom spoke with them except during my once-a-year visit because long-distance phone calls were expensive. I had asked Michael about his future. He told me he wanted to enlist in the Army. I wished him luck and spoke with Mama, who caught me up on everyone else.

Now, Daddy was telling me that a young, vibrant man whose laugh I still heard ringing in my ear was dead. Drowned? "What happened, Daddy?"

"Well, Michael and one of his cousins took one of the little fishing boats out on the lake this morning. Afterward, they sat on the bank laughing and talking and suddenly noticed the boat spinning away. Michael jumped in and tried to rescue it, unaware that the power company had opened the dam. A strong current took him under, and he never resurfaced." The rescue squad dragged the lake and found Michael's body hours later.

The following day, Casanova invited me to his home. We held each other and I cried on his shoulder. "I'm flying to Alabama for my brother's funeral. Will you come with me?" He refused and reminded me how much he hated flying. That was one of the first times I felt that he was selfish and self-centered. At the funeral, I stood alone with my family, mourning Michael.

I'll never forget how my young brothers who slept beside Michael wept and tried to console one another. They were lined up like cadets across the front yard next to a long black hearse parked on the red dirt road with its engine running. The church was full of weeping young people, classmates, and students from Michael's high school. But it took years for me to unhear Mama's haunting screams ringing around Mt. Zion Baptist Church as she hollered, "Lawd have mercy, Jesus; Michael is gone," and tried to

My Son

throw herself into his casket, suffering the loss of yet another child. Afterward, I called Mama weekly and tried to help her talk about something besides her son's death, but for more than a year, she was inconsolable; she even told me once that she'd rather die than suffer the loss of another child. Years later, she told me she dealt with Michael's death by writing letters to and about him, expressing her thoughts and feelings about his life and death.

While I waited at my home for Casanova, I was furious, thinking about how casually he had rejected me the one time I needed him most. I imagined him cheating and disrespecting me while I was busy building my life and career, too trusting to notice. When I opened my front door, unlocked the storm door, and Casanova walked in, I slapped him across the face with all my might. Seeing his shocked expression, eyeglasses askew on his face and him on one knee, I began to tremble, afraid of what would happen if he hit me back. Instead, with a look of bewilderment and in that kind voice I had come to love, one that threatened to break me, he said, "Why did you hit me? I would never strike you."

I wanted to slap myself for being pregnant, feeling like shit, and standing there crying, but I refused to back down. "How *dare* you disrespect me, lie to me, and lead me on. If you'd said the word, I would've been gone. I don't need you; I chose to be with you." He told me straight-faced that he was not a married man. "You're right," I said and asked him to leave. I didn't hear from or see him again until the day after I drove myself to the hospital while in labor.

After the baby was born in February, five weeks early by C-section, I called Casanova, told him he had a son, and asked if he cared what I named him. "Yes. I'd like for him to be a junior." His response surprised me because he had shown no interest in me or the child after learning I was pregnant. I liked that he wanted his son to be his namesake; I thought every child should know his father and have a close bond. I agreed to give our son his father's name. "Casanova was not his father's legal name but perfectly describes his character. I refer to my son as Richard throughout this text." He came to the hospital, took a cursory look at his child, and asked, "Why is he so dark?" I ignored that ignorant question and gently stroked my son's face, smooth as a Hershey's Kiss like my father and Casanova's mother.

Casanova signed all birth certificate documents and accepted paternity. When I contacted him three days later to say we were going home the following morning, there was that cold silence again. "What? Do you need a ride?"

"*Of course, we need a ride*. Did you think I would walk home in the snow with this child?" I did not expect anything of the man for myself, and after that day, I would only insist that he support his child financially. He dropped us off, placed the baby into his crib, and drove away. He didn't ask, and I didn't say whether I needed help.

With my gut slashed from pelvic bone to pelvic bone from the C-section, the doctor had instructed, "No driving, heavy lifting, or steps—only bed rest." I didn't tell him I was a woman alone and could not avoid those things. I had rushed out of the house five weeks before my due date, leaving an almost empty refrigerator. But, that evening, home alone with my child, I bundled him up, slid cautiously on my backside down the steps one at a time, holding

My Son

him in my arms, and drove to Kroger to stock the refrigerator. I had never operated in such pain. I prayed with each movement that I would not burst a stitch.

I parked in a handicapped space, the closest spot to the door, and crept across the icy parking lot to grab a shopping cart. I placed the baby in the top part of the buggy and leaned heavily on it to support myself while I stocked up on enough food to last a couple of weeks until I was stronger. A woman at the cash register asked if I was okay and offered to help me to my car. I accepted. I couldn't even get angry about the citation on my windshield for parking in a handicapped spot. I deserved it but have never done so again.

The Saturday before our son's first birthday, I invited Casanova, his mother, sister, brother, and their children to my home to celebrate with dinner and a cake. Monday, February 25, our son's actual birthday, his father and I met at the daycare to share cupcakes and ice cream with his little schoolmates. We hadn't seen each other for months before the baby's party weekend. Casanova, whom I had caught eyeing my well-toned legs, breasts, and butt the whole afternoon, was the perfect gentleman, opening doors for me, touching the small of my back, and treating me like his mate. "Say, Mil, why don't you stop by the house? We can spend a little time together before you bring the baby home." It was storming out, and I would rather have gone home. Casanova didn't know it, but he and I had unfinished business.

"Sure," I said. I declined the offer to park in his garage "to avoid getting soaked" and thought, *No, thank you; I'd rather drown than tread where your floozies have lain.*

"Come on, Mil. Let's get comfortable in the family room, maybe grab a bite," which meant me cooking and him watching television. I suggested we talk in the formal living room. Eyeing my breasts, he patted a spot on the sofa beside him and spread his long arm across its back. I chose a Queen Anne chair across from him. "What's going on? You seem a little tense." *We hadn't had a conversation or been a couple for months. Now, he wanted to be cozy?*

"Casanova, we've been in this relationship for seven years if you want to count the last two. Today, you're behaving like we're a couple. What do you want from me?"

He took a deep breath, sat forward, propped his elbows on his long legs, and his shoulders relaxed. "You know, Mil. I want no strings attached." The pleased look on his face was startling. "Yeah, that's what I want. No strings attached."

Damn, that hurt. I sat on that straight-backed chair and pretended I hadn't felt the scab ripped off a heart that I thought had healed.

"Just so there is no misunderstanding, please tell me what that means?"

He stood and used his hands like a professor at a lectern explaining a complex problem to a first-year student. "You and I will always be together. I love spending time with you, and we have a son together. But I think, if we see someone we want to spend time with, we should be able to do so without anybody getting upset. Don't you think that's fair?"

Fair, my ass, you conceited phony. I gazed around the living room at the snow-white French Provincial sofa, pinch-pleated curtains and sheers, and thick wall-to-wall carpet. The familiar smells

My Son

of candles burning, our favorite food, and air fresheners all but choked me as I stood and smiled at Casanova.

"Well, that doesn't work for me, Casanova. But for the first time in a long time, you're being honest with me. Thank you for that. I've allowed you to disrespect me for far too long, and it ends today. I will never keep you from your son, but *please* call before stopping by. And, Casanova, I've never loved anyone as much as I love you. For a time, I thought we had something special."

The look of confusion on his face spoke volumes. I realized he didn't know me at all. He'd had no clue the impact his words would have. He stood, attempted to embrace me, and blocked my path. I walked around him and turned the front doorknob.

"Mil, where you going? What did I say wrong?"

Dark clouds hung overhead. Lightning flashed, and thunder rolled, but I had to get out of there. I could no longer breathe. On the two-mile drive home, the wipers struggled to clear the rain from my windshield, and I struggled to see through eyes flooded with tears. That was the last time I wept for Casanova or any man, and it was one week before I began my new job at Hobart.

Later, I shared with Casanova my leaving GM and taking a job eighteen miles away. I asked for his help if the daycare center needed a quick response for our son. "Only a fool would take a job so far from home," he said. I was only thirty-three, but I hung up the phone and swore off male relationships, declaring if a man ever parked his shoes under my bed again, he'd be gone before daybreak.

CHAPTER 20
New Love and Turmoil

Driving the eighteen miles to Hobart that chilly March morning, I allowed seeds of doubt to take root, seeds planted by Casanova when he called me a fool for taking a job so far from home. I began questioning why I had left the comfort of my old job. How could I get to work if I had car trouble? How long would it take me to reach my child if he needed me? What if I was fired? I didn't know a soul at this new company, and I had never felt so alone. I pulled into the parking lot, stared nervously at all the cars and trucks, and didn't recognize a single one. The steely eyes in the rearview mirror chided me. "O, ye of little faith. You can slap a two-hundred-pound man to his knees and cut your daughter to the quick with tough love, yet you're afraid of changing jobs? Get your ass out of this car, into that building, and do what you signed up for."

On my first day at work, I was at the salad bar, forking lettuce and hard-boiled egg pieces onto my plate, when a warm voice from behind me spoke. "Mildred, what are you doing here?" I turned and looked into the friendly face of an old friend.

"I have a job in data processing, and this is my first day. What about you?"

Dale, a friend from college, was the HR director at Hobart. We hugged, grabbed lunch, sat at the same table, and caught up on old friends and news. I was gazing across the room, watching people at the self-serve hot food bar, when a young man with a gigantic afro grabbed a plate and piled on a spoonful of glazed carrots. *Hmmm, what a nice butt. Somebody sewed those pockets too close together in the back. He's cute, but why is such a young man wearing those big old Herbie Hancock eyeglasses?* I looked the other way when he walked toward our table.

"Hey, man. Come over and join us," Dale said. I wasn't one bit embarrassed for having enjoyed the view from behind. Up close, the man's smile was warm, eyes syrupy brown, and the chip on his front tooth and his shoulder were endearing. His name was Darryl. He and I became fast friends when I learned he lived in an apartment complex less than a mile from my house. "If I ever have car problems, would you give me a ride to work?"

"Of course," he said. I scheduled my car for maintenance two weeks later, and he picked me up in his red Corvette. I learned Darryl had an eight-year-old daughter, was HBCU educated, hailed from Philadelphia—which explained the chip on his shoulder— and his parents had southern roots. Weeks later, when we began dating, him working on the ground floor and me on the third floor in different departments was a plus; we seldom saw one another at work. But our first date was almost our last one.

Darryl had invited my son and me to a picnic and stopped to visit afterward. At my son's bedtime, I strapped the baby in his car

New Love and Turmoil

seat for a drive around the block, his favorite way to fall asleep. I left Darryl in my bedroom with his shoes off, watching television. When I returned to my street, Casanova's unoccupied red and white Cutlass was parked in my driveway. *Oh, shit*, I thought, and kept going, afraid to face whatever was happening inside.

Fear was my constant companion inside the car as I drove around the corner and hid until I saw Casanova back out of my driveway. Then I pulled into the garage and hurriedly closed the door. Inside, Darryl was hustling down the stairs with his shoes in his hands. I liked this guy because he was funny, I enjoyed his company, and he showed me more concern than anyone in a long time. He stole my heart one evening as lightning flashed, thunder roared, and power lines were downed in a torrential rain. My telephone rang. "Hey, you guys okay over there?" *This man is a keeper*, I had thought. But after one lousy date, the way he moved down those steps, it looked like my new friend was slipping away.

"Where are you going?" I asked anxiously.

"I'm getting out of here. You may not be married, but you might as well be." He stopped, wrinkled his brow, and looked back up the steps like he had fled a ghost. "Can that man see into your bedroom window from the ground?" I was holding my sleeping thirteen-month-old and watching Darryl, thinking he'd lost his mind.

"*What?* What person can see through a second-floor window from the ground?" I later learned from a neighbor that he yelled at a man standing on top of the air-conditioner. Darryl said Casanova had clawed at the window like Spider-Man, screaming my name. I couldn't believe what I heard but asked him, "Will you ever come back?" He said maybe, but not right now.

Within weeks, he was staying at my home, parking inside my warm garage on cold winter nights, and enjoying fried chicken and scrambled egg breakfasts in bed. I accepted a management position at Wright Patterson Airforce Base in Dayton six months after Darryl and I met, unsatisfied with my Hobart job. Within eighteen months, we had moved in together and were engaged to marry. The next few years were the most spectacular and tragic of my life.

When my daughter was fourteen, less than a year after she moved out, she had been so disruptive at her father's that he returned her to me. "From now on, you, *not I*, will do your laundry, iron your clothes, and clean your room. You'll do everything for yourself except cook your meals," I told her because I feared she would burn the house down.

One Friday evening, when she was supposed to be at her father's, I came home from work and noticed a worse-than-usual pungent odor creeping into the hallway outside Ashaki's closed bedroom door. Inside the room were clothes, shoes, and food wrappers strewn over the floor and bed, and chewing gum smashed into the carpet. Soiled sanitary napkins, rotting peels from a five-pound bag of white potatoes, and an empty, half-gallon ice cream box were underneath the bed. I slammed the door and called her father. He said she wasn't there. "Would you have her call when she returns?"

"What do you mean?" he asked. "I haven't seen Ashaki since I brought her back to you." Every other weekend since she'd returned, Ashaki had gone somewhere, and as was the rule, she called me at work to say she was leaving with her father. I beat myself up, asking, "*How the hell could this happen?*" Ashaki had been a latchkey

New Love and Turmoil

kid since age ten. She was home from school every day by two, and her dad picked her up religiously every other weekend before I arrived at five. Out of respect for his visitation rights, I seldom called when she was with him.

At five o'clock that Sunday evening, I rushed out the front door and confronted a woman in a raggedy gray Buick full of girls. The woman accused me of being too strict. My daughter had lied, claiming she had permission to spend weekends with this lady and her children, who, according to Ashaki, "could do as they pleased," primarily unsupervised. Furious that this person hadn't contacted me before taking my child, I threatened to call the authorities. I never heard from the woman again.

Unfortunately, by then, Ashaki had a taste of freedom, running wild at her dad's and other places in the streets, which I wouldn't tolerate. For the next two years, I tried but failed to corral a willful child who continuously ran away, skipped school, and stole from me, Darryl, and others. Even psychiatric help and family counseling failed. "Your daughter is irredeemable, a pathological liar incapable of redemption. Take her home and *never* bring her back," a psychiatrist told me after our last family counseling session. I believed removing her from a toxic environment where she had found cracks to hide in and moving closer to family down south was the answer.

In 1987, Darryl and I quit our jobs and packed up, and moved to Atlanta, near one of my sisters and closer to my parents. After a few weeks, I was promoted to management in a new job and kept my professional life on track. But over the next two years, Ashaki found similar people in the Atlanta area and ended up at a court hearing for theft and truancy. "You can't control this child, can you?" a judge asked.

I stood before the judge in open court dressed like the young mother and successful professional I was, struggling to hold back tears. I confessed to my parental failings. "No, your honor. I've tried tough love, gentle caring, and family involvement. I even uprooted my family and moved closer to relatives for assistance. But nothing I've done has had any impact."

The stout white judge, wearing a crisp white shirt, red tie, and V-necked black robe, sat silently for a moment, looking as perplexed as I felt. He peered over his horn-rimmed glasses, first at me and then my daughter, before he banged his gavel. "Get her into a group home until she can straighten up. I suggest Anneewakee Treatment Center," a place for emotionally disturbed youth, a sentence that would cost me almost four hundred dollars a month. But finally, I could sleep at night and not worry about her dying in the streets. My son and I visited her as frequently as allowed. She complained about torture, and the administration reported that she was purging at Anneewakee, so I moved her to a cheaper place closer to home.

CHAPTER 21
Marriage and Separation

Despite the turmoil with my daughter, we had joy in our lives. On July 2, 1988, Darryl and I said our vows in downtown Atlanta at Big Bethel AME Church in front of two hundred guests. I had suggested a small wedding at the courthouse. "I've never been married before and won't ever again. I want my family and friends present," he'd said. I wore an ivory gown and veil with tiny pearls, and he donned a dark gray pinstripe tuxedo with a white shirt and pink cummerbund. We each had six attendants. My court wore teal gowns with pink corsages and his were in gray pin-striped tuxedos. When I surprised Darryl by singing "You Are the Love of My Life" by George Benson and Roberta Flack, tears flowed, including his.

I sewed a stunning pink and teal gown for sixteen-year-old Ashaki, who was still sheltered in a group home but allowed to attend. She sang angelically two duets with one of my choir members, "Always" by Atlantic Starr and "How Do You Keep the Music Playing" by James Ingram and Patti Austin. Handsome, four-year-old Richard was our ring bearer. He sported a tuxedo that matched his pop's, whom he lovingly calls "D." Although he spent summers with his father, who has always supported and been in his life, Darryl played a crucial role in raising "our son." We invited Darryl's young daughter to the wedding, but she was unable to travel to Atlanta with her grandmother and attend the ceremony. The reception at a Holiday Inn ballroom in downtown Atlanta featured an open bar, full buffet, live band, and family and friends from across the country who partied well past midnight.

Near the end of the evening, Daddy strutted across the dance floor—a peacock in a black suit—and sat at a table with me, Darryl, and my new in-laws. "Make sure y'all go out dancing regularly. It'll keep your marriage fresh." He gazed at the silky red hair of my thin mother-in-law, a light-skinned woman with freckles who cautiously studied Daddy. I wouldn't have been more stunned if he had handed me a suitcase filled with hundred-dollar bills.

Other than sixteen years earlier at my first wedding reception, I had never seen my parents dance or known them to attend such functions. "Well, I probably won't see y'all in the morning. We gonna head home 'fore day to make it to Sunday school. Y'all enjoy the honeymoon cruise." Daddy dashed across the dance floor and side-eyed Mama, who slid off her chair and—slightly stooped—hurried behind him as they left the room. I shook my head, thinking, *Daddy is full of surprises.*

One evening in July 1989, a year after our wedding day, Daddy called with an even bigger surprise. Darryl and I were sitting at the dining room table, celebrating our anniversary and eating year-old wedding cake. "How Do You Keep the Music Playing" by James

Marriage and Separation

Ingram whispered softly from the stereo. A brilliant sunset winked through the sliding patio door overlooking a grove of pine trees in the backyard, where a white hammock swayed gently in the breeze. The shrill ring of the telephone ripped through the peace in our home like a tornado warning.

After a quick greeting, Daddy said, "Babe, me and your Mama got this balloon payment past due on the property, and the folks at the bank claim they gonna foreclose on the farm if we don't come up with the money next week. Since you're the family leader, I need you to call the chillun, collect the money, and send it to me. We'll pay you back soon as we can." It had been a long time since I'd heard that cunning voice that tricked little girls. Suddenly, I was five again, holding back tears as Daddy slipped a nickel I had earned picking cotton back in his pocket and laughed, enraging me. Now, holding the phone against my ear, before I realized it, I went from being a calm wife laughing with my husband to a fire-spitting dragon raging at my father, something that had never happened in my thirty-nine years.

"What are you talking about? You've been in that house for forty years. Why do you have a mortgage? And when did I become the leader of this family? Those are *your* children, and that is *your* debt. If you need help, *you* call them."

I could almost feel the telephone wires shaking from Alabama to Georgia as dishes rattled when Daddy banged his fist against the dining room table, hurling insults at me. "This place is gonna be *yours* when I'm gone. It's your legacy." Daddy called me a fool who lacked business sense, too stupid to realize the value of his property. "That shitty place where you live in Atlanta ain't worth a damn," he shouted.

"Guess what, Daddy. This shitty house is mine, and nobody is threatening to foreclose on it because I pay my bills. If there's a fool on the line, it's you, begging *me* to bail *you* out." I hadn't forgotten how Daddy stiffed B. F. Goodrich when I was three.

Half an hour later, with us still shouting uncontrollably over one another, I was startled by the angry reflection that glared from a large gold-framed mirror on the wall as I marched through the living room. How could I have broken a promise I had made and kept for years—to always have peace in my home—ever since I had left the hell-raising in Daddy's house at eighteen? I screamed, "Pay your own bills and leave me alone." I slammed down the phone and massaged the headache shooting from behind my eyes.

Tuesday, a week later, Mama called, bawling. "Mildred, if we don't get that money to the bank by Friday, we got to find somewhere to go. Them folks already sent the notice. We can't raise that kinda money in a few days, not no five thousand dollars. I'm pleading with you—will you do this for me?"

She whimpered as I asked scathing questions and refused to let her off the hook for foolishly agreeing to a mortgage. "Do you have a job somewhere I don't know about? Knowing you could not pay a mortgage, what possessed you to scribble your name on that note?"

She claimed Daddy forced her to sign the papers, arguing so fiercely on the way to First National Bank that Daddy crashed into a bridge and wrecked the car. "I wasn't gonna sit in front of them white folks at that bank fussing, so I signed them papers."

I didn't know whether to be angrier with myself or Mama when I said, "Get me that bank's name, the account number, the amount

Marriage and Separation

owed, and the address. I will *never* put a dime in Daddy's hands." I hated myself for feeling guilty, imagining her homeless. "Mama, you two deserve each other. Sign your name to another loan, and you *will be* outdoors," I warned her. She promised they would pay me back, which they never did.

My husband and I had been married only a year, yet he agreed to loan my parents almost four thousand dollars, every dime we had saved, while a few of my siblings pitched in to help pay off the debt. So conflicted about my feelings, I refused to speak to Mama or Daddy for more than six months, feeding them with a long-handled spoon, using childhood advice Mama suggested on how to treat those who mistreated you.

The same year Mama and Daddy almost lost the farm, within days of arriving at a new group home, Ashaki stole the administrator's money and ran away with another girl. I found her and brought her home. She hadn't been back for one week before she dropped out of school and ran away for good. She was seventeen.

Several weeks later, I was vacuuming the living room carpet when my phone rang, and it was Ashaki. She was bawling, screaming, calling out to me in a shrill voice. "Mom, Mom."

"Who is this?" I asked in a frozen voice that I hardly recognized. I was tired after spending sleepless nights, thousands of dollars, and noticing new gray hairs every day, worrying endlessly about a child who defied all rules. I had found peace when she was gone all those weeks.

Back then, I'm ashamed to say I didn't want her back. But, years later, my sister, Rachel, asked Ashaki why, as a child, she treated me as she did. "I had decided by the time I was thirteen that it didn't matter what anyone said. I was going to do what I wanted," Ashaki told her. Then, I knew I had made the right decision not to allow her to return home.

"Mom, it's me, Ashaki. I just wanna come home. It's horrible out here, and people do bad things to you. I'm tired of running, Mom." I said nothing. She was seventeen, and I was at the breaking point. "Please, Mom. Can I come home?"

It took every bit of restraint in my soul to say these words: "Call home and find out."

"What do you mean?" She screamed louder.

"You don't live here anymore. You've told me to kiss your ass for years, and I'm sick of it. Now that you're almost grown, you want to come home? Leave me alone."

"Mom, I never said that to you. I would never do that."

I told her she'd done far worse, and her actions were harsher than any words. After over five years of crying, praying, and trying everything to help my child, I hung up the phone, too weary to worry, while she screamed. I put up the vacuum cleaner and held my five-year-old, who I didn't realize had sat on the bottom stair step and heard every word.

Two years later, my son and I sat at the dining room table across from one another. I worked while he did his homework. "Mom," he said softly. I answered yes but kept pecking on my keyboard. "Mom, look at me." I stared into my son's eyes through his wire-framed glasses and saw an earnestness I hadn't seen before. "I'll never give you any trouble. You've had enough trouble already." I watched him for several moments as emotions twisted me in knots, wondering

Marriage and Separation

if he remembered his sister, whom we hadn't seen in two years. She now had a child.

"I will remind you of those words when you are a belligerent teenager." I chuckled, trying to lighten the moment.

"You won't need to remind me," he told me, and I never did.

I was thirty-nine when my son made that declaration. Holding back tears, I couldn't believe how much he reminded me of my young self, putting the welfare of others above my own.

I had lived independently of my parents for twenty-one years—more than half my life. Yet, I had never given them trouble as a child or an adult. Of course, I had made mistakes but never wallowed nor depended on them for advice, money, or anything else. They pushed me into the world at eighteen, leaving me there as I shouldered life's knocks and kept moving. Even when I could barely afford to do so, I sent money home monthly, unsure whether it was out of some tucked away guilt or if I thought it my duty. Either way, my parents never refused or discouraged my giving. They had come to expect it. One time, on the phone with Mama, she said after I had sent money, "Your Daddy sure be looking forward to that check every month. He grins and says, 'That's our Ant Babe.'"

More than six months after I stopped speaking to them, Mama called. "Mildred, me and your Daddy really miss talking to you. We was wondering if you was okay since we hadn't heard from you."

"I've never been better," I told her.

During my six-month hiatus, I wrestled with feelings that my parents had used me most of my life, shouldering enormous responsibilities like caring for their children while Mama and Daddy slept. Yet, as an adult, I continued this behavior, denying myself by regularly sending money home, although I needed it. I even shouldered the expense of long-distance phone calls, denying myself extras while trying to help my parents. But having that extra money for the past six months was like getting a raise.

Like a drug addict who quit cold turkey, I had cut them off and never sent them another nickel of my monthly salary. Maybe I *had* been the fool Daddy called me, but no more. I decided I could not change how my parents treated me, but I could change how I treated myself and my husband, a man who quietly and unconditionally supported me. So, I went to the scripture for guidance. Mark 10:7 says, "For this cause shall a man leave his father and mother, and cleave to his wife." I thought the same was true of a woman. I soon learned that by distancing myself from my parents, we all grew more respectful of each other as adults. While I would always love and respect my parents, I would never again put them ahead of myself or my husband.

In 1990, less than two years after we married, Darryl lost his job to a downturn in the economy. "I have bad news," he told me at the dinner table one Monday night. "There was a big layoff today. I won't have a job after Friday." After months of cleaning carpets, delivering furniture, and not finding another purchasing position, I admired how hard my husband worked to help support our family. Yet, I noticed the inability to find gainful employment wearing on him.

"Please call Rick, your old Ohio boss, and check if the position you vacated is still open," I suggested, not for the first time. Darryl named all the reasons why that wasn't a good idea: we were newlyweds, he feared the marriage would suffer, and he didn't

Marriage and Separation

want to leave me. But I urged him to get his career back on track and assured him that if we were committed to the relationship and each other, the distance wouldn't matter. He reluctantly returned to his old position in Dayton, and I remained in Atlanta. For eighteen months, I waited excitedly at home for the garage door to go up, announcing Darryl's arrival, or we met at the halfway mark in a Knoxville, Tennessee, motel, never spending more than two weeks apart.

Nobody looked forward to those reunions more than our six-year-old son, who stared out the window until he spotted his pop's black Ford Ranger pulling up to the front of the hotel. He dashed outside screaming to his "D," helping bring in the dirty laundry, excited to inform him how fast Mommy drove from Atlanta to Tennessee. Those magical Tennessee nights were like mini-honeymoons as Darryl and I bonded, folding clothes in a steamy laundromat or eating my delicious home-cooked meals like meatloaf, mashed potatoes, and string beans on the picnic grounds. After our son wore himself out frolicking in the park with a new friend, he showered and immediately fell asleep, allowing Darryl and me time to make memories and keep our marriage fresh in a Knoxville motel room. But that lifestyle was unsustainable long term. As the leading spouse, I landed an excellent, well-paying job at a research and development (R&D) software company and moved to Houston in August 1991. Darryl joined me after securing a position with an excellent company.

CHAPTER 22
Stinging Words

Four years after I moved from Atlanta to Houston and joined the software corporation in 1991, I successfully performed several technical and management assignments, including customer service and quality assurance. I had doubled my salary, and the company promoted me to an executive-level position.

On a warm October 1995 day, Mama and Daddy traveled from Alabama to Houston so Daddy could "see where Babe was making the big decisions." That morning, I completed my forty-five-minute exercise routine of sit-ups, jumping jacks, and thirty minutes of cardio and hopped in the shower. I quickly looked in the mirror, ensuring every stitch of my navy-blue slacks, red silk blouse, and white blazer was in place. I could not believe how nervous I was to see my parents, whom I hadn't seen in almost a year.

Now, I noticed them across the hall. Daddy, always the soldier, wore black Johnston & Murphy shoes and a long-sleeved plaid shirt tucked in his creased black dress slacks. Even from a distance, my eyes skittered around the thick leather belt that used to terrify me.

Daddy stared at the stories' high ceilings, marble floors, and the glass and granite wall angles like the brick mason and carpenter he was, sizing up the work. Mama looked like a stouter version of Queen Elizabeth, sweet with curly hair fanned out under a fancy hat. She wore common-sense shoes, a no-frills royal blue skirt and jacket, and a pink cotton blouse.

Something internal pulled me across the lobby like a lodestone. The child inside me still wanted to please my parents. I grabbed them both and held on, thrilled that they had traveled nearly seven hundred miles to see me at work—something they had never done. "Let's go," I said. "You didn't come this far to hang around in the lobby." I hooked my arm in the crook of Daddy's and walked to the elevator.

When the steel doors slid open, welcoming us inside, Daddy dropped my arm and jumped back like lightning struck him. The black and white cowhides stretched across the elevator cab stopped him in his tracks with his mouth hanging open. *"Great day in the morning!* Will ya' look at that?" I was thrilled to see him so excited.

"Come on in, Dad; they won't bite." Daddy slid his large, rough hands across the shiny cowskins, studying them like one of his newborn calves, and contemplated how he might get in the cowhides-for-elevator business.

We strolled down a wide hallway on the seventeenth floor, where custom Gorman artwork decorated the walls. In a brightly lit break room where refreshments were on display, I handed Daddy a Dr. Pepper and Mama a Sprite. I took a Pepsi. Mama said, "How much do these cost?" When I told her that free snacks and drinks were perks of working with this company, she opened her oversized purse and slipped in a few bags of peanuts, popcorn, and M&M's. A little something "for later on," she said.

We passed programmers who wore cutoffs and T-shirts. "*They* don't work here, do they?" Mama asked with a disapproving frown. I told her that although I dressed professionally, a casual dress code was another job perk.

I pointed to the chief architect sitting in his office. "That guy and most others on this floor are brilliant computer scientists, architects, and coders behind the company's many products. They report to me but are smarter than I will ever be." I explained to Daddy that the architects produced blueprints for writing code comparable to those he used in carpentry and brick masonry jobs to build physical structures. He nodded, but I knew he wanted to learn more.

When we reached my seventeenth-floor corner office with floor-to-ceiling windows, Daddy clapped his hands and grinned, oozing pride at the daughter he once told, "You was always our favorite." At the time, I could not appreciate the unearned grace he bestowed upon me in my early twenties, but as an older woman, I embraced it and appreciated it as the gift he intended. I strolled around my office, pointing out local artists' original artwork on the walls. "The CEO is the man handing me the award and shaking my hand. I won two Caribbean cruises for being a top-ten performer." Mama studied cheerful family photos that were on my desk.

Daddy held the plaques I had earned like they were Oscars or Emmys. "Babe, you've always made us proud. From the day I dropped you off in Ohio, I never worried 'bout you handling yourself." I didn't remind him that I hadn't forgotten how, as a child, he once told me I'd never amount to anything. But since the day Daddy called me stupid when I was four, deep inside myself, it mattered that he thought I was smart. Out of fear of rejection, though, I refused to admit it. I despised the man who had called me names but admired the one who taught me determination. Seeing his face then, I knew I had earned his admiration.

We stood at the window, marveling at traffic jams on the freeways. Beltway-8, I-59, and the 610-Loop wrapped around themselves like a bed of snakes. Mama said she wouldn't like to be on those highways every day and asked me if I ever got lost coming to work. It was funny until Daddy said, "You'd have to be stupid to get lost going somewhere you go every day." I quickly changed the subject and pretended not to notice the hurt in Mama's eyes.

I sat on a high-back executive chair behind my cherrywood desk and credenza while Mama and Daddy watched from colorful armchairs on either side. "Sitting here, typing on this keyboard is equivalent to riding on your John Deere, planting a crop; you put seeds in the ground, and with enough nurturing, a harvest grows. Let me show you." Using the mouse and keyboard, I typed *World War II* into Yahoo search and printed the results for Daddy. He sat on the edge of his seat, eyes racing across the page. I captured a German chocolate cake recipe for Mama, and she folded the paper and stuck it in her purse. I guided Daddy's large index finger and typed *Abraham* on the keyboard.

When the screen filled with biblical and historical facts, Daddy said in a barely audible voice, "Well, I'll be Joe Bob. How much would something like that cost?" I chuckled and told him it was expensive. He beamed. "Babe, from when you was a little

Stinging Words

bitty girl, I always knew you was somebody special and would be running a outfit like this." Mama smiled, taking it all in and deferring to Daddy, until later that evening when she placed her hands on my shoulders, looked into my eyes, and told me she was proud of me.

In the office, I caught a whiff of farmhouse mold on their clothing, saw more gray hairs around their temples, heard the pride in their voices, and couldn't have loved them more. I was humbled. As though I had something to prove, I'd been showing Mama and Daddy that the hard work, time, and money they invested in me had paid off.

Sixty-nine and seventy-four, respectively, my parents were beautiful. While they were still in reasonably good health, I intended to continue repaying their love by spending more time with them. At home after work, my husband, who I had married twelve years after divorcing Peter, and my eleven-year-old son entertained Mama and Daddy, listening to stories about Alabama and their Texas visit. I prepared fried chicken and gravy, mashed potatoes, green beans, and cornbread and basted in the glory of their stories from back home.

After that visit, I flew Mama out to see me many times, and Daddy, who seemed to have mellowed a bit, allowed it. In October 1998, when she was seventy-two and I was forty-seven, I treated Mama to a three-day mother-daughter vacation in our home—Sunday to Wednesday. I arranged with Continental Airlines to meet her at the gate because she used a walker after having open-heart surgery earlier in the year. I hurried through the airport well before schedule, excitedly anticipating our girl time. The small plane taxied to the gate but stopped on the tarmac short of the door. Portable stairs snaked out of the plane. "My mother, who uses a wheelchair, is on board. How will she get down those steps?" I asked the gate agent.

"We'll get your Mama off the plane," the friendly woman said. After the last passenger deplaned, I noticed attendants wrestling with an electronic lift, attaching it to the railing like an escalator, facing sideways. Suddenly, Mama appeared like a queen perched on that chair, wearing a Sunday hat, waving, and smiling at the workers on the ground.

I was learning that Mama was starved for affection. I didn't know whether to laugh or hide my face when people at the gate asked, "Who is that lady?" Mama was quite the spectacle, soaking up the kindness of strangers.

When she saw me, her eyes lit up. "Mildred, did you see me in that wheelchair coming down that ramp," she asked, grinning and talking to people who greeted her, shook her hand, and spoke kind words.

"Mama, who *didn't* see you in that wheelchair?" We hugged, and I rolled her to baggage claim, where we picked up her luggage, a tiny bag, and a huge one tied together with a rope. I handed her the small suitcase and tried to lift the large one, which must have weighed fifty pounds because I could hardly pick it up. Before I knew it, I had snapped.

 "Mama, what's in this thing, and why did you bring all of this stuff?"

"Well, I didn't know what all I might need, so I brought a little bit of everything."

Stinging Words

Helping Mama empty the suitcase that night, I found three towel sets, two pantsuits, a church dress, and matching church shoes. "Mama, there's no need to pack like this when you visit me. I want us to relax and enjoy each other." During her visit, she told everybody she spoke with how the big, strong men picked her up "just like a baby and carried her" to a wheelchair.

Later in the week, Mama and I sat on padded chaise lounges on the covered porch by the pool at the back of my two-story house. We ate lunch, drank iced tea, read, and chatted like we had many times in her dining room. "Mildred, I'm so proud of you." She paused a moment. "When I was a girl, I read about the tumbleweeds in Texas but never thought I'd ever see the place, much less have a daughter living like this in Texas."

I looked around the all-brick custom home my husband and I had designed and built earlier that year. There was an outdoor kitchen with a stainless-steel grill and rotisserie outside a bay window. Birds chirped in the water oaks along a ten-foot brick privacy wall separating our expansive backyard from golf course estate homes. Our yellow Labrador retriever, Max, was stretched out, nodding underneath a pecan tree in the corner of the yard. The smell of fresh mulch around sago palms, shrubbery, and black-eyed Susan's wafted on a light breeze from the ceiling fan whirring slowly above our heads. The four-bedroom, five-bathroom home with a three-car garage tucked behind a wing wall was a far cry from the two-bedroom cinderblock house where I grew up. Yet, I felt humbled and embarrassed to live in such a house and was glad when Mama changed the subject.

"You got any light bread? Maybe I can make me a sandwich." Instead of the healthy choice of grilled chicken and a tossed salad, I made Mama a chicken sandwich on whole wheat and refreshed her sweet tea. "The crepe myrtles sure is pretty. Did you plant the mums, and what kind of flowers is the black and yellow ones?" Mama loved plants so much that she could have had a horticulture career in a different life. After we finished lunch, I held her arm and helped her stroll around the gardens, stopping to discuss each new freshly planted flower, including fall shrubbery.

After our walk, I asked Mama if she'd ever bathed in a Jacuzzi tub. We laughed when she gave me a blank look and said she'd never heard of such a thing. I threw my arm around her. "Well, today is your lucky day. Every girl should feel Jacuzzi jets on her body at least once." I ran a warm bath, added Epsom salt and bubbles to create a heavenly aroma, and helped Mama lift her arthritic legs into the tub. I placed a soft pillow behind her neck and turned on the jets.

Relaxing in the deep, oval-shaped tub with bubbles covering her body, Mama looked like a Black woman with her head sticking out of a pile of snow. I rested on the tub's wide ledge with my legs crossed at the ankle and back against the wall and read Maya Angelou's poetry to Mama as chamomile scents wafted from the steamy bath and water gurgled like ocean waves against her flabby skin. She listened intently, saying more than once, "This sure feels good." I felt I'd offered her a little slice of heaven.

After she had soaked for a half hour, I washed Mama's back, feet, and legs as the water drained from the tub. "Okay, beautiful. Bath time is over." I caught hold of her hands and pulled, but she

Stinging Words

slid around, slippery as an oily pig. I dried and gripped her arms with a beach towel and pulled, but that five-foot-three, 230-pound woman was stuck. Before her bath, I hadn't realized the bathtub was too deep for Mama to climb out easily.

I pondered every possible scenario for getting her out of that tub as sweat ran down Mama's face and her hair lay flat against her head. She sat naked and erect with one knee pulled up to her chest and the other slightly bent—helpless. While I wrestled for several minutes trying to get her up, Mama laughed so hard that she fell backward. "Just wrap a sheet around me and wait for D to come home." I looked at Mama sitting there like a fat Buddha and at the clock, noting my husband wouldn't be home for four hours. I saw nothing funny.

I am ashamed to say that I was furious that my mother was obese and too large to help herself. She had high blood pressure, diabetes, a cholesterol problem, and recently had open-heart surgery, yet she refused to change her diet to live healthier. When I was growing up, she often told me, "Never ask anyone to do for you what you can do for yourself." When she was first diagnosed with diabetes in her fifties, she said, "That doctor said I couldn't have but one slice of bacon. I'd rather not eat no bacon if that's all I can have." When I said she should stop eating it, she said, "I'll just take my medication, and I can eat whatever I want," which defied logic.

My love and disgust for Mama were churning in me like gumbo, and I couldn't separate the two. I loved my mother and hated to see her suffer at her own hands. I looked at the stitches running down her chest from triple bypass surgery like crossties on a railroad track. I wanted to yell at her, "Please stop killing yourself!" I said none of those things.

"Mama, you *know* I'm *not* leaving you sitting there all day." I strapped on my gym shoes, placed a step stool behind her, and stood directly above her head with my feet braced on each side of the ledge. We locked hands at the wrists, connecting our limbs like chain links. "Mama, try to sit on the bottom of the stool when I lift you." I gave her a good tug, and she swung her butt onto the lower step. Another pull, and she was on the second rung. After a quick pause, I said, "Mama, wrap your arms around my neck." I stood in the bathtub, gripped her waist, and twisted, sitting her backward on the edge of the tub. Within minutes, I had combed her hair, pampered her with Fashion Fair lotion and a dab of perfume, and put her to bed for a nap. I needed to be alone; time to come to grips with feelings I didn't know I had for Mama.

Daddy used to say, "Eat like you're gonna live to be a hundred and start right now." I disliked him most when he would tell Mama, "You're digging your grave with a fork." I was not even six years old when he said those things, but I had held on to his words and noticed he lived by them. And now, I'd more or less adopted them as my own.

That night, Mama sat at the glass-top dining table laughing and eating smothered pork chops and gravy, rice, and string beans that I had cooked—foods she should not have, but I knew she loved. She told my husband, son, and then later, Daddy on the telephone, that I was too weak to pick her up. Mama even compared me to another daughter—her words stung. I felt like asking if she remembered Daddy's quotes from all those years ago. Instead, I got up from the table. "You're not still in that tub, are you? How *dare* you mock me. That's how Daddy treats *you*."

I took some satisfaction from the hurt look on her face. Walking away, I counted the hundreds of hard-earned dollars I'd spent bringing her to Houston, shopping for lovely clothing at Dillard's, and eating at excellent restaurants—an overall experience she'd never had. I was furious that, of all women, my mother seemed not to appreciate my devotion to her or how hard I had worked to make something of myself and share it with her.

CHAPTER 23
Hard Drinkin' Lincoln

Two years before the corporation promoted me to director of product development, one of my managers, Sonya, the company's lone female R&D director, who had never entered my office before, moseyed in and asked, "Where do you get your work ethic?" I was forty-four years old and had never considered not working hard. *Doesn't everyone work hard?* I thought.

I regarded this sharply dressed woman whose tough-as-nails approach to problem-solving had earned her the title of "emasculator" among her male peers. I had admired her for years, yet we had never held a one-on-one conversation. While Sonya stood before me with her arms folded beneath the Chanel scarf wrapped around her shoulders, I considered quoting one of Mama's favorite sayings. "Anything worth doing is worth doing to the *very* best of your ability," but telling her where I came from seemed much more significant.

Sonya was five feet tall. In heels, I was five-nine. To be at eye level, I sat on the edge of my desk. "I grew up on a sixty-acre farm." I described how I had cooked meals, washed clothes on a scrub board, and picked over two hundred pounds of cotton daily as a child. If I fell short of Daddy's expectations, I had a meeting with a leather strap. I credited him for my dogged approach to work.

I thought about how I had seen Mama saddled with a house full of babies and dependent on Daddy for every dime. Sitting at the dining room table the day before I left home, Mama told me that once, when she was pregnant and craving something sweet, she asked him if he would buy her a Baby Ruth. She stared in the distance, her shoulders slumped as if she could still hear him say, "There's plenty Baby Ruth's at the bottom of that outhouse. Go get yourself one." I thought I'd dig ditches to make my own money before relying on any man for my well-being. I told Sonya I was running from the harshness of farm life and the fear of losing my independence.

She studied me with eyes that zeroed in on mine like magnets. "Hmmm," she said, in a voice as soft as my mama's. "No wonder you're so tough; you'll need that scrappiness to succeed in this good-old-boy network."

We bonded over being Aries women—according to her, "natural leaders." Then I asked, "Does it bother you that your male counterparts snicker behind your back and call you a ball buster and man-eater? How do you deal with the disparaging words?"

"Mildred," she said in a southern drawl for which she was well known, "I've been called worse by better," then sashayed out the door. Several weeks later, Sonya was walked out of the building by security—fired. We never spoke again.

Hard Drinkin' Lincoln

My scrappiness did me well when the company promoted me to director a couple of years after firing Sonya. Under my leadership, my team stabilized an optimization product line, the worst one the corporation had ever built, causing significant daily outages to banks and financial institutions. Bank presidents frequently called senior management, screaming about downtime and business losses. I attacked assignments with the tenacity of a little girl terrified of a beating if she missed her quota. Year after year, in the "strengths" section of performance evaluations, my managers wrote: "Mildred has 'maniacal focus,' is a 'problem-solver,' and, for her, 'no job is too complicated.'" In the "areas for improvements" section, they wrote, "Must learn to not measure others against her own high expectations/standards." For nine years, according to my reviews, I was a "rising star" with a "bright future." Then, the corporation acquired a small-town Georgia company, integrating me with people whose styles were more unprofessional than any I had experienced.

One day in early April 2000, I arrived to work more than an hour early, preparing for a meeting with people I would name The Georgia Three. The Three were Karen—a white woman—and two white men, who, along with me, were on the leadership team assigned to bring a new product to market. Since they'd ignored most of my meeting invitations, I did not expect them to show up at this one. I was always the first to arrive on my floor, so I was surprised to hear laughter. I gripped my briefcase and purse tighter. The glorious smell of sausage, eggs, and jalapeno kolaches drifted up from a box I balanced on my palm and caught in my throat. My high heels fell silently against the plush hallway carpet like they were sneaking up on someone. The cackle that had stolen my coveted early morning peace could have come from only one person.

As I turned the corner into the wide hallway leading to my office, I looked into the beet-red face of Cain—one of The Three. He was pacing outside of an office designated for visitors. How his hair stood on his head, and the slant of his eyes reminded me of Jack Nicholson in *One Flew Over the Cuckoo's Nest*. Cain stepped into my path. "You got a minute?" He walked into the room toward his laptop and said, "I got something to show you. Something you'll really like." I hesitated, said nothing for several moments. Did I dare believe that after months of being disruptive, Cain suddenly had something to show me? Something, according to him, I'd "really like?"

When I saw Duke, another of the Three, inside the office stuffing his laptop into a case, I swallowed a wave of fury. These two were always up to something nefarious, and our encounters never ended well. Duke's eyes skittered around like twin squirrels in traffic. He tucked his PC under his arm and hustled out of the office. "You kids play nice, ya' hear," he said. The back of his head bobbed down the hall like a kite in flight. Cain fidgeted with his laptop, apparently searching for whatever I'd "really like."

I did not see Karen that day but had met her previously at a reception welcoming her, Duke, and Cain to the corporation. Soft music played in the background of a large conference room. The mood was festive as waitstaff, dressed in black slacks and white tops, served cocktails and soft drinks, and offered light hors d'oeuvres like pigs in a blanket, cheese, and fruit from silver

Hard Drinkin' Lincoln

trays. When Chuck, who was across the room, pretending not to gaze down Karen's low-cut blouse, saw me, he waved, and they strolled toward me and one of my peers—a blonde-haired white woman. He gestured toward my friend and me and said, "Karen, meet Mildred, your partner for the new project." With a warm smile, Karen reached past me, pumped my peer's hand, and said she was looking forward to working with her.

I laughed and offered my hand. "Don't worry. Most people can't tell us apart." A crimson curtain lowered from her forehead and slid past her exposed cleavage. Karen ignored my hand, and my dark complexion hid the blood that boiled beneath my skin. I had known women like Karen before and knew the best way to deal with them was to be direct.

"Let me get this straight, Karen. You were 'looking forward to working with' Sheila until you realized *I, not she,* was your peer?" I expected Chuck to speak up about our roles. He gulped his Budweiser, shoved a hand in his pocket, and skulked across the room.

I stepped close enough to Karen's smug face that I smelled her strong perfume. "You and I are partners here. I'm responsible for development; you have marketing. What am I missing? I expect you to invite me to your meetings. The sooner we're on the same page, the better."

Before the evening ended, Karen had asked me why I was on the project and told me she didn't need me at her meetings, stating she would work directly with my lead developer, not me, to do her job.

The following morning, Cain burst into a conference room, followed by the other two Georgia folks thirty minutes late for a meeting. He slung his knapsack on a table and tipped over a pitcher of ice water. "Can't take you nowhere, Bubba. Now, look what you done gone and done," Duke said. Cain laughed that now too-familiar cackle. Just when I thought he had settled down, he snapped his PC closed and walked to the back of the room with a pompous look. That Cain moment crept into my memory when I saw Donald Trump skulking over Hillary Clinton during the 2016 presidential debate. I moved the pointer of a laser beam across my PowerPoint presentation but kept an eye on Cain.

When I scheduled planning sessions, The Three did not show up. When Karen *did* invite me to her meetings, she did not share the agenda, leaving me unprepared for assignments. I confronted her about the lack of communication, and Karen waved a dismissive hand, claiming she had sent me invites to all meetings. She suggested I check my junk mail: "Maybe the messages are there."

Cain offered me one of the two chairs in the room, the only furniture in the windowless office except for a small table. I didn't trust him as far as I could kick him, so I stood near the door, held on to my briefcase and purse, and set down the kolaches. I was curious to see what had him so excited. I thought he'd decided to change his ways, stop being an asshole. He sat on one of the chairs, clicking away with his mouse, mumbling to his monitor, "Come on, baby; where you at?" Then he swung his laptop toward me, laughed, and said, "Oh, here it is. Come look at this."

I stepped closer and sat on the edge of a chair. A bright screen popped on Cain's monitor with the title "Hard Drinkin Lincoln" splayed across the top in flashing red and blue letters.

Hard Drinkin' Lincoln

Beneath that was a black stovepipe hat perched atop a green whisky bottle. Bold red words, "The Rocky Hitler Picture Show," bled into a yellow background. A video unwound slowly, playing a musical version of "Battle Hymn of the Republic." A drunken Abraham Lincoln— "a public masturbator"—staggered up to the counter and belched. In a slurry voice, he asked to purchase a movie ticket. A Black woman with a broad nose and kinky hair, with the name "Sholita" pinned on her dress, was in the ticket booth. When she informed Lincoln that the movie he wanted to see was not showing, he pointed his finger at her face and shouted, "None of your backtalk. *I freed your black ass, Missy.*" Sholita jammed one fist on her ample hips and, with bulging eyes and thick lips, wagged her finger at Lincoln and did a neck roll. "Oh no, you di'nt. Uh ugh," she said.

I jerked backward as if Cain had slapped me, then rushed toward him in a blind rage, intent on smashing his brains with my Ralph Lauren briefcase. Suddenly, I was back in elementary school, where Willie Isaac—a second-grade bully—had tried to impress his friends by snatching my braid so hard my head snapped back. I had hurled my books into the red dirt in the schoolyard, smashed my fist into his nose, and knocked him to the ground. When I closed my eyes, punching his face repeatedly, I imagined myself hitting Daddy for all the times he had struck me until my younger brother pulled me off the boy. After it was over, I'd looked at my bloody fist as if it belonged to someone else. I would surely get a beating when I got home, but I was tired of Willie Isaac's shit. Now, within a foot of Cain on his chair—red-faced and laughing so hard his big belly jiggled—I turned, grabbed my food, and rushed out the door. My office seemed miles away. I moved fast. I needed to get to a safe place behind my locked door.

Inside, I tossed the kolaches in the trash can, fired up my laptop, and canceled all meetings for the day. Later that day, when I knew my manager would be in his office, one floor above mine, I took the steps two at a time, huffed through his open door, and closed it firmly. In the three months since the corporation had acquired the small Georgia company meant to escalate entry into new cutting-edge technology, I had complained, but this time was different. "Chuck, we need to talk." He was lazily flipping through the pages of *Computerworld* and pinching off pieces of a cinnamon raisin bagel. Steam piped out of a large cup of coffee on his desk while stock market quotes scrolled across the color television screen on the wall in front of his desk. I said, "Listen. I am *not* whining in your office. I have a formal complaint." He finally looked up, surprised.

Chuck closed the magazine and beckoned me to a visitor's chair across from him, a place that had become far too familiar.

I swallowed frustration and sat ramrod straight on the edge of the seat. "Chuck, for months, I have brought you complaints about the lack of cooperation, hostile treatment, and exclusion from crucial meetings by The Three." He squirmed, and his six-foot-five body, especially his stomach, slumped forward like a big fluffy pillow. I choked back tears and described the earlier "masturbator" incident in great detail. "Chuck, *please*, as unintentional as it may have been, I believe you have set me up to fail." I also told him he had the authority to get the team working together, even though I knew that would never happen.

Hard Drinkin' Lincoln

Chuck was known for being a conflict-avoidance manager. When he had a team so screwed up that it became dysfunctional, the company moved him to a different assignment. I told Chuck that he never provided any feedback after our meetings, even though his pat answer was always, "I'll look into it." At least this time, he changed it up. "I'll take care of it."

As the sun reflected off the gold frame around his thick eyeglass lenses, I saw no indication in Chuck's blank gray eyes that he took my grievances seriously. My spirits sunk each time I waltzed out of his office. This time was no different, except when I stood up to leave, I said, "Chuck, I'm taking the rest of the day off. I'll see you tomorrow." I did not tell him he had twenty-four hours to get off his ass and do something, or I would. I *did* tell him, "These people are literally making me sick."

That afternoon, I had a follow-up appointment with a gastroenterologist. "Tests reveal that you have severe cases of gastroesophageal reflux disease (GERD) and irritable bowel syndrome (IBS)." He handed me several bottles of Nexium and some Xanax samples and instructed me on what dosage to take.

After seeing Mama take handfuls of pills morning and night, I had worked hard all my life to live a healthy lifestyle and avoid taking medication. I exercised at the gym four times a week, walked or ran outside regularly, and ate a nutritious diet, including fresh fruits and vegetables. I stared at the pill bottles and asked, "How long will I need to take these meds?"

"You'll need Nexium for the rest of your life," he told me. "Any time you feel anxious, just pop a Xanax on the end of your tongue without water. It'll dissolve. Relief is almost instant."

I couldn't wait to try this miracle drug. With the tip of my tongue, I lifted the pill from my palm. A sweet burst, fizzing like Alka-Seltzer bubbles, lit up my mouth as tension melted like water down a fall. That night, and for months afterward, my body ached, and my stomach and bowels involuntarily purged themselves of the bitterness I experienced that day.

Two days later, Chuck "took care of the problem," as promised. The company demoted and stripped me of most of my responsibilities—but not my title, giving me a less prestigious position managing the quality assurance department. "We have nothing else for you. Take it or leave it," Chuck said. The following week, my primary care physician diagnosed me with fibromyalgia, and I had lost five pounds. I made an appointment with a psychiatrist and went on short-term medical leave before attempting to return to work. Long-term disability followed in October of 2000, never to return to that job again.

CHAPTER 24
Retaliation and Depositions

While still employed, in the fall of 2000, I sued my employer for race discrimination, retaliation, and wrongful demotion. Winning such a lawsuit in Texas, a "right-to-work state" run by conservative judges, was next to impossible, but my failure to fight back against bullies was not an option. "If we were in a jurisdiction such as the Southern District of New York, we would win this case hands-down," my attorney had told me.

Almost a year after I filed suit and was placed on long-term disability, one bright spring day in 2001, I sat in a small, poorly lit room at a rectangular table next to my attorney, armed for battle. Tom, who looked and dressed more like Jerry Lewis in *The Nutty Professor* than the legal eagle he was, sat protectively at my side, scribbling notes on a yellow legal pad with a fluorescent light reflecting off the top of his bald head. I wore a solemn black suit, a tailored powder blue blouse with a button-down collar, and black pumps. I sat erect on a straight-back chair. The defense attorneys, dressed in custom-made dark suits, expensive ties, and spit-shined Italian shoes, marched back and forth across the room like Baptist preachers, firing questions at me in a two-day deposition totaling ten hours, including short breaks.

During much of my deposition, the defense grilled me on several topics unrelated to the lawsuit's racism charges. The lawyers produced an internal investigation, which the corporation had provided, and instructed me to read excerpts that deemed me inflexible, incompetent, or mentally ill. I sat up straight on my chair and articulated every word while I boiled inside:

"There was no race discrimination," the report read. "Mills was treated badly because she was hard to get along with. These colleagues appear to have been motivated not by racism but rather by a strong disrespect and dislike for Mills." According to the report, " Chuck," who was my manager, "Should have taught them how to behave. They didn't know how to behave. They came from a culture where they didn't know how to behave. That's why they behaved that way. Well, they've admitted they did things wrong to you. They've admitted that they've treated you badly. What else do you want? You're just difficult to get along with." I read in the report that I responded to those allegations with my own questions in a heated exchange with Human Resources and Charley, a manager in my chain of command.

"Are you telling me this corporation hired director-level people who don't know how to behave? My parents taught me manners as a child. In my ten years of employment here, I have never heard, nor has it been documented, that I was difficult to get along with." Reading that report, I believed I had nowhere to turn for support

Retaliation and Depositions

while the company surrounded and protected those who practiced bigotry. "Keep reading," the defense attorney instructed.

I read that Charley and The Three—people who had been with the company only a few months—accused me of being paranoid, incompetent, and litigious. Yet I had filed only one complaint in thirty years of employment, other than the current one.

In the 1970s, while working for General Motors, I was standing at a podium teaching a seminar when a male colleague walked behind me, pinched my rear end in front of a room full of peers, and laughed. I immediately reported the incident to my management, who interviewed me, the witnesses, and the accused. GM's management swiftly disciplined the employee by placing a written warning in his personnel file. Rather than perform similar due diligence, my latest employer excluded me from critical parts of the investigation and blamed *me* for my unfair treatment.

I complained that the company lawyer investigated my racism grievance and, without speaking to me, concluded that Cain's actions were unintentional. The defense attorney seemed incredulous that I believed the lawyer should have questioned me. "What would you have said if the lawyer had asked you, 'Ms. Mills, what else do you have to tell me about this situation?'"

I wanted to slap the shit out of him for mocking me. Instead, I said the accuser and accused had a voice in criminal or civil complaints. He snapped around, red-faced, and I was glad I had slipped a Xanax under my tongue earlier when he launched a different line of attack.

"Has the frequency of your sexual relationship decreased?" he asked and wanted specifics about how often my husband and I had sex. "I hate to have to ask you personal questions, but I feel like I need to relating to this case. Have you ever been diagnosed with any form of herpes?"

I sat forward on my chair and buckled up for a nasty ride. "Years ago, I had a sore, and my primary care physician said he thought it was herpes, but I've had no further occurrences."

"Any infidelity in your marriage?" I told him I didn't know of any.

"Do you like your psychiatrist?"

"I don't like or dislike her," I said, "But I *do* respect her," *which is more than I can say about you*, I thought.

"I assumed your father was in the home as you grew up?" He asked if Daddy was in the military and if I knew his rank. I answered yes, he was in the home and served in the military, but I didn't know his rank. "Did he bring his military ways into the home? Was he a strict father? Was he a disciplinarian?"

"Define disciplinarian," I said, and my heart danced joyfully when the man glared and changed tactics.

"Let me ask it this way: Did he—was he a strict father in ways that one in the military would normally be? Was he regimented, did he talk about chain of command, did he focus on those kinds of things?"

I wrinkled my brow as if deep in thought. "He didn't speak of chain of command, and I was never in the military, so I can't say that he had a military style."

"Okay. Is your father still alive?" He asked when I'd seen him last and whether we had a good relationship now and when I was growing up.

Retaliation and Depositions

I said lovingly, "Yes, Daddy is very much alive; we have a great relationship, and of course, we had a good relationship when I was growing up."

The lawyer asked if "stressful events" or "problems" existed with either of my children and, if so, what problems. He questioned when I had last heard from or spoken to my daughter.

The agony I felt answering those questions was more jarring than the labor pains I experienced bringing Ashaki into the world, opening old wounds that festered just below the surface that had just begun to heal. Still, I refused to perjure myself. I told him that my twenty-nine-year-old daughter was a teenage runaway, stole from people, including myself and her father, and was a compulsive liar. I heard from her on Mother's Day but had last spoken with her eighteen months earlier at Christmas.

"What message did she leave you on Mother's Day, and did you call her back?"

"She said, 'Happy Mother's Day.' No, I didn't call her back; she didn't have a phone."

"What other problems does she have?"

I spoke as if it was the most natural thing to discuss the pain of raising a troubled child, but I refused to shrink from truthfully answering questions meant to rattle or disturb me, questions to which I knew they had the answers.

"My daughter has many problems," I told him. "She has abandoned her children and left their care to her father, me, and our spouses. She was arrested several times for theft in Hamilton and Montgomery counties in Ohio, and went to jail but has never been in prison. She committed identity theft by opening up credit in my name. She confiscated my American Express business credit card number from a receipt when I helped her rent a car. She then charged more than five thousand dollars in merchandise online from Saks Fifth Avenue."

He stepped back and gazed around the room at a nonexistent audience, like someone should be outraged at such behavior. "She essentially stole from you, right?"

"*Absolutely,* she did," I told him and hid the blood boiling underneath my skin, remembering sleepless nights and the fear of a phone call announcing her death.

"Have you ever contemplated suicide?"

"*Never,*" I answered. I contemplated my fist going through those straight, white teeth as he wrapped up his questioning but felt suddenly calm when my psychiatrist walked into the room and raised her right hand.

For months, I had felt isolated and alone, and I hovered near my closest family members, including Mama, Daddy, my spouse, and my son. Yet, I felt pride when my German-accented psychiatrist—a poised, stout woman—took the stand to answer questions and defend me against insanity claims. I wanted to leap from my chair and cling to her oversized floral dress.

"Have you ever diagnosed someone with paranoid personality disorder, and what is it?"

"Well, it has to be an entrenched style that damages your social and occupational functioning and must be present before age eighteen and is thought to be determined by nurture, not nature."

"They consistently bear grudges, are challenging to get along with, and may be litigious, frequently becoming involved in legal disputes, right?"

Retaliation and Depositions

"Now, you can't call it a personality disorder unless you have damaged social and occupational functioning. They very often will not be employed. Can't get a job, can't keep a job. That's not the situation here. Women are often paranoid about men, and I have dealt with those situations for women who can't sustain a marriage for any length of time. Still, I don't believe that applies to Mrs. Mills because she was a director with a superior level of occupational functioning."

"Okay. Just so I'm clear, if you have paranoid personality disorders, you can't sustain a marital relationship?"

"Right. See, paranoid personality probably we all have. You know, many people are suspicious of, say, the government, particularly veterans. But it doesn't become a personality disorder until it disrupts social or occupational functioning. If you have a track record of sustained occupational functioning, then it's not a disorder."

"For any of the people who you've diagnosed with that condition, did they believe that their phones or that people were watching them?"

When that lawyer launched into this line of questioning, my blood ran cold. The company had subpoenaed my records from the psychiatrist. It spewed my most personal thoughts, including how I thought the company had bugged my line after I heard unusual clicking noises on my home phone. My psychiatrist said, "My explanation about the emphasis on whether the phones are bugged is because there is an adversarial relationship here, and one wonders what level the employer will resort to in order to prevail in an adversarial relationship."

Mildred J Mills

"So, I guess your contention is that it's natural for Ms. Mills, given what she's been through, to assume their phones are bugged?"

"Well, whether it's natural or not is a whole different thing." I was pleased with my doctor's valiant defense against the insanity and paranoia claims the company aimed at me, attempting to dodge the actual race discrimination suit. I pretended not to notice the wink from my psychiatrist as she marched triumphantly from the stand and out the door.

Two months after my deposition, I sat beside my lawyer in a small windowless room, awaiting the first defense witness—Cain—to show his face. The court reporter sat on a three-legged stool facing the lawyers' tables. A fluorescent light hung from the ceiling, winking like an eye with a nervous tic and making a buzzing noise. I pulled my tailored navy suit jacket tighter to ward off the chill from the air-conditioning, making it cold enough to hang meat. The defense attorneys were huddled at a table across the room, flipping legal pad pages, whispering in low voices, and nervously cutting their eyes toward the open door.

Cain rushed into the room at nine o'clock with a loud cackle, and his hair stood wildly about his head. He appeared thinner than I remember, and rather than his typically sloppy clothing, he wore dress slacks and a white shirt. "Boy, that Houston traffic is something else," he said. Nobody responded. When the court reporter told him to raise his right hand and swear, he slid a cocky smirk my way. I sat on a cozy leather chair and thought, *Let's see who gets the last laugh.*

In less than five minutes, Tom, a portly grandfatherly type, had peppered Cain with so many questions about the website that

Retaliation and Depositions

he was squirming on the hard wooden chair with sweat rings forming under the arms of his wrinkled white shirt. Tom moved in close, jammed his hands into his loose-fitting black slacks as if to restrain himself, and glared through his horn-rimmed glasses. "Was the website you showed Mrs. Mills so offensive that no Black person would see it without wanting to advise the company that this is what somebody in the company is showing to Black people?"

Cain's face turned red like a crab in a pot of boiling water. After the defense counsel objected repeatedly, he stammered and didn't answer the question. I had to remind myself of God's words, "Vengeance is mine." Yet, I enjoyed his apparent discomfort as he scowled at the lawyer, who was unrelenting in his attacks as he stalked back and forth, the soft soles of his brown shoes inaudible. "What did Mrs. Mills say when you showed her the racist website?"

"She said, 'Oh my.'"

Inside my head, I yelled, "WHAT! I never say, 'Oh my.' You're such a liar." But thanks to the Xanax, I doodled on a yellow legal pad and calmly waited for my attorney to pounce.

Tom stopped pacing and stared, incredulous. He rubbed his hand across his bald head and snapped, "So, you thought she was *happy* to see that website?" When Cain refused to answer, he shouted, "Answer the question!" Cain's attorney objected again, and he never responded.

When Tom finally said, "No further questions for this witness," there was no cackling. Cain jumped off the chair and tore out of the room like bloodhounds were chasing him. I sat erect on my swivel chair for four days while Tom fought for me. He shot questions at white men in rapid-fire succession while their heads snapped back and forth like a whipsaw, especially my managers, Chuck and Charley, who had created a racist and hostile work environment by their lack of leadership. In his deposition, Chuck admitted that Karen discussed removing me from my position and replacing me with Cain, which did happen when they demoted me.

CHAPTER 25
Women and Children

Three months after the depositions, while still awaiting the verdict, my heart raced when the phone rang one night later than usual.

"Babe, is everything alright? I been thinking 'bout you all week," Daddy said. I told him I had wanted his opinion about racism in the workplace but didn't want to worry him and Mama about my problems. They knew of the lawsuit and were supportive. Still, Daddy's wisdom as a successful Black man in the South, never arrested while carrying a .357 magnum underneath his car seat "in case of trouble," was invaluable. I listened to Daddy's voice and envisioned him sitting on the edge of his bed near the gun rack that held a double-barrel shotgun and a rifle. I had never fired a weapon nor wanted to, but lately, the thought of grabbing one had crossed my mind, especially leading up to my testimony.

Days before I was deposed, I stopped at the dry cleaner's, wrote my check, and waited as colorful garments spun around the clothing carousel like children on a merry-go-round. A skinny white woman looking for my order suddenly turned and said, "By the way, I met your sister the other day." I snapped to attention, confused by that statement.

"What do you mean you met my sister?" The defiant look on my face must have startled the woman.

She stepped back from the counter and spoke cautiously. "Someone came in here and said she was your sister. She was real friendly. Asked when I had seen you last and other questions like that. I didn't think nothing of it."

"Well, you *should've* thought something of it before discussing my business with a stranger. I have seven sisters, and none are in Houston, nor have they been here recently." I ripped the check from my checkbook, paid for my clothes, snatched them off the hook, and rushed to my car, looking over my shoulders for a fake sister.

When I couldn't sleep a few nights earlier, I had gazed from my second-floor window at 2:00 a.m. and saw a chubby Black woman skulking like a possum away from my trash can at the curb. While I thought it was odd, I didn't tell my husband because, months earlier, when I had mentioned that I believed someone was following me, he said I must have been paranoid.

I told my attorney about the stalking incidents. "That's to be expected. You're making them nervous. Just keep doing what you're doing." I had no idea what that meant. I told him that hiding in my home and looking over my shoulder each time I went out was unhealthy. "Be strong," Tom said.

I told Daddy I had lost fifteen pounds in the past year and regularly saw a gastro doctor. I didn't mention the psychiatrist. Over the years, I had heard him say that only nut jobs took their troubles to a shrink. He listened without interruption. He calmly but firmly said, "Babe, you got everything you need to handle whatever news that phone call brings."

The following morning, I woke up soothed by Daddy's words but also puzzled that such a disagreeable person could deliver comfort. I was in the master bedroom, the most peaceful place in my home. A ceiling fan whirred slowly overhead. The waterfall from the swimming pool hummed like soothing rain. My reflection appeared in the mirror over the fireplace mantel next to my wedding portrait above the headboard, and I stopped short. The woman in a flowing ivory-colored gown with a radiant smile vaguely resembled the one staring back with hollow cheeks, sunken eyes, and a black nightgown. I grabbed the bedpost, gripped it tightly, and cried out, praying more fervently than ever before, no longer able to hold back the wall of tears or be the strong woman everyone expected.

"Oh, God, please, Father. Help me release the stress of this lawsuit. If my life continues this way, I won't see my son graduate from high school, go to college, marry, or have a family. Lord, my child needs me. Please, God. *Help me NOW!*" Suddenly, with the bedpost as my wailing wall, all the tension I had felt began melting like candle wax flowing through my body, and every muscle relaxed. I opened my eyes, and a vision like bright sunshine had engulfed the room, replacing confusion with peace and light.

I released the bedpost, and almost immediately, the telephone rang. It was Tom. "Mildred, I have bad news."

For the first time, he couldn't say anything to upset me. When he said the case would not proceed to trial because, on its face, it didn't meet race discrimination standards, I shouted, "*Thank *you, God, for answering my prayer.*" Tom hesitated and asked if I understood what he said. "I sure did, and I appreciate you letting me know." The attorney told me that the judge admonished the corporation. She stated that my lawsuit alleged and presented some facts supporting prima facie showing of race discrimination and retaliation but not enough to prevent summary judgment. According to Tom, the lead defense lawyer complimented me, stating that I was the most competent and bravest client he had ever met. *Fuck that smug bastard and his compliments*, I thought.

After that phone call, I felt the shackles unlock that I'd worn in corporate America's male-dominant IT industry for thirty years. Stepping back from that place allowed me to make time for myself, find my softer side, be a more attentive wife and mother, and nurture others.

I volunteered at my son's school, something I had never done. Every evening, I sat at the dinner table and attentively listened as he shared the events of his day, like details from baseball practice or some story about Iman, a cute girl one year older. And he never failed to ask, "Mom, how are you doing? I mean, how are you really doing?"

I was touched by how in tune my teenage son was with my suffering through a rough patch in my life. With his kind spirit and gentle manner, Richard allowed me into his space at an age when many young people avoid their parents. Even going off to college at the University of Michigan, my son welcomed me to parents' weekend every year, where California Pizza Kitchen became our favorite meeting place. My son and I were always close, but I cherish those last months of high school as our most precious time together. His kindness taught me to be kinder to myself. After he went away to college, I took an English class at Houston Community College and later enrolled at the University of Houston to help fill my days.

After praying my stress and anxiety away, I walked out my front door for the first time in months. I didn't look over my shoulder for the unknown or jump out of my skin when a squirrel scampered across the yard, or a dog barked. The sun hung high in the sky. Birds chirped, and neighbor ladies pushed babies in strollers and threw up their hands. "I haven't seen you in a while. You look lovely," they said. I walked briskly past the Sweetwater Golf & Country Club and waved at familiar landscapers tending manicured lawns and planting spring flowers, and I enjoyed watching bumblebees pollinating blossoms. *Not winning in court wasn't a loss at all,* I thought. I had stood against an oppressive system and fought for myself, Mama, and every other woman who had no voice and lacked the means to hit back, women terrified of facing their oppressors.

For years, I had written checks and provided charitable gifts but seldom gave the gift of time. The same day I heard from the attorney, I contacted a women's shelter and the Children's Hospital, seeking volunteer opportunities. After a few hours of orientation, I donned khaki slacks or skirts, a white shirt, and a red vest with a name tag and worked two-hour shifts three afternoons per week. I walked the bright hospital corridors, searching for young patients who needed a kind word. I carried my Bible, delighted when a parent was present. "Would you like me to pray with your family or read scripture passages?" My favorite children's verses were Mark 9:36-37: "*He took a little child whom he placed among them. Taking the child in his arms, he said to them, whoever welcomes one of these little children in my name welcomes me; and whoever welcomes me does not welcome me but the one who sent me."*

Most families gladly accepted the prayer offer and chatted openly about their child's illness's effect on their daily lives, while others preferred solitude. I listened to parents' concerns about a lack of financial and emotional support at home while caring for a hospitalized family member. I had chosen to volunteer in the cancer ward, which included children with chronic illnesses like sickle cell anemia and certain forms of cancer. "Would you like me to read a story?" I would ask.

One little girl with sickle cell disease snuggled up to me and said she never had visitors. "Will you read *Snow White*?" she asked. I read it repeatedly while she clung to me, asking that I not leave her. I looked forward to those hospital visits, witnessing children's bright and hopeful smiles despite suffering.

After contacting the women's shelter, I snatched every dress and work suit I had from my closet and gifted them to the organization. The first thing that hit me was the gloominess of dim lights and no windows inside the building. Ladies eyes darted on high alert at a strange face.

The first time I sat down with one of the women, she asked, "Why should I trust you?" In a soft, non-threatening voice, I told her of my childhood—as one of seventeen children growing up on a cotton farm—and how I had sued my company for egregious treatment in the workplace. I mentioned that my father hit my mother and his children. The next time I showed up, she had a group of women waiting to hear my story and encouraging words.

Women and Children

Standing amid those women—most broken and afraid—I thought of Mama's Friday night prayer meetings. I said, "Let's pray. Afterward, each of us will share a story."

I grabbed the woman's hand next to me, and we sat cross-legged on the floor, asking the others to join us. In our tight circle, some women cried softly, others embraced, and I hugged those on either side of me. "Thank you. No one has ever prayed for us, and the white women who come here don't touch us, and they sho' don't hug nobody," one woman told me.

"Not everyone is a hugger, but *someone* prays for you daily," I said. I heard harrowing tales of sexual assault, domestic violence, child molestation, and the shame of being in a shelter. "You are so brave to leave an abusive situation and face your demons. I still pray my mother will leave my father," I said. Unfortunately, many of the women returned to the abusers, including my mother.

One evening, several years after I divorced Peter, Mama called me collect, sobbing so hard, I couldn't understand a word she said. "Mama, calm down, please. What's wrong?" I was terrified of the danger lurking on the other end of that phone. I was twenty-nine, she fifty-four, and there were still six underaged children at home.

"Mildred, I want a divorce. Can you help me? I don't know nothing about getting no divorce, and I ain't got no money to pay for one," she said. I had wanted Mama to leave my father for as long as I could remember, but this was shocking news.

"Of course, I'll help you, Mama. What happened?" She described continued physical and emotional abuse and said Daddy now slept in a separate room, whispering on the telephone late into the night.

I was thrilled that Mama had finally decided to leave an abusive relationship, so I was happy to help. I researched attorneys, paid the retainer, and spoke to her often, reassuring her that this was the right thing to do. I offered to assist in finding housing and assured Mama that her children would take care of her and the babies still at home. But she remained with Daddy, who soon moved back into their bedroom.

Several weeks later, she called, and the enthusiasm I had heard before had disappeared. "Mildred, them white folks gonna take everything your daddy got. They said we have to split all the assets between us." I pulled the phone from my ear to keep from screaming. "They said Abraham got to buy me out of the house and farm. He can't run that farm with only half of his equipment." I was furious but did not say a word until Mama said, "Mildred, I just can't do that to him."

"Well, for years, he has done plenty to you. You deserve each other. Don't ever ask me for help again," and I hung up the phone, pissed that she had fallen for Daddy's charm and screwed me out of hundreds of dollars. But years later, I realized Mama was wiser than I knew.

In 2007, while traveling as a missionary with my church to Eastern Africa, I encountered impoverished women who had to choose between maintaining their dignity and feeding their families. We arrived in Nairobi, Kenya, to visit orphanages and provide food, clothing, and other supplies to orphans, recovering teenage addicts, and women and girls living with HIV/AIDS at the height of the epidemic. But nothing could have prepared me for the number of orphanages, which was as startling as the number of prisons in America.

Women and Children

"Why are there so many orphans, and what happened to these children's parents?" I asked, astonished. The stories of a deteriorating education, health, and social services system, which led to poverty, affecting mostly women and children, brought tears to my eyes. With limited economic opportunities to provide for their family, many women became sex workers, selling their bodies to long-haul truck drivers passing through the region.

Watching women stretched out in the open on pallets amid swarming gnats and flies, dying by the thousands or too sick to care for their children after being infected with the disease, was gut-wrenching. I was most troubled by the impact on children who lost one or both parents and ended up in orphanages.

Yet, the brilliant smiles of children with so little ignited an explicable light inside me. With bright eyes, dazzling smiles, and tattered clothing, they danced and sang barefoot on grassless dirt. Their voices, as pure as the driven snow, still ring in my heart like church bells.

The faces and smells of those sun-kissed boys and girls reminded me of my childhood, growing up on the farm in a close relationship with my brothers and sisters, only taking baths on Saturday nights. One would think living in miserable conditions would cause sadness or despair in a child. But I understood the joy in those happy feet. The children spoke the perfect Queen's English, their faces radiant as they shouted, "Black Americans, Black Americans" (accustomed to mainly seeing white missionaries). When their small hands reached out and touched my skin—black like theirs—a sensation like bumblebees touching flower petals buzzed through my body, stamping a life-altering impression forever in my memory. It is only now that I realize that Daddy brought the bricks, and Mama was the mortar, and as rough as their relationship was, they built a family that held together.

After four years and hundreds of stories with women in abusive relationships and performing countless interviews assisting them back into the workforce, I conducted one last interview. Although I'd been writing my thoughts on slips of paper, in letters to myself, or on my computer to express love, pain, joy, sadness, or other emotions that overwhelmed me, I had not considered writing a book. I was an avid reader who fell in love with the written word before I could even read, but I had not thought any part of my life was interesting enough to write about.

Under pressure to find a short story topic for a community college English class assignment, I wrote "*My Wall of Shame*," a tale about domestic violence. At the end of the semester, my professor asked me to remain after class. She contemplated me for several moments before saying, "This is one haunting story with a ring of truth. But you don't look like a woman who would tolerate abuse."

"Trust me, lady, I'm not," I told her as my whole body tensed up, angry, thinking of my mother, the character I wrote about. The instructor encouraged me to write my story with the same passion I'd written the essay. Her words frightened and delighted me, for it was the first time I thought I had something worth writing about. I wanted to tell that story, but I feared the repercussions from family members who feel the past is irrelevant and should remain hidden. So, I ignored the professor's advice for years, even after interviewing Mama.

Still, on March 21, 2006, I drove more than 650 miles from Houston to Alabama and sat across the dining room table from the

Women and Children

first domestic violence victim I had known, the subject of my essay and the only person qualified to tell her story. I pulled a cassette recorder out of my handbag and placed it on the table.

Mama eyed the machine laying between us like Aladdin's lamp with magical powers, and I reached for her, loving the feel of her wrinkled hands. We sat in the quiet of the dining room, just touching, the hum of the Frigidaire the only sound, an occasional housefly the only distraction. "Mama, I want to know your story. Will you tell me about your happiest days, saddest times, and everything in between?" I especially wanted to know when Daddy first hit her and if the abuse continued. She was eighty; I was fifty-five.

Mama sat quietly, studied me with kind eyes, and glanced at the recorder. Then she rolled her wheelchair closer to the table and crossed one hand over the other. I braced for rejection. Mama folded her lips and shook her head from side to side, slow like waking up from a long nap. "Mildred. I'll answer your questions."

I reached for the recorder before she could change her mind. "Thank you, Mama. Let's pretend I'm Oprah, and you're a special guest on my show. Do you mind if I record our session, so I won't misquote you or forget anything?"

Mama leaned forward, relaxed her shoulders, and joy radiated from her face, reminding me of a line in an old hymnal, "Gonna lay down my burdens, down by the riverside." Her steady gaze met mine, and in a firm voice, she said, "You can record our talk, Mildred. It's time I told somebody. But, first, put me a little wine in a cup wit' some ice cubes and Pepsi."

My eyebrows shot up. "Mama, I didn't know you drank wine." I poured Mogen David Concord grape into a red Dixie cup, and we giggled like schoolgirls. Mama swirled the beverage slowly, and the clinking ice cubes sounded like unlocking chains. "Mama, I will ask you tough questions about your life and some of your choices. If you get tired or need a break, just let me know. If there are questions you don't want to answer, I won't force you. Are you ready?"

Mama nodded. I pressed record and stated the date, time, and place.

"Do you remember the first time Daddy hit you?"

"I'll never forget it. The first time ya daddy laid his hands on me was the summer of 1947. Brother was about four or five months old." Mama spoke softly as the wine loosened up her tongue. She told me how, early one morning on the way to the cotton field, she sat on the bench next to Daddy in a horse-drawn wagon. The last thing Mama heard before Daddy slapped her so hard across the face that she fell headfirst onto the dirt road was that he had told her to be in the wagon *before* sunup, not a minute after. When her eyes finally focused, Mama could barely see Daddy's straight back and the horse and mule's rear ends swishing down the dirt road, pulling the wagon toward the cotton field. "I had a miscarriage that day," she told me, and even though her mother made her file a restraining order against Daddy, two days later, Daddy drove her to downtown Wetumpka. She dropped the charges and rode home with him. She and I sat unspeaking for several moments, me staring speechless at her and her avoiding my glare.

In silence, I asked God to hold me with His mighty hand and bridle my tongue until I found the courage to ask the next question. "Mama, *why on earth* did you stay with him?"

Women and Children

There was anguish in her voice when she wrang her hands and wailed, "Where was I going wit' a house full of little chillun, Mildred?"

"You didn't always *have* a house full of children, Mama. First, you had one. Three years later, you had another. If Daddy hit you once, you had to know he'd keep hitting you. Why didn't you leave?"

I realized I was yelling, and Mama looked like a cornered animal, so I refreshed her drink and took a deep breath.

"I'm sorry, but I *must* understand why you exposed your children to such violence. It's no wonder all your children except two who were ever married have divorced at least once. I'm surprised your sons don't beat their wives and that your daughters aren't in abusive relationships."

True to form, Mama was like a heavyweight boxer, skillfully weaving and dodging questions she didn't care to answer. "Now, Abraham was a hardworking man and a good provider. I don't think there was nobody worked no harder than him."

I ignored that response and decided that, unlike her mother, who was widowed once and divorced two husbands, Mama stayed in a toxic relationship to avoid the hard job of taking care of herself.

Years earlier, she described her mom when I asked her to tell me about Big Mama. "Momma almost worked herself to death," she said. "Always pulling in behind a old plow or washing clothes and cleaning up for white folks. I just didn't wanna work like that by myself." Remembering that conversation, I thought, *Mama would sacrifice her soul to keep a roof over her head and food on the table.*

I asked her why she had tolerated Daddy's philandering. "He wasn't always so bold wit' his fooling around," she told me. Mama sat across the table from me, wearing a black satin bonnet on her head, a pink, green, and white duster, and black old folks' comforts. When she reminisced about being in the cotton field with Daddy and how he asked what she'd do if she learned he was cheating, she told me, "I didn't say nothing 'cause I didn't know what to say."

Mama kept wringing her hands. I could not comprehend being speechless if a man asked me such a question, so I silently prayed I'd have happier stories if I lived to eighty.

"Some men they say whatever they wanna say to they wives 'cause they can't do nothin' about it anyway." Then she bowled me over, stating that her mother told her all men cheat, but the good ones come home at the end of the night to sleep in their own bed. As conflicted as I was about this thinking, I felt pity for Mama that she thought so little of herself and accepted such shabby treatment.

After they bought the farm, Mama tried to assert some authority, telling Daddy there would be changes. She threw up her hands and said, "You see how that worked out." Mama seemed at peace when she propped her elbows on the table and rested her chin on her clasped hands. "Every day of my marriage, I've prayed and asked God to let me live long enough to see Abraham keep his hands off me—*both ways*—and He finally granted my wish."

"*Mama*, you sat here for sixty years doing nothing to escape Daddy's hands but praying while he attacked you whenever he felt like it? How many times did you quote James 2:25 to me: 'Faith without works is dead'?"

Mama laughed to herself and ignored those questions. But I recognized pain when she recounted once when Daddy fumed because she denied him sex. He was in his eighties and told Mama,

Women and Children

if women knew she was denying him, they would be scratching at windows and tearing the hinges off the doors trying to get at him. She lowered her head. "Humph. Well, look at him now; ain't no woman of no kind trying to get to him or me neither. Time sho' brings about a change now, don't it?"

I reached for her hands and squeezed them tight, realizing not every question had an acceptable answer. "Mama, I'm glad you've found peace. Now, I've saved the easiest question for last. Tell me about your most amazing day with Daddy, when he swept you off your feet, made you feel drunk with love."

Mama wrinkled her brow like that was the most challenging question she'd ever heard. She asked me what I meant. We stared at one another, completely confused, and then I explained. "You know, Mama. Tell me about a time when Daddy told you how beautiful you were, how lovely your hair looked, that he loved you or your dress or the shape of your legs—*any compliment at all, Mama.*"

Her shoulders—no longer relaxed—were scrunched around her ears, and her eyes skittered around the dining room like she'd been caught breaking one of the Ten Commandments. In my mother's expression, I suddenly saw an unappreciated woman who hadn't known she deserved kindness or compliments. "What you mean? There ain' been nothing like that."

"Are you telling me that in sixty years of marriage, Daddy never told you that you were beautiful, that he loved you, or appreciated that you gave him seventeen healthy children?"

"Naw, Mildred. Whenever I put on a little lipstick or powder, he say, 'There you go puttin' on that clown face again.' Sometimes I just don't even bother, 'cause I don't wanna hear his mouth."

With such a stunning revelation, I pressed stop on the recorder.

I tried to think of something soft and kind to say to show that I thought she was beautiful and adoration-worthy. I had drilled Mama for hours and filled two four-sided cassette tapes with her voice. Her unabashed laugh and a few tears as she told stories full of the joys and pains of marriage and motherhood and hope for the future of her descendants was like a sugar high, sweet and thrilling, a place where she and I had never gone. Mama's words, animated and clipped, glided through the air, and her eyes danced as if she had been held captive, and I was Harriett Tubman shuttling her to freedom on the Underground Railroad. At the end of my interview, her brown eyes twinkled like stars in a midnight sky, a child's smile on her face begging the question, *Now what?*

I tucked the cassette player and tapes in my handbag as if they were top secret, dangerous if found in the wrong hands. "Mama, you can trust me with your words. I have no idea when it will happen. But someday, I will write my memoir, and I promise to share your words and mine inside the pages of my book to help others."

Then I thought to tell her, "Every morning before he leaves, and every evening when he returns home, my husband greets me with a warm hug and a kiss."

At Christmas, nine months later, with all of their children and some grandchildren gathered at the house, a fire crackling in the fireplace, and exquisite aromas piping from the kitchen, for the first time in my life, I saw Mama and Daddy holding hands. They sat side by side on a new leather sofa from their children, and Mama was grinning like when he gave her that fake rose more than fifty

Women and Children

years earlier. I was as shocked by my parents' display of affection as I was by Mama's blank stare when, months earlier, I had asked her to describe a romantic day, and she couldn't.

I pitied my mother, a sheltered woman yet devoted and loyal wife, who allowed her husband, a man she gave seventeen babies and whose home she kept for more than sixty years, to hand her crumbs when she deserved a cake. I was furious that Daddy, a worldly World War II veteran and charismatic businessman admired by men and women alike, showed his cows more affection than his wife. I remember the beating he gave me for striking a cow that kicked me when I was a girl. And every morning, in his old age, Daddy sat on the tailgate of his truck, calling lovingly to the herd that gathered around him, mooing like lovers while he smiled and fed them hay. I couldn't help but wonder how long before Mama would again be bitten by the sting of his hurtful words or struck by the hand she held.

CHAPTER 26
Secrets Revealed

The day I interviewed Mama, I had absorbed each word as a river of hurts flowed from her lips, purging her of personal, private, and sordid details, locked away like hidden treasures in a pirate's trunk she'd never shared with anyone. Mama had given much and asked little that day. She was a woman trapped in a life that would have crushed most people, but there she sat with the strength and dignity to bare her soul to a trusted daughter, but not strong enough to walk away from an abusive husband.

Driving back to Houston, I kept envisioning the image of Mama's tired profile as she sat in a wheelchair, hands resting on a sagging bosom. I had wrung truths out of Mama, shown frustration and impatience with her choices, but I never told her how much I valued her as a woman, mother, person, and friend. I did not tell Mama that the pearls of wisdom she had shared with me as a girl, like "Nothing beats a failure but a try" or "Do the best you can with what you have right now," still guided my daily life.

A bright sun shining through the window usually cheered me up, but back home in Houston, another conversation with Mama after the interview kept nagging at me. We'd been reliving milestones and comparing our first few years as married women and mothers when she suddenly stopped talking and gazed at me with a tender expression—resembling pity. "What is it, Mama?" She didn't answer but kept staring. "*Mama*, you're scaring me."

She lowered her head and wrung her hands, a habit when contemplating how to break bad news. Suddenly, she leaned forward, babbling. "I know you won't remember this, but when Rachel was born, you was thirteen months old. Yet, *you couldn't walk*." She studied my face with pain in her eyes. "There wasn't nuthin' wrong wit' you; you just couldn't walk. Your daddy's bricklaying buddy, Harold, and his wife, Matilda, wanted a girl. They kept telling us how much they wanted a little girl."

"What does that have to do with me, Mama?"

"Mildred, you couldn't walk. You was thirteen months old." Mama stressed the words slowly as if I could not comprehend them. "I had Brother. He wasn't quite five yet, and Bunny had just turned two. You was almost thirteen months old, and now a brand-new baby coming! Your daddy came home one day and said, 'Harold and Matilda want a baby girl real bad. Let's go 'head and give Babe to them.' I just didn't know what to do wit' all them babies, and we was struggling just trying to make ends meet."

Daddy wanted to give me away? The Mama I thought I knew would never have agreed to that. But Mama looked like she was back in that place, resigned to handing her child over, too overwhelmed with life and motherhood. She couldn't even look at me.

Secrets Revealed

"Mildred, I didn't know what else to do, so I said that would be alright with me. I agreed to give you away. Harold and Matilda lived over in Montgomery."

"*What? You gave me away?*"

She kept talking as if I had not said a word, telling me how Rachel was born on Monday, May 5, and a few days later, she dressed me in an outfit she'd made and handed me over to strangers. "That was a sad day for me," she said, and I sure cried about it, but at least I could handle Rachel better. Abraham said it was best 'cause we needed to try and get back on our feet."

I sat in a stupor, unsure of what to think or how to feel. "Mama, *how* could you discard me? Why didn't you give that baby away?" She didn't acknowledge me.

"I thought about it and thought about it, you being gone, and wondered what you was doing and whether you was eating alright or crying. You was just a baby, but I wondered if you missed us and wanted to see us or if you even knew you were with another family. I tried to tell Abraham how I felt, but he said, 'Harold and Matilda can afford to take better care of her.' Somehow, I just wasn't satisfied hearing that."

I watched Mama—incredulous, hearing such a story at age fifty-five and unable to comprehend why she was telling me now. Three months after they gave me away, she got religion one night. She thought she heard me crying clear as day and couldn't get back to sleep. It was a Sunday in August, nearing Daddy's birthday. "I woke Abraham up and told him I wanted my baby back. You go pick her up today after church," she told him. Daddy protested, and they argued as he dressed for church. "She can eat what the rest of the chillun eat and wear whatever we have to put on her. I done made up my mind."

She rocked a while before speaking again. And then she smiled, our eyes met, and I sat in stunned silence, allowing her to finish the story. "Mildred, I stood up to your daddy that day. When he walked back through that door after church, you was in his arms. You was dressed in a pretty blue dress with ruffles and little white flowers and had on new black patent leather shoes and matching light blue socks. Your hair was combed real pretty. You looked right sad. Abraham put you down, and you got on your hands and knees like you was gonna crawl. I reached out my hands to you, and, *Mildred*, you stood up and ran toward me like you figured out why we sent you away." She told me that after that day, Daddy looked at me differently. He always said, "Babe is daddy's little girl."

If Mama had whipped a Colt 45 pistol from her bra, it would not have stunned me more than that story. I didn't know whether to shake or thank her, so I could only stare, bewildered, unsure what to feel. "Mama, standing up to Daddy would have meant you didn't give me away. I mean no disrespect, but I bet you were his 'little girl' or something besides a punching bag early in your relationship. Look what it got you."

Mama bristled. "Watch your mouth, Mildred. I thought you might want to know what happened. We really was in a bad place back then. You don't know how hard it is for me to sit here and tell you we gave you away, but I hope I made it right by getting you back and raising you the best I knowed how. I didn't want you to find out about this somewhere else when I'm gone." She lowered her head,

Secrets Revealed

stared at her hands on the table, and rocked gently back and forth. "Mildred, I hope someday you'll realize how hard we tried over the years to make it up to you."

I wondered about the long-term impact of such an abandonment on me. I wasn't sure what to do with that information. Did it matter that my parents gave me away? They brought me back, right? I had no conscious memory of the time away from my family. Could I have subconsciously remembered the trauma of being taken away? Is that why I overachieved, always tried to please, and never complained when asked to do so much?

Still, I tried envisioning a twenty-six-year-old mother, overwhelmed by a life she never planned, struggling to catch one small break, and desperate enough to give away her baby. I pondered this for a while. I could not fathom Mama's agony after another child was born the following year, and then she had twelve more. Yet, I thanked her for her honesty, unearthing a truth she could have taken to her grave. I couldn't help thinking that Mama and Daddy were the same—they told lies.

I rolled my suitcase across the kitchen floor and thought, *It is a merciful God who protects us from our most devastating memories.* I wondered about the impact of knowing this story earlier. On my way to the door, I bent to kiss her cheek and was surprised when she almost whispered, "Can you stay a little while longer?" Mama rubbed her hand gently across my face, "Mildred, I'm glad I named you after me." I threw my arms open—already forgiving her for giving me away—and squeezed her tight, thinking, *So am I.*

She sat quietly for a few moments. "You don't know this, but your Daddy wanted to name you Jezebel."

I folded my arms and stared. "Mama! How could *anybody* look at a newborn baby—their daughter—and want to call her Jezebel? It's no wonder you all gave me away. You didn't want me in the first place."

I hadn't heard of anyone with that name other than the brazen and shameless woman in the Bible. Mama hung her head. If I'd had any sense when I stood up as a baby, instead of running into her arms, I would've run away from both of them as fast as my little bowlegs could take me. I walked out the back door and drove home to Houston, wondering what other secrets an eighty-year-old woman carried, waiting for the right moment to unburden herself.

CHAPTER 27
A Memory Returns

The next day in Houston, when I stepped into the La Madeleine restaurant to meet a prospective employer—a woman small business owner—the heavenly smell of French bread, olive oil, and exotic spices almost made me forget Mama's disturbing disclosures. I was searching for a "white woman," the only description from a mutual acquaintance, but every female was white. I finally spotted a short lady who looked like a spymistress with a blonde ponytail. She wore a long, colorful dress, sat in a far corner with a paperback book watching the door, and rose as I approached her. "Are you Dee Pipes?" I asked. Her eyes were sharp and watchful with a bit of mischief, but her smile was instant. She reached up, embraced me warmly, and offered me a seat at her table.

We quickly ordered soup and sandwiches, and Dee zipped into business mode, telling me she had numerous projects in flight but wasn't finishing any of them. She owned a staffing firm, needed to find candidates for her clients, and was writing her first novel. Dee wanted to hire a part-time but trustworthy business operations manager to oversee her finances. "My husband is unhappy with me because we haven't vacationed in two years." I swung my head side to side while Dee jumped from one topic to another, sucking iced tea through a straw from a large plastic cup labeled Whataburger. "Tell me a little about yourself."

"I worked in the IT industry for over thirty years, am performing volunteer services, and attending classes at the University of Houston. But after a four-year hiatus from corporate America, I'm ready to reenter the workforce but never again for a corporation." I quickly disclosed the details of the lawsuit against my employer.

The eye twinkles sprung to life, and she chuckled. "I also worked with IT companies, which is why I greatly appreciate owning my own business."

Dee trained those caramel-colored eyes on me through spotless eyeglasses, and we shifted to personal lives. I described my large family growing up on a farm; her only remaining blood relative was a nephew. She spoke fondly of two "nephews" from underprivileged families she had "adopted" through the church. We were both married and Christian. Then she surprised me. "I'm prejudiced against Hispanic men."

I thought, *Oh, no. Not a racist.*

Before I could question her prejudice, Dee said, "My husband knows where I am every minute of the day. I was kidnapped once."

While this woman described an abduction that occurred years earlier when she was in her mid-twenties, I sat riveted on the edge of my chair. After she entered her husband's sports car in their apartment garage one morning, a man who smelled like horses and

A Memory Returns

had a Spanish accent directed her—at gunpoint—to a construction site and attempted sexual assault. While I absorbed the impact of this woman's incredible escape by kneeing a would-be rapist in the groin, an inexplicable alarm went off, sending a cold chill scampering down my spine.

That morning, after I met Dee and she hired me on the spot, was only three days after the unsettling conversation with Mama where she'd spilled her secrets. I was home alone, gazing out my second-floor office window. Down below, all makes and models of cars and trucks pulled into the landscape and design business at the corner of Saint Street and West Alabama with their trunks and tailgates open. The muffled music from car radios thrummed against my windowpanes like a drumbeat. Brown-skinned Hispanic men wiped glistening sweat on their shirt sleeves and loaded sod, shrubbery, mulch, and blooming plants before shutting vehicle doors and trunks.

The sights and sounds of bustling spring activity outside my window always cheered me, reminding me of new life. But today, the image of me as a fifteen-month-old baby, scrambling from my knees into the arms of a mother who had rejected me but whose longings brought me back, was tangled with Dee's telling me about her escape from a serial rapist. Against my chest, I held an unaddressed invitation filled with pictures and happy notes announcing my son's college graduation, an invitation with no destination. It was for my daughter, now an adult, whom I had not heard from in months, but I recently learned was in jail again for theft. I stepped to my desk, fired up the computer, and wrote another entry in my diary, a section where I poured out my heart to a daughter who had rebuffed me since birth, always seeming out of reach.

April 2006: "Ashaki, you may find this hard to believe, but before I was your mother, I was a little girl who dreamed of freedom from your grandpa's cotton fields and strove to make good choices, maneuvering life on my own. Lord knows I have made mistakes and the occasional poor choice, but none have landed me in jail. I worry about your incarceration, but at least I know where you are, and thank God you are off the streets."

After writing those last words, laughter drew me back to the window. Down below, four Hispanic men jostled back and forth, carrying a magnolia tree. Hearing their laughter and Spanish banter caused a hard knot to form in my stomach. The magnolia tree's wide white blossoms reminded me of bed sheets, of me in a hotel room more than eleven hundred miles and thirty-six years ago. It reminded me why I left Arthur, my good job and recording contract, and ran from Columbus to Dayton. That image at that moment awakened memories I'd buried so deep in my soul they'd all but disappeared.

And now, clear as day, it was 1970, and I was nineteen again. A bright, sunny day that began with work and a brisk walk across Ohio State University's campus, sharing a peanut butter sandwich and laughter with my friend, Lillian ended with me spread eagle, wearing one black platform shoe strapped on my foot, face down on a king-sized bed in a pie-shaped room with floor-to-ceiling windows. Twelve men devoured a buffet of breast, legs, buttocks, and thighs with wooden instruments drinking from my core. Bright sun in a cloudless sky cast shadows across cotton sheets

A Memory Returns

crinkled beneath my body and caught sweat, drool, and cum on the sixteenth floor. Fluffy white pillows muffled moans and tears. Heavy curtains pooled on the carpet resembled swirls of vomit near a lone chair centered on a pale wall holding pictures of old white men. A nature scene of wild animals stared dead-eyed at the girl—a sacrificial lamb draped across the bed.

The men slapped, bit, spanked, and pulled me apart like a Thanksgiving turkey as their salty rancor filled my nostrils, and guttural sounds assaulted my ears like an untuned pipe organ rambling around a packed church on Sunday morning. I absorbed semen from prickly spears like a pincushion swallowing needles.

And then, I refused to be raped—a victim. "*Fuck it*; it's only sex, something I enjoyed, but on my terms." I became every Black girl, surviving the Middle Passage, young, strong, defiant on the trading block, sold, surviving white men's rape in cotton fields. Harriett Tubman, conductress of the Underground Railroad. The last passenger aboard got the ride of his life when, trapped on my stomach, I moved my ass like a bucking bronco, reached back, gripped his butt, and my feet flew up, nailing the back of his head with a platform shoe. The rider came fast—left even quicker. Olive-skinned men, once bold and boisterous, scampered from the room like thieves in the dark as the sun set, hiding cowardly behind clouds in a black sky.

The memory had returned suddenly, a dark, fierce pop-up storm bending me at the waist—confused but unbroken. I wondered how I could have forgotten something so traumatic. Yet, sitting in silence, I remembered: me unwashed, snatching on clothing, racing from the room, tears spilling, asking God to send radiation to the cancerous poison that had entered my cavity. Riddled with shame and guilt, I would *never* report that crime.

In 1970, I did not believe anyone—not the police, friends, strangers, no person—would think a girl in a mini-skirt, "showing all that flesh," wasn't "asking for it." The only exception was Arthur—the one man I thought would believe, protect, and defend me—whom I couldn't contact. So, I prayed fervently: *Please, God, help me forget.* Walking in the dark—fast—toward my empty apartment. Then, I swallowed the evidence, buried my secret, refused to be raped again in the court of public opinion and even in my own memory. I chose to love again, not cower in fear.

My first reaction after the stabbing memory returned was shock. Then I wept, remembering horror tales from women in a homeless shelter, Mama revealing her shameful story, and how bravely Dee Pipes chronicled her abduction and escape. These women spoke unabashedly and shamelessly and formed a protective shield around me, which allowed me to remember the disgrace and shame I had buried so deep that it had all but disappeared. I continued weeping, remembering my adult daughter, whose father, just that morning, had informed me that she was homeless and addicted, subjected to the cruelty of the streets. I tried to imagine what decisions went into choosing disconnection from family and one's support system. Now, I thought of telling my husband of eighteen years—a kind, loyal, and supportive man who had entered my life when my son was thirteen months old and assumed the role of father, then husband.

In bed that night, he watched a Houston Astros game on television. I held a book, not reading it. I breathed deeply and

A Memory Returns

searched for words. "The weirdest thing happened to me today," I said. Then I told my husband of the suppressed memory and my remembering it.

He put down the TV remote and turned to face me, questions hiding behind confusion written on his face. I braced for rejection, repulsion. But he pulled me into his arms. "I'm so sorry that happened to you." He held me tenderly while our hearts beat as one. I wondered what questions he buried to preserve a love stronger than ghosts from the past.

Long after my husband fell asleep and the music of his soft snores quit playing in my ear, I gazed into the darkness and thanked God for Darryl. I replayed memories of how one month after I resigned from GM, a week after I left Casanova, and the day I began a new job, God blessed me with a man who made and kept his vow "to have and to hold from this day forward, for better, for worse, for richer, for poorer, in sickness and in health, until death do us part."

CHAPTER 28
Precious Lord, Take My Hand

Two years later, as the light faded from Mama's eyes on her eighty-second birthday, I drove from Houston to Baptist South Hospital in Montgomery. I stood at the door and studied the woman who had given me life, sleeping in the fetal position, lying on her left side, her back to the door. She wore a blue, floral hospital gown open down the back, revealing her nakedness. Mama's eyeglasses were askew on her face, and her hair—unbrushed that day—was standing in all directions. The five o'clock news played on a television screen. I walked around the bed.

"Mama," I whispered and straightened her glasses.

I will never forget her smile when I came into focus. She was beautiful. Her face lit up, and I folded into the loose skin of her open arms. "I didn't know you was coming today."

"Well, it's your birthday. I needed to see you."

She scooted over on the narrow bed with much effort, moved her hand slowly, and patted the mattress. I squeezed into the tiny space and felt warmth radiating from her body. Clear liquids dripped slowly from a bag through an intravenous line in the top of her hand. Various monitors chirped, and the smell of anesthesia hovered in the room like a ghost. A clear oxygen tube snaked into each nostril, and I rubbed her soft, wrinkled hands, gazed at the ceiling, and thought of everything I wanted to say. "Mama, I have something to tell you."

"*Oh*?" she said in her singsong voice.

"I don't know if you remember being upset when I suddenly quit my job at Ohio State, but there was a reason. I left what you called 'that good state job' in Columbus and moved to Dayton because I was gang raped." I turned to her. "One evening after work, a man I had seen before but didn't know kidnapped me, drove me to a hotel, and sold me to men who spent the evening raping me." Mama gripped my hand, moaned low in her throat, and held on with a strength I didn't know she still possessed. "Mama, a merciful God scrubbed my mind of that evening until a few days after I interviewed you. Then I relived the entire night as if it had just happened."

"Lawd, have mercy, Mildred. I thought I'd been through some thangs, but I sho' can't imagine nuthin like that. Ugh, ugh, ugh. Is you alright?"

I told Mama how, at first, I was sick to my stomach, had tried to banish the memory back to where it came from, and doubted whether anyone would believe I had forgotten such a thing. I realized that her raw story of abuse and neglect was the catalyst that erased my fears.

"Mama, I'm fine. I've wanted to tell you since I remembered, but you've had enough worries lately, in and out of the hospital.

Precious Lord, Take My Hand

I wanted to meet you at our favorite spot across the dining room table from each other, but I now doubt that ever will happen."

Mama gave me a knowing look, folded my hand inside hers, and our eyes met. She was my young mother, protecting her girl from the horrors of a world where men rape and pillage, and I was safe in her hands. Now, she fell asleep with worry lines between her brow, and I protected her.

For the remainder of my stay, I spent every day in Mama's hospital room, advocating for her, fixing her hair, or giving her sips of water when she was awake. At night, sterile smells kept watch while I slept on an oversized plastic chair next to Mama's bed, and she labored to keep up with the C-PAP machine smothering her face. I wondered how long before congestive heart failure would win the race.

Two days later, on May 5, 2008, Mama woke up around 2:00 a.m., peering through the window of the C-PAP contraption, and yelled. "Mildred, that doctor said you could take this thing off me." I jumped up from the chair, disoriented and exhausted, and clicked on the overhead light. My mother, usually kind and gentle with a sweet voice, glared, too tired and angry to speak. I held her hand and spoke softly.

"Mom, I realize the machine is uncomfortable, but I can't remove it. You know the doctor did not tell me to take it off." Mama peered through the large mask that caused her watery eyes to bulge, rolled over, turned her back to me, and pretended to be asleep. The noisy pump—a suffocating pillow—slammed against her frail body, shoving air down her throat faster than she could absorb it. We both lay awake, unspeaking, as congestive heart failure, like termites, destroyed her from the inside out.

By noon, a nurse had replaced the C-PAP with a thin oxygen supply threaded into each nostril. I watched Mama toss and turn, restless, as I packed my Hartman suitcase and contemplated leaving her to catch a flight back to Houston. I rubbed her soft hair, still mostly black, and kissed her warm cheek. We stared into each other's eyes like one could read the other's mind. I thought, *I will never see my mama alive again. I need a lasting memory.*

I sat on the bed and folded her palms in mine. I studied the wrinkled hands with fingernails—thick and hardened by age—painted red like vibrant roses, and I knew what I had to do. "Mom, what should I sing for you?"

Without hesitation and quicker than I imagined she could speak, she whispered firmly, "Sing 'Precious Lord' for me." I stood up, released her hand, and rubbed her back like a young mother walking the floor, soothing her teething babies.

"Precious Lord. Take my hand, lead me on . . ." In a weak, sweet voice, Mama sang along for two lines and drifted off like an empty vessel along a wavy seashore. Her chest moved slowly and rhythmically. I finished the song and rubbed her back, ensuring she remained asleep.

While I sat on the lounge chair in her room and watched my mother rest, I prayed against hope that God would allow her one more recovery—one more trip home. At two o'clock sharp, I tiptoed across the room, pulling my roller bag behind me. For a brief moment, I stood. I watched her chest rise and fall as she lay in the fetal position. I said a mental goodbye and thought of another of her favorite sayings: "Once a man, twice a child."

Precious Lord, Take My Hand

I reached for the doorknob and was startled when Mama asked in a sweet, gentle voice, "It's time to go?"

I dropped my luggage, raced to her bedside, and squeezed her as tight as possible without cracking a rib. "I thought you were sleeping, but I should have known you wouldn't let me go without saying farewell."

"I was sleeping, but I could sense you leaving. I wanted to say goodbye and that I love you, Mildred." I told Mama I loved her but batted back tears that threatened to fall.

Two days later, Daddy called. I was alone in my Houston office. "Well, Mama's gone. When can you come?"

I hung up the phone and screamed, a primal wail for all of Mama's suffering. I cried because I'd lost the woman who gave me life and her name. "After all, you looked like a Mildred," she once told me. I instantly missed the woman who, for the last years of her life, was a dear friend with whom I could share anything, one I called every day at five o'clock because I knew Daddy was watching the news and wouldn't answer the phone or smother her, listening to the conversation. "What you cooking today?" she would ask and exclaim, "Ooh, that sho sounds good," regardless of what I prepared. I wept, angry at God that he took Mama instead of Daddy, not allowing her to spend one lousy day knowing the feeling of freedom from sixty-two years of oppression. Even in the hospital, she couldn't escape his temper.

One morning, I had dolled Mama up, given her a sponge bath, rubbed body lotion on her arms and legs, and brushed her hair. Daddy had walked into the room while two nurses held each of Mama's arms and struggled to transfer her from the bed to a chair.

"Naw, naw," Daddy yelled. "Y'all don't know what the hell you doing. At home, I pick her up a certain way. Thas what you need to do. You better not fool around and drop my wife." (He didn't tell the nurses he had dropped her on the concrete floor one night, couldn't pick her up, and had to call one of his sons to help.) The women skittered out of the room with fear in their eyes.

Mama had flared her nostrils and pinched her lips into a knot, and her eyes became tiny slits. I had never seen such a scornful look on her face. "Abraham, after that accident, I thought you woulda changed. But now I know, you ain't never gonna change."

A few months earlier, on the way to a church meeting, Daddy had hit a deer that crashed through the windshield and kicked Mama in the face. Daddy lost control of the car. The car was stuck in a ditch far off the road, hidden by bushes, with all four doors jammed shut. When Daddy saw Mama's eye swollen shut and her face bloody, he had kicked out the back window, crawled out of the car, and walked almost a mile to seek help. He was eighty-seven. After the sheriff arrived and noticed the dead deer on the back seat, he asked what had happened. He said it was a miracle they survived. Mama had to have eye surgery but couldn't stop talking about Daddy's bravery.

In the hospital that day with the nurses, if Mama's looks could kill, he would be a dead man.

We buried Mama six days after she passed on May 14, 2008, but not before I leaned over her casket and kissed her cheek—now cold and lifeless—for the last time. I walked to the podium and marveled at the walls of flowers around her coffin. She loved flowers of any kind and would have been so happy. Daddy sat on the front pew, looking lost—a shrunken shell of himself. Mama's children were

Precious Lord, Take My Hand

all dressed in black except me. I wore a cream-colored dress, her favorite color. Old and young ladies with assortments of church hats honored my mom. I felt a tearing of hearts between mother and daughter as I cast my cares on Jesus, looked heavenward, and sang a unique rendition of *"Precious Lord, Take My Hand"* with all my soul. I improvised between the verses, stating words I thought Mama felt as she took her last breaths.

"I imagine as my mother lay dying, too tired to take another breath, she reached her hands to the heavens, saying, 'Precious Lord, take my hand / Lead me on, let me stand, / I am tired, I am weak, I am worn.'" I swallowed the tears that threatened to fall. "Perhaps, when Mama knew she had done all she could on Earth, she closed her eyes, rested, and held on until the last of her children, Sonny, arrived to say goodbye after driving all night from Texas. Then she took God's hand and reached the other side. 'Oh, at the river Lord, I stand / Guide my feet, hold my hand / Take my hand Precious Lord, lead me home.' And then Mama closed her eyes and let go of the world."

Later that day, Daddy and I stood in the backyard at the cinderblock house, chatting about how pleased Mama would have been to see her homegoing celebration. Her fifteen children, several grandchildren, nieces, nephews, one brother, and many friends (more than a hundred people) had gathered at the farm for a repast, marveling at fat, black cows grazing in the pasture or drinking at the edge of the lake where cotton once grew. Her children fed the masses who ate, laughed, talked, remembered Mama, and greeted Daddy. "Babe," he told me, smiling, "I think 'Precious Lord,' not 'Amazing Grace,' is now *my* favorite song."

CHAPTER 29
A Return to Daddy's House

After we buried Mama, Daddy lived eight years. I had begun writing this book, painting him as an irredeemable antagonist, but I did not have the heart to continue in that manner after witnessing his brokenness. A week after the funeral, Daddy and most of his children walked across a massive parking lot to his granddaughter's graduation ceremony in Atlanta. He squeezed my hand tightly and stumbled along, reminding me of a small child unable to keep pace with its mother. His eyes were like spotlights, moving side to side, searching for something lost. We surrounded Daddy and tried to fill the empty place Mama had occupied for sixty-two years.

For the first few months, I checked on him daily. "I saw ya' mama last night," he often told me. He excitedly said how she spoke to him and told him things, but he refused to share them, saying, "Well, that's me and Mama's secret." I visited Daddy four or five times a year, helping around the house and keeping him company. He raved over my food, especially fried bone-in striped bass or catfish. Daddy would call me later. "Babe, I been trying to make that fish nice and tender like you do. Some people cook it so hard that it hurts my gums. Do you put a little water in it?"

"Oh, no, Daddy. I don't overcook it." I enjoyed our time together and felt closest to him during such conversations.

We sat side by side at the dining room table, playing dominoes. A Christian TV show played softly on the television, and a commercial-sized fan chased hot air around the room. I spun side to side in a swivel rocker. "You remember the milk route, Babe?"

"Yes, sir. How could I forget my first job?" I smiled.

"You had a good business head on your shoulders, even back then. You wouldn't let nobody cheat me." He studied the dominoes, rocked slowly on his chair, and chuckled, a faraway look in his eyes. "It tickled me when you would say, 'Daddy, that lady didn't pay you last time. Remind her she owes you double today.'" He slapped his right knee, reared back, and laughed, happy at the memory. "I thought I'd give the lady a break, but you nagged me until I collected from anyone who owed money."

I didn't remember any of that, and I thought about the secrets Mama and I shared in this very spot on the same chairs. "Daddy, Mama told me you guys gave me away to the Hendersons when Rachel was born."

He hesitated, cleared his throat, and shifted his eyes. "I don't remember that."

We were both silent for a while, counting dominoes. "You were the one who called me when Mama died. 'Babe, when can you make

A Return to Daddy's House

it home?' you asked. You also said you and Mama had something for me. But when I arrived, you were so sad. I didn't mention it." I told him how Mama said they intended to make it right by me for giving me away. "What did you and Mama have for me?"

"Hmmm. I don't remember saying that." I was disappointed but not surprised that Daddy would not honor any promise between himself and Mama. We continued our domino game, him keeping score and sometimes taking an extra point for himself, but I pretended ignorance.

I was immune to his deceptions and betrayals; he couldn't help himself, and as Mama had said, he was not likely to change. Daddy had a funny way of showing love, but I knew he loved me, and I enjoyed his conversations about the past.

I admired so much about my father: his flawless skin—chocolate like Hershey's Kisses—the quiet way he entered a room and earned immediate respect, how he minded his own business, his self-assuredness, and more than anything, his work ethic. Of all those attributes, I often focused on the flaw that, in my view, overrode all his good qualities—his raging temperament at home. Daddy adored me and, more than once, told me I was his and Mama's favorite.

He called me one Saturday morning to thank me for the money I sent home after each paycheck when I finished tech school. Daddy surprised me when he whispered lovingly, "You know you was always our favorite." He told me again when I was in my twenties—after a promotion at General Motors, to which I responded, "I am not interested in being your favorite. You have fifteen other children. Treat us all the same." In hindsight, I wish I had just said thank you and enjoyed the grace. I had rebuffed his feelings to keep the peace, concerned about what my siblings may have thought. But I honored my father all the days of his life.

Eight years after Mama passed, one month after I had last seen him, and less than a week since I'd spoken to him, I walked into the bedroom of the most powerful man I have ever known. A man I had adored and despised. In less than two weeks, he had gone from caring for himself with little assistance to requiring around-the-clock hospice care and regular morphine. Kidney damage was winning the battle.

Choking on oppressive heat from the open flame of a propane heater, I envisioned the times I stood outside this same bedroom door as a little girl. I tapped lightly and said, "Good morning, Daddy," before preparing breakfast for the family. The familiar sounds caught me first. Gospel music played from a transistor radio. Crickets chirped outside. The whir of a fan moved hot air. Then came the smells of sixty-six years of living in the same place. The fresh scent of Pine-Sol mixed with the stale smell of urine. The musty odor of mold on cinderblock walls. And last, I felt the pain.

A torrent of feelings washed over me—a little girl traumatized by blows from a leather strap. Still, my heart filled to bursting when I looked into his cataract-ridden eyes. Lying on a hospital bed—with protective bars—wrapped in a homemade quilt pulled up to his thin neck, he watched me in silence, a look of confusion on his face.

I dropped my Hartmann luggage on the worn wood planks, rushed to his bedside, wrapped him in my arms and kissed his dark cheek. I whispered, "Hey, Daddy!"

A Return to Daddy's House

His hand brushed through the air like a broken windshield wiper. A weak smile crossed his face. "Hey there," he said in a barely audible voice. I wanted to hear Daddy call me Babe, the childhood name only he used. He studied me, seemingly unknowing, with those deep brown eyes clouded by ninety-four years of life. His body was frail, but his chocolate skin firm, unwrinkled.

I stood in the tight space beside his bed and talked to Daddy about nothing at all. His voice, now soft, his few words seeming to come from a place far away. I remembered scathing words, "How could you be so stupid? Look at your socks," after I had dressed myself as a four-year-old and wore my socks upside down.

Daddy closed his eyes, soothed by the familiar sounds of bullfrogs croaking, cows mooing, and the wind rustling tree branches against the window. I sat swaddled in the comfort of my childhood home, staring out the window into pitch darkness, mesmerized by the sounds of Lake Jordan. The peaceful waters of this forty-mile lake rested at the edge of Daddy's property, which turned a dead-end road at the butt end of the earth into a stunning lakefront property with small cabins nestled on a hill when Alabama Power built Walter Bouldin Dam.

Absent from that night's serene view were squawking chickens, geese, the barn, the cotton patch, and cornfields. There was no garden, only cows—the assets my parents set aside to bury themselves—which my sister and her husband tend. And, although my father failed to honor many of his promises, he and Mama had executed a will, leaving the house and land to their children. A crescent moon and twinkling stars cast light on the black cows standing behind a barbwire fence, their eyes shining like headlights. I tucked the quilt around Daddy's shoulders and smoothed his head full of gray hair. "Daddy, it's my turn to care for you. I'll be here for four days. Then, I will go home."

"Alright," he said, his voice raspy like rusted metal.

Later that night, I tiptoed past Daddy's bedroom on my way to bed and heard an unfamiliar sound, whimpering, like a kitten's cry. Curious, I eased the door open. From the light of a bedside lamp, I noticed a jerking motion beneath the covers. He was weeping, a pitiful sob so wispy I could barely hear it. I stepped closer and wiped the tears spilling down his cheeks. He whispered through breathless sniffles, "Lead us not into temptation, but deliver us from evil," the final words of The Lord's Prayer, the same bedtime ritual he and Mama taught me to say as a child.

I grabbed his hand, no longer the rough, calloused hand of a working man. Not a hand capable of beating welts across the back of his eighteen-year-old daughter in a prom dress because she came home a few minutes late. It was the soft, warm hand of a man near death. I stood stoically and held back tears as we both said, "Amen." As he wept, I tried not to.

I rubbed his back with gentle, circular motions and sang *"Amazing Grace."* My insides lit up as he joined in with a determined voice and sang every word of two verses. Whatever pain he had felt drained from his face as he fell into a quiet slumber. I scurried around his room, putting it in order. I set the propane heater on low, cleaned and emptied the bedside pot, and tucked the covers around his body. I emptied his colostomy bag and left Daddy to sleep in peace.

A Return to Daddy's House

At sunrise the following day, I stood at his bedroom door observing the man who gave me life. Sunrays cast a peaceful glow across the room. I took it all in. The gentle rise and fall of his chest as he breathed through his mouth. A whistling sound escaping through the gap where a front tooth was missing. The beautiful aroma of his foul breath. All were signs that he was still alive. I smiled and exhaled. *"Forgive so you may be healed."*

I walked the short path from the bedroom to the kitchen, the squeaks from old planks loud and noticeable. I switched on the Hotpoint stove's one operable burner and prepared Daddy's favorite breakfast: soupy oatmeal with honey, cinnamon, and raisins. I set the table and prayed he would have a good appetite.

I bounded into Daddy's bedroom to say breakfast was ready and stopped short. He was propped on two pillows in the middle of his bed with all the covers strewn to the floor. He covered his nakedness with a diaper that he meticulously picked small pieces from and placed in two neat piles. One on his right side. Another on his left. I opened my mouth to say something; I had no idea what. Daddy kept his gaze on me, grinning with one front tooth missing. "Howz everybody doing this morning?" he asked. Every instinct in me wanted to laugh at my father, who, at that moment, looked like a toddler building a magnificent LEGO structure. I marveled at his hairless chest—smooth and brown like a Milk Dud, thinking I'd never seen his nakedness except his legs, arms, and face. Then, I unearthed a memory from sixty years earlier.

I was five or six, squealing through the backyard and being chased by Sonny. I raced up the back porch steps through the kitchen door, laughing and trying to escape my little brother.

When I slammed into the kitchen, I stopped, stunned to see Daddy standing in a #3 galvanized washtub, butt-naked, drying off with a white hand towel after bathing. I'll never forget the shock as we stared at each other, bug-eyed and mouths gaped open. Daddy quickly turned that wet washrag into a whip and popped me hard enough to draw a welt across my bare arm. "You knew I was taking a bath, and you ran in here looking at me," he said. I had no idea Daddy was bathing and was confused by his accusation. As a child, I didn't know why he hid behind that small towel, but vulnerability, a word I did not know then, covered his face as he searched the kitchen floor for clothing that wasn't there. So, I raced out the back door, terrified and confused, yet knowing the unlikelihood of any nude man making a spectacle of himself chasing a child through the backyard. I didn't laugh when I found my bedridden father tearing up his diaper, but giggles bubbled inside me, remembering how baffled he looked standing in that bathtub.

Swallowing my laughter, I gathered the covers from the floor. "Daddy, were you hot? Where are your clothes?" I asked.

He kept stacking up diaper pieces. "Huh?"

I wondered what magnificent structure the brick mason and carpenter thought he was building.

I swung his bony legs off the bed, wrapped him in his housecoat, and placed the bedside stool behind him. "Daddy, hold on to me. Let's get you on the pot." He wrapped his thin arms around my neck and hung on, trembling with such force that I could barely stand up. After he sat on the stool, I reached for the tape of his Depend. He grunted and stiffened. "Are you okay?" I asked. He stared at me with a look of manly pride. I handed him a clean Depend and Johnson's Baby Wipes, and Daddy watched me until I was out the door. After several minutes, I knocked. "May I come in?" In a breathy voice, he told me yes.

I followed close behind my father to catch him if he fell on the way to the kitchen while he held himself upright by pushing the metal contraption with two wheels and two rubber feet. He gripped the bars of his walker, wobbled, and shuffled along, taking one painful step after another. His frail body was crooked, and he dragged his feet as if they were in leg irons.

After he had walked twenty-five feet from the bed to the dining room table, I rolled Daddy's swivel rocker behind him, and he flopped onto the chair like he had run a marathon. He took a long breath. "Whew!" he said. I placed the oatmeal in front of him, poured a glass of chocolate Ensure, and set a handful of pills in a small Dixie cup beside his plate. He picked at his breakfast and stared out the glass patio door. Sitting before his oatmeal, Daddy watched his black cows grazing in the pasture and stared at a man on a fishing boat drifting on Lake Jordan.

I watched the man who taught me toughness, independence, and how to stand up for myself become more dependent on morphine. He slept peacefully and seldom woke up. On my last full day with him, I swung Daddy's arm around my neck and practically carried him to the dining room table. He could no longer walk and seldom spoke.

After the four-day visit, I rolled my luggage across the wooden planks of the kitchen floor. I switched on the dining room light and took a mental snapshot of what Daddy saw each day as he'd sat alone for eight years since Mama died. Medicine bottles, medical books, Ensure cans, and old rusted tools stacked in neat piles on the dining room table. Mama's ladder-back chair was next to his rocker as if she might stop by for breakfast. I gazed around the living and dining rooms and studied years of family pictures hanging from the walls. Daddy in his World War II army uniform. Mama's high school graduation. Mama and Daddy on matching lawn chairs under the pecan tree, celebrating their fiftieth wedding anniversary with their fifteen children grinning in the background. So many graduation and baby pictures. An old gospel hymnal lay open on Daddy's electric organ with missing keys.

I thought of the first time he and I had teamed up to perform, him playing piano, me singing *"Precious Lord."* It was the fall of 1970 after I had won Miss Talent and moved to Dayton. I stood in the choir loft next to Daddy and faced the congregation while he sat at the piano, searching for the right chords with his back to the audience. That Sunday, at my childhood church, I sang with unabashed freedom, a freedom I hadn't felt since winning Miss Talent in New York.

The congregation rose to their feet, clapping and rejoicing in the aisles. Sitting on the front pew, Mama and Aunt Willie Alice shouted so hard they almost flipped over a church bench and nearly scared me half to death. I swore I would never sing at Mt. Zion again, yet Daddy beckoned me to his side every time I was home. That Sunday, he had hopped off the piano stool, a broad smile across his face, and said, "I had heard her sing before, but I sho' didn't know she could sing like that."

A Return to Daddy's House

After that day, I sang most Sundays and weekends at funerals, weddings, or in my church choir. My love of singing flew back like a dove with an olive leaf, returning me to where God needed me most at that time in my life.

I parked my suitcase outside his door, slipped into Daddy's bedroom, and watched him sleep on his right side, hands folded like a praying child. I studied my father's frail body, reluctant to wake him, but I had to say goodbye. I touched him gently. His eyes fluttered open, and he searched my face intently but said nothing. The way he stared, I was sure he didn't know me.

"Morning, Daddy. It's time for me to go." I leaned over, kissed his cheek, and said, "I love you, Daddy." In a swift and surprising move, he hooked his bony arm around my neck. I stiffened; the little girl inside me frightened, prepared to fight back against his stranglehold.

But then he loosened his grip and began to speak. In that powerful voice that once commanded field hands and directed church choirs, a sound I thought he'd lost forever, Daddy said, "I *sure* am glad you came. Tell D (my husband) I said hello." I threw my arms around his neck and felt the faint drumbeat of his heart as we held each other. Daddy didn't call me Babe, but I know he knew me as he gazed into my eyes for the last time.

I traveled through my best and worst times with Daddy for four days. But at the end of the journey, I did what God put me on Earth to do—help others, including my father. Did I believe he deserved such treatment? It doesn't matter because I love God. I thought of 1 John 4:20: "If anyone says, 'I love God,' yet hates his brother, he is a liar." In loving and caring for my father, I found peace and the strength to forgive the most contrary man I'd ever known.

Growing up, I wanted nothing more than to move as far from Daddy, his house, and that farm as the earth is from the sky. But watching my twin headlights slicing through the early dawn, I realized Daddy, the master manipulator, had saved for last his cruelest trick. I could almost see him clapping his hands and laughing, saying, "You thought it was your idea to leave my house? I purposefully made it unbearable for you to stay, shoved you out of the nest, and forced you to stand on your own." The thought of Daddy believing he got the last laugh brought a wide grin. *It's hard to shove someone from a place they were hell-bent on leaving, especially when it was the last place on Earth they wanted to be.*

When I drove away from the cinderblock house, pea gravel crackled beneath the tires, a lone owl hooted in the distance, and a crescent moon stood guard. I watched through the rearview mirror, a single light growing dim, thinking that many would believe Daddy deserved to suffer, lying on his deathbed, writhing in pain. But I swallowed memories of a little girl who had wished her father would burn in hell and embraced the woman who turned the other cheek, honored her father, and refused to deliver an eye for an eye.

The call came three weeks later, on April 8, 2016, two days before my sixty-fifth birthday, while I watched a tennis match at Farmington Valley Racquet Club in Connecticut, where my husband and I had relocated after he accepted a new job in 2011. In a soft voice, sounding eerily like Daddy's, my brother, James,

A Return to Daddy's House

said, "Well, PawPaw's gone." I didn't shed a single tear. Yet the human side of me the that feeds the homeless and donates to charities benefitting people I don't know, thanked God that hospice care and chronic pain were no longer constant companions of the man whose blood was coursing through my veins. A soothing calm washed over me, remembering my last trip to Daddy's house, where I healed and forgave while we held hands and said, "Amen."

Printed in the USA
CPSIA information can be obtained
at www.ICGtesting.com
LVHW091557230424
778174LV00007B/687